Microsoft® Exchange 5.5 Administrator's Pocket Consultant

Kathy Ivens

PUBLISHED BY
Microsoft Press
A Division of Microsoft Corporation
One Microsoft Way
Redmond, Washington 98052-6399

Library of Congress Cataloging-in-Publication Data
Ivens, Kathy.
Microsoft Exchange 5.5 Administrator's Pocket Consultant / Kathy Ivens.
p. cm.
ISBN 0-7356-0623-4
1. Microsoft Exchange server. 2. Client/server computing.
I. Title.
QA76.9.C55I96 1999
005.7'13769--dc21
99-13768
CIP

Printed and bound in the United States of America.

1 2 3 4 5 6 7 8 9 MLML 4 3 2 1 0 9

Distributed in Canada by Penguin Books Canada Limited.

A CIP catalogue record for this book is available from the British Library.

Microsoft Press books are available through booksellers and distributors worldwide. For further information about international editions, contact your local Microsoft Corporation office or contact Microsoft Press International directly at fax (425) 936-7329. Visit our Web site at mspress.microsoft.com.

Acquisitions Editor: Juliana Aldous
Project Editor: Susan S. Bradley
Technical Editor: Anoosh Ghazi

To Fred, Teri, and Raisa, because having bright, interesting people in your family, who know about computers, and who ask questions and make suggestions, is just terrific.

Contents at a Glance

Table of Contents

Part II
Client Software

Tables

Preface

This book is designed to be a quick reference guide for maintaining an existing Microsoft Exchange Server system, rather than a complete tome on installing, configuring, and using Microsoft Exchange Server 5.5. *Microsoft Exchange 5.5 Administrator's Companion* by Rick Greenwald and Walter J. Glenn should be referenced for complete information on installing and configuring Exchange Server.

I selected the specific subject matter by asking lots of Exchange administrators to keep track of how they spent their days. The tasks that occurred most frequently made it into the chapters of this book. Of course, no two organizations or Exchange Server configurations are the same, so your list of things you do over and over may differ. But I'm confident that my nagging questions to administrators will mean you'll find plenty of useful information in the pages of this book.

I hope you find *Microsoft Exchange Server 5.5 Administrator's Pocket Consultant* both useful and easy to use.

Acknowledgments

I drove a lot of Exchange administrators and trainers crazy, badgering them for information and opinions about what's important to the maintenance of an Exchange System. A couple of them cooperated in a way that was over and above my requests, so I feel the need to express my gratitude. Paul Begley, of Wolff Data Systems (*http://www.wolffdata.com*), used the expertise he's gained in training Exchange administrators to answer questions, give examples, and make suggestions. Chris Scharff provided great information about Web services and interacting with ISPs. John McCrae, of Data Return web hosting/development (*http://www.datareturn.com*), was a font of information as he manipulated public folders all over the immediate world to test and document the results for me. My favorite geek in the Microsoft Exchange group, David Madison, was his usual patient and funny self in response to my many "why does this work this way?" questions, and also in response to my frequent comments that started with "here's my suggestion about how it should work."

At Microsoft Press, Juliana Aldous is a real gem of an acquisitions editor, who is always a delight to work with. Tracy Thomsic's considerable gifts in managing the book's content were exceeded only by her ability to provide a wonderful atmosphere of teamwork. Maureen Zimmerman and Susan S. Bradley brought a great deal of expertise, efficiency, and patience to the production of this book (and I didn't always make it easy), for which I'm extremely grateful.

Introduction

Microsoft Exchange Server 5.5 Administrator's Pocket Consultant is a resource for Exchange 5.5 administrators who need to respond quickly to user and system needs. This book is filled with information and instructions that will help you get through the maintenance and troubleshooting chores you face on a daily basis.

You won't have to struggle through pages and pages of nonessential information because this book is focused on maintenance, and it's filled with the information you need to keep an existing Exchange Server system running smoothly.

You'll find a great deal of information on client software issues, in addition to those tasks you need to perform on the server.

Who Is This Book For?

Microsoft Exchange Server 5.5 Administrator's Pocket Consultant is designed for the people who keep the company mail system running. If you hold any of these roles, you'll find valuable information within these pages:

- Organization administrator
- Site administrator
- Server administrator
- User software administrator
- Helpdesk personnel

I made some assumptions when I wrote this book, which really means I presupposed there was information it was safe to omit. I think this makes it easier for you, as an administrator, to find what you need. Here's what I assumed:

- You have a basic understanding of Microsoft Windows NT.
- You know how to create and manage Windows NT user and group accounts.
- Exchange Server 5.5 is installed and deployed.
- Some of your users (perhaps not yet all) are working with Exchange client software.
- You understand the administrative jargon for Windows NT and networking (which means I don't have to explain the word "protocol").

How Is This Book Organized?

Microsoft Exchange Server 5.5 Administrator's Pocket Consultant is organized around the Exchange components you work with every day. This book is the down-and-dirty, in-the-trenches manual for getting your administrative work done quickly and accurately. For those times you may need a more comprehensive tutorial and reference volume, *Microsoft Exchange Server 5.5 Administrator's*

Companion, also from Microsoft Press, is the perfect accompaniment to this Pocket Consultant.

This book has a table of contents and an extensive index that are both designed to get you to the information you need in a split second. Other useful ingredients are step-by-step instructions, tables that make complicated issues more comprehensible, and commentary about shortcuts and tricks other companies that use Exchange have discovered.

This book is arranged in parts and chapters, and each part contains an opening paragraph or two about the chapters it holds.

Part I, "Private Information Store and Mailboxes," covers the heart of your Exchange system, the mail. This is what your users care about. Chapter 1 is all about managing mailboxes. Chapter 2 is an easy-to-use guide for managing the Information Store. Chapter 3 is a troubleshooting guide for mailboxes, providing information and tricks I learned on my own system and on my clients' systems. There's also a lot of good information I gathered by picking the brains of lots of other Exchange administrators.

Part II, "Client Software," is filled with essential information you need to support and assist users, as well as troubleshoot the problems they encounter. Chapter 4 is filled with hints, suggestions, and information for maintaining client software and helping users get the most out of it. Chapter 5 is a comprehensive troubleshooting guide for Exchange client software.

Part III, "Site Components," is all about the tasks you perform in the Exchange Server Administrator's window. Chapter 6 is chock-full of information and tips for maintaining and troubleshooting sites and the Exchange servers on those sites. Chapter 7 is all about public folders, covering maintenance, troubleshooting, and lots of hints about getting your public folders under control. It includes plenty of information about handling those folders that are exposed to the Internet.

Part IV, "Appendices," provides information you'll probably need to check out frequently, if not daily. There's a copious amount of resource data as well as information about some utilities you may find helpful as you perform your administrative tasks. Appendix A is all about the "other" components in client software. Users care more about mail than they do about any other utility, but you need to be prepared to assist them with Calendar, Tasks, Contacts, and the other client components. Appendix B takes a comprehensive look at some of the most helpful utilities in the Microsoft BackOffice Resource Kit. Appendix C covers some of the nifty software available in the Windows NT Resource Kit. (A Windows NT system, with extra functions and features that are useful to Exchange and Exchange administrators, makes your life easier.) Appendix D is a collection of resources you'll find helpful. Most of them are Web sites that provide a rich and varied aggregation of information about Exchange Server. Appendix E is about some of the outstanding add-ons available to you as you seek to enhance the power and efficiency of your Exchange system. There's also detailed information about the Exchange Server Service Packs.

Conventions Used in This Book

I've used a variety of elements to make it easier to use this book efficiently. Code terms and listings are printed in monospace type. Any text you need to enter in a dialog box or at the command line appears in bold type. In addition, the following easy-to-spot (and therefore easy-to-use) elements are scattered throughout the pages:

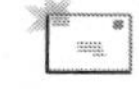

Notes These are items that give you additional details about a subject.

Tips These are exactly what the name implies, a bit of helpful information.

Cautions These indicate something you need to watch out for, or a task you need to perform very, very carefully.

Support

Every effort has been made to ensure the accuracy of this book. Microsoft Press provides corrections for books through the World Wide Web at the following address:

http://mspress.microsoft.com/support/

If you have comments, questions, or ideas regarding this book, please send them to Microsoft Press using either of the following methods:

Postal Mail:

Microsoft Press
Attn: Microsoft Exchange Server 5.5
Administrator's Pocket Consultant *Editor*
One Microsoft Way
Redmond, WA 98052-6399

E-mail:

MSPINPUT@MICROSOFT.COM

Please note that product support is not offered through the above mail addresses.

Part I

Private Information Store and Mailboxes

The heart of your Microsoft Exchange Server system is the Private Information Store. Users care more about e-mail than they do about any other service Exchange Server provides.

The volume of mail, the propensity of users to make mistakes, and the urgency with which they appeal to you to fix the mistakes, add up to quite a workload for Exchange administrators.

Add to that the need to baby-sit the health and efficiency of the Private Information Store, and you begin to wonder how any Exchange administrator can maintain any level of pleasant demeanor (or sanity).

The chapters in this section are designed to give you some insights into the care and feeding of the mailboxes you administer and the Private Information store that houses them.

Chapter 1

Managing Mailboxes

Mailboxes should just exist, behaving properly, accepting mail, and generally giving users what they expect. Of course, it doesn't always work that way. Microsoft Exchange administrators must spend time managing mailboxes as a result of user requests, user problems, or company policy decisions. Managing mailboxes also includes managing the Private Information Store.

Maintaining Mailbox Permissions

You might need to add or change permissions on a mailbox for any of several reasons. For instance, company policy may dictate that certain mailboxes should have additional users, and you must assign rights to those users. You may want to permit other administrators to help manage mailboxes. Permissions are commonly manipulated on mailboxes that don't belong to individual employees but are instead specialized. Mailboxes are often needed for conference rooms, for supplies (people need to request the overhead projector for a meeting), for the company suggestion box, or for the receipt of articles for the company newsletter.

Displaying Permissions

You encounter a problem when you open a mailbox to change the permissions attached to it—there's no place to perform this task. No tab on the mailbox dialog box contains permissions entries, and no button will lead you to a permissions dialog box.

By default, Microsoft Exchange Server does not display a Permissions tab on objects. You must turn on this function, and you do that in the Administrator window. From the Tools menu, select Options, and then move to the Permissions tab (see Figure 1-1, on the following page).

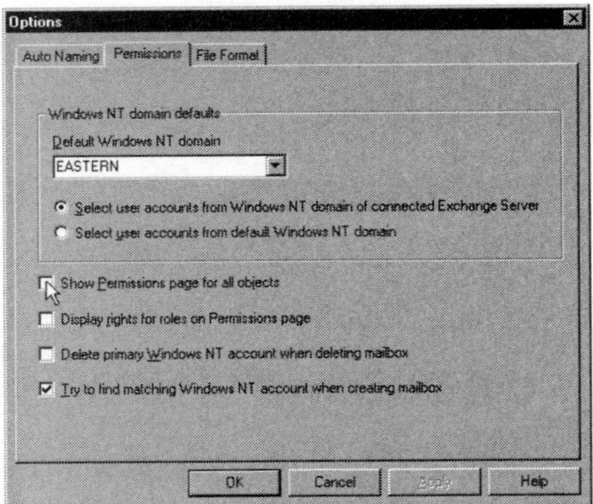

Figure 1-1. *Use the Options dialog box to configure the display of permissions for all container objects.*

You can configure the display of permissions and rights as follows:

- Turn on the display of the Permissions tab for all objects that have one available.
- Display the rights attached to roles on the Permissions tab (you need this information when you're assigning rights, unless you have an incredible memory).

Tip There is no way to turn on the display of a Permissions tab on one type of container object without turning on the display of the Permissions tab for all objects that have a Permissions tab available. The same rule applies, of course, if you turn off the display of the Permissions tab.

Giving Mailbox Permissions to Additional Accounts

An administrator commonly adds permissions to a mailbox because the mailbox requires multiple users to manage its contents. This is the case with groupwide mailboxes that hold information (rather than individual mailboxes owned by users). For example, the mailbox for your Help Desk or for the Human Resources Department is a candidate for multiple administrators.

You may, however, want to grant additional personnel permissions to particular user mailboxes, either at the request of the mailbox owner or as the result of company policy.

The mailbox object's Permissions tab, as seen in Figure 1-2, displays two different sets of permissions: inherited permissions and accounts with permissions.

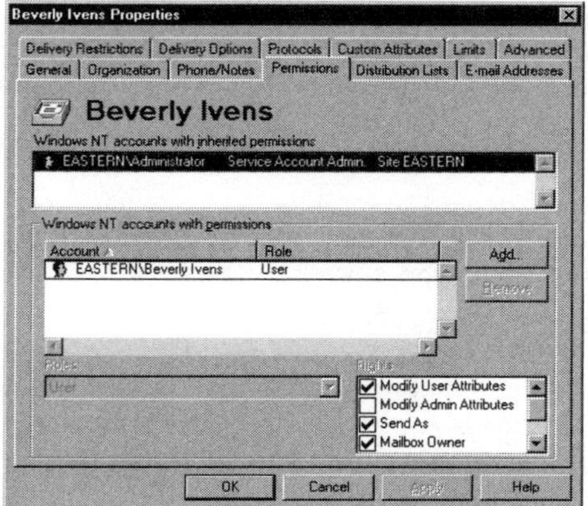

Figure 1-2. *Mailboxes have inherited permissions and account permissions.*

Adding and Changing Inherited Permissions

The inherited permissions are read-only and cannot be changed in the mailbox dialog box. The permissions are inherited from the permissions granted at the site level; this means that at least the account name used when Exchange Server was installed has administrative permissions. If additional accounts were given site-management rights, those accounts show up in the inherited permissions portion of the mailbox Permissions dialog box.

If you want to extend inherited permissions to additional administrators so that they can help you administer all the mailboxes on your site, follow these steps:

1. Select the site container.
2. From the File menu, choose Properties to open the Site Properties dialog box.
3. Go to the Permissions tab.
4. Choose Add, and then select the account(s) to whom you want to give site administrative permissions.
5. Click OK.

Adding and Changing Account Permissions

Adding mailbox permissions for other users or groups is beneficial for two reasons:

- Multi-user mailboxes for shared resources can be checked by anyone with responsibilities for that resource.
- Mailbox owners can delegate mailbox chores to other users.

Multi-User Mailboxes I've seen some inventive examples of multi-user mailboxes at client sites, and you might want to think about applying some of this creative thinking to your own company. These mailboxes are created so as to avoid having one person receive tons of e-mail; they instead distribute the workload throughout a department.

One company created a mailbox (named Library) for the research library to which employees direct inquiries. All employees in the research department share mailbox permissions and answer queries.

Within Human Resources Departments, I've seen mailboxes named Pension, Benefits, HR Policies, and so on. Employees send e-mail asking about pension plans, benefits, promotion policies, merit evaluation policies, and other HR issues. Replies are generated by the appropriate member of the department, or on a round-robin basis that the department members work out.

Another company created a mailbox named HelpDesk, to which non-urgent requests for information about using software are directed.

To give a Windows NT account or a group permissions on a mailbox, click Add on the Permissions page. The Add Users and Groups dialog box appears, displaying groups and individual user accounts. Select the account you want to add to this mailbox. You can repeat this as many times as you need to.

Tip If you're planning to give identical mailbox permissions to all members of a specific department, you might want to think about creating a group for that department in User Manager for Domains, and then selecting the group for mailbox permissions. Creating a group is easier than selecting each person for mailbox permissions and defining a role for him or her. This technique also makes it easier to change permissions or otherwise manipulate that group.

Understanding Roles and Rights

For each new account, select a role from the drop-down list in the Roles section of the dialog box, or select specific rights from the choices in the Rights box. Notice that mailbox permissions do not have a role named Custom in the Roles drop-down list. However, if you select a group of rights from the Rights list and that group doesn't match an existing role, the Custom role is added to cover your selections.

Table 1-1 lists the rights involved in each role available for mailboxes.

Table 1-1. Predetermined Roles and Rights

Role	Rights
Admin	Modify User Attributes; Modify Admin Attributes
Permissions Admin	Modify User Attributes; Modify Admin Attributes; Modify Permissions
Search	Search
Send As	Send As
User	Modify User Attributes; Send As; Mailbox Owner

These rights are specific to mailboxes, and they include the following functions:

- **Modify User Attributes** This is the ability to change user-modifiable properties. Such changes are usually made at the client software window and include the right to delegate mailbox chores and to give mailbox access rights to other users.
- **Modify Admin Attributes** This is the ability to change any property that can be modified at the Exchange Server window by an administrator (for example, the display name or size limit).
- **Send As** This permits the selected account to send messages as this mailbox owner. When you give this right to an account in addition to the mailbox owner, the recipient cannot tell that the message did not originate with the mailbox owner.
- **Mailbox Owner** These are the same rights as those granted to the person for whom the mailbox was created. An account granted this right can read, send, and forward messages.
- **Modify Permissions** This right enables the user to change any entry on the mailbox's Permissions tab.
- **Search** This is a new right, introduced in Microsoft Exchange Server 5.5. Technically, it provides Read access for the Microsoft Exchange directory. For mailboxes, it's specifically used for running Exchange Server with the Microsoft Outlook Web Access (OWA) component. If a user wants to access a mailbox through a Web browser, this permission must be granted.

Setting User Permissions in the Client Software

The mailbox owner can change permissions directly from the client software. The permissions and roles are different from those presented on the Permissions tab of the mailbox that's available in the Exchange Server Administrator window. Users can grant rights to create, read, edit, and delete items.

To set user permissions in client software (assuming Outlook as the client), follow these steps:

1. Right-click on Outlook Today in the Outlook Bar, or on the Mailbox object in the Folder list, and then select Properties from the Shortcut menu.
2. In the Mailbox Properties dialog box, go to the Permissions tab (see Figure 1-3).
3. Click Add to open the Add Users dialog box.
4. Select the list you want to use (usually the Global Address List or the Recipients List for the site).
5. Select the user to whom you want to give permissions for your mailbox, and click Add to place the user name in the Add Users list (see Figure 1-4).
6. Click OK to return to the Permissions tab.

Before you leave the Permissions tab, you may want to examine and reconfigure the roles and rights for the users to whom you've given mailbox permissions.

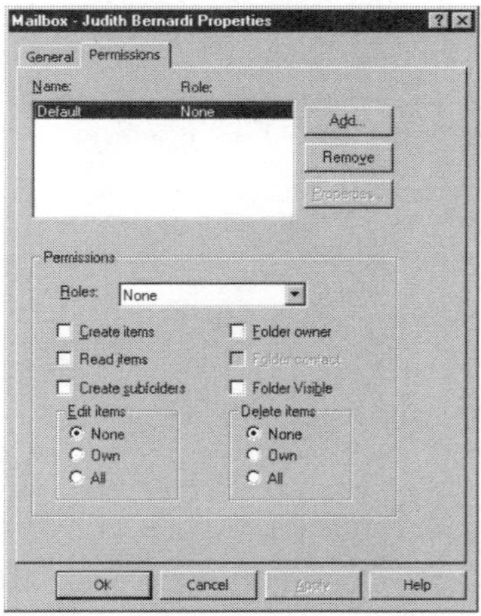

Figure 1-3. *The permissions in the client software are different from and more granular than the permissions available in the Exchange Server Administrator's window.*

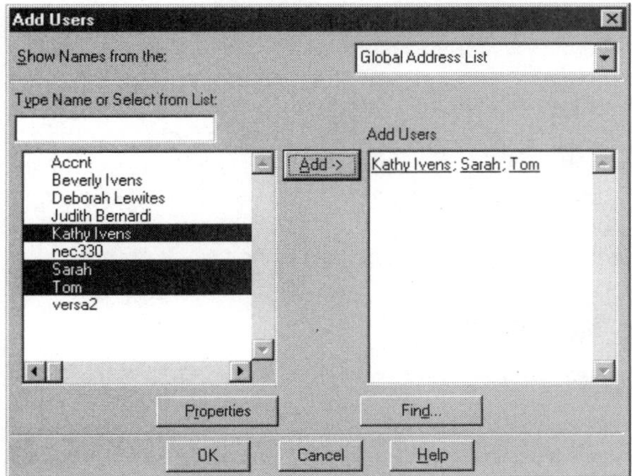

Figure 1-4. *Select the users to whom you want to give access permissions for your mailbox in the Add Users dialog box.*

Opening Another User's Mailbox

After you've given permission to User A to open and manipulate the mailbox belonging to User B, the task of opening that mailbox occurs on the client software. Assuming Outlook as the client, here are the steps that you, as User A, take to open User B's mailbox.

1. From the Tools menu, select Services to open the Services dialog box.
2. Select Microsoft Exchange Server in the Services tab.
3. Click Properties to open the Properties dialog box for Exchange Server.
4. Move to the Advanced tab.
5. In the Mailboxes section of the dialog box, click Add.
6. Enter the name of the mailbox you want to open. There is no browse feature; you must know the name of the mailbox you want to open.
7. Click OK three times to return to the Outlook window.

The mailbox is in your Outlook window, in the Folder List (display the Folder List to see it). You can create an icon for this mailbox in the Outlook Bar (in the Folder List, right-click the mailbox and then click Add To Outlook Bar). After you've placed the icon on the Outlook Bar, however, be sure to rename it—or you'll have two objects named Mailbox.

Caution The mailbox appears in your Outlook folders list even if you didn't have permissions to access the mailbox. When you add a mailbox to your list of mailboxes, as long as you spell the name of the mailbox properly, Exchange Server is very accommodating. If you don't have permissions for that mailbox, you're not warned, you're not told, and there's not a murmur of protest. When you attempt to use the mailbox, however, you see an error message telling you that the mailbox cannot be opened. There's still no explanation, no message telling you that you don't have permissions to open the mailbox. It just won't open.

Controlling the Size of Mailboxes and Messages

It's a universal problem—users want to save every message they've ever received and sent. This fills up the hard drive that houses your Information Store, it makes backing up a longer procedure, and also makes replication more onerous for the system.

It's a good idea to notify all users in your organization that there's a policy about saving mail. Then you can outline the guidelines, which include the fact that there's no particular reason to keep a message in the Inbox unless the user plans to reply to or forward the message. In all other circumstances, messages should be moved to folders on the user's local drive.

It's a bad idea to believe this is going to work. Like many Exchange administrators, you'll probably find that the only way you can keep user mailboxes under control is to apply size limits. Then you can shrug and say, "Hey, the computer does that automatically," when users lose functionality because they haven't followed your guidelines.

In fact, many Exchange administrators tweak the system by changing mailbox sizes periodically.

Setting Default Mailbox Size Limits

The default limits for mailbox sizes are set in the Private Information Store object. Select it and choose File, and then choose Properties. The General tab contains the storage limits, as shown in Figure 1-5. All mailboxes assume these default settings, but you can override the settings on a mailbox-by-mailbox basis.

The limits are set in kilobytes, and you can set the following criteria:

- **Issue Warning** This is a size limit for the total storage space used by the mailbox. When that limit is exceeded, the system issues a warning to the mailbox owner.
- **Prohibit Send** This is a size limit for the maximum amount of space a mailbox can occupy before the owner will be unable to send messages.

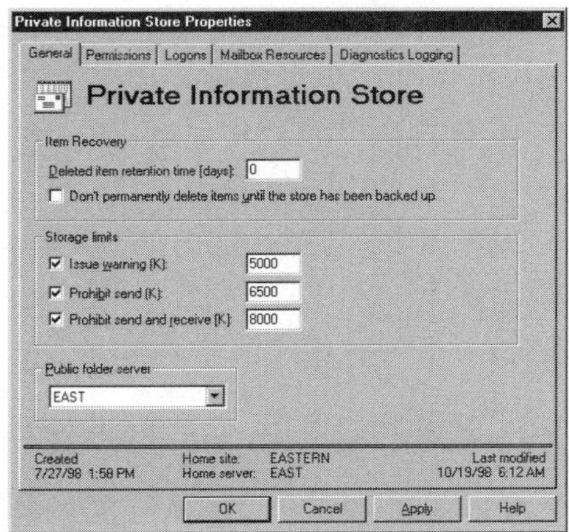

Figure 1-5. *Set a default size configuration for all mailboxes under the General tab in Private Information Store Properties.*

- **Prohibit Send and Receive** This is a size limit for the maximum amount of space a mailbox can occupy before the owner will be unable to send or receive messages.

Tip The prohibitions for messages do not apply to messages sent via Post Office Protocol 3 (POP3) or Messaging Application Programming Interface 4 (MAPI4), because those protocols don't support these functions.

When a user attempts to send a message after the Prohibit Send limit is exceeded, he or she receives the message "The item could not be sent. You have exceeded the storage limit on your mailbox. Delete some mail from your mailbox or contact your system administrator to adjust your storage limit." The message remains in the Outbox; it's not deleted.

When a message is sent to a mailbox that exceeds the Prohibit Send and Receive limit, the sender receives a standard nondelivery report (NDR). As with any bounced mail, the sender must retrieve the message from the Sent Items folder in the client software and then resend it after the problem is resolved.

When users reach these limits and are unable to use the Send or Receive functions, you can increase the storage limits, or you can explain the virtues of archiving to local folders. You can even try to explain the virtues of deleting mail (although this probably won't work).

Setting Individual Mailbox Limits

Some mailboxes cannot operate effectively with the default settings for size, and you can override those settings with more appropriate limits. Open the mailbox

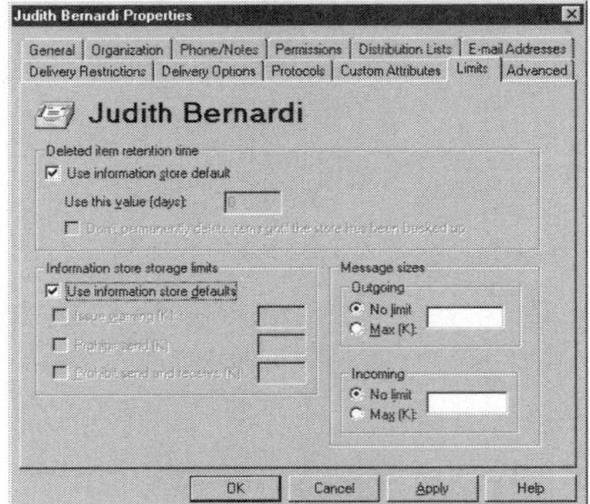

Figure 1-6. *Use the mailbox Properties dialog box to set limits on the mailbox size as well as message sizes.*

and move to the Limits tab (see Figure 1-6). Deselect the Use Information Store Default check box and then specify limits for this mailbox.

The Limits tab also provides an opportunity to set the size of individual messages that can be sent or received by this mailbox.

Tip Client software has no capacity for imposing or changing limits; you must perform this task from the Exchange Administrator window.

Retaining Deleted Items

As you work with the dialog boxes that permit you to set limits on sizes, you see references to the amount of time that the Information Store holds on to deleted items. Like decisions involving mailbox sizes, decisions about time limits on the retention of deleted items can be imposed globally or on a mailbox-by-mailbox basis.

Tweaking the retention time for deleted items is an ongoing maintenance chore, and you'll probably find you're constantly fine-tuning the numbers to keep your system running smoothly.

On the General tab of the Properties dialog box for the Private Information Store, you'll find a text box in which you can specify the number of days that deleted items are held before they're really deleted. By default, the number of days is zero, but Exchange administrators change this after they've been the target of whining and begging users who have inadvertently deleted items.

Be sure to select the option to retain items until you've backed up your Information Store. Regardless of the number of days you specify for holding on to deleted items, they won't be deleted permanently until you back up.

On the Limits tab of the Properties dialog box for individual mailboxes, you can override the deleted item retention setting in the Information Store. Some Exchange administrators use the mailbox setting to return the number of days to zero after specifying a number of days in the Information Store. Some administrators do it the other way around, leaving the Information Store set at zero and giving individual mailboxes several days to hold onto deleted messages.

Cleaning Mailboxes

You can clean mailboxes from the server with the Clean Mailbox command on the Tools menu. Select the Recipients container for the site you want to use, then select one or more mailboxes (use the Windows standard Ctrl or Shift key actions to make multiple selections). Choose Tools, and then choose Clean Mailbox to display the Clean Mailbox dialog box seen in Figure 1-7.

Choosing the Cleanup Options

This tool provides enough options to make the procedure both safe and efficient. Follow these guidelines to avoid problems:

- **Age** Specify the number of days to use as the criteria. All messages older than your specification are removed. Specify a size (in kilobytes) to remove all messages larger than this maximum. These are independent settings; the size is not a subgroup of the age.
- **Sensitivity** Specify the sensitivity level to be deleted (see Table 1-2, on the following page, for details). The sensitivity level is applied to outgoing messages.

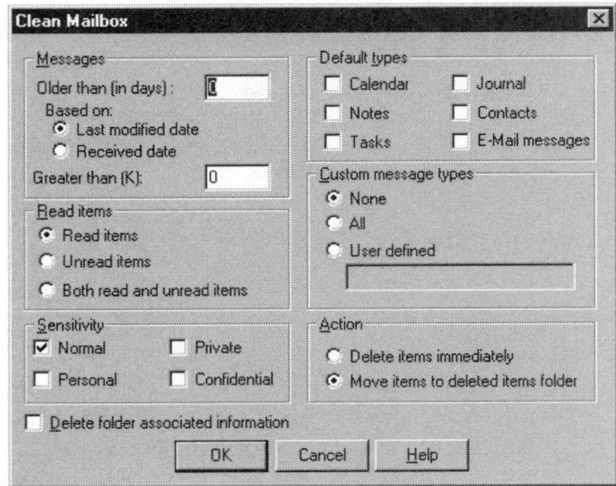

Figure 1-7. *Use the Clean Mailbox tool to reduce the size of the Private Information Store.*

- **Read Items** Select the read/unread status of messages you want removed.
- **Delete Folder Associated Items** Select this option to delete views, deferred messages, or any other rule-based items that meet your other specified criteria.
- **Default Types** Select the types of items you want to include in the deletion.
- **Custom Message Types** For Outlook clients, select the custom message forms and user-designed templates you want to include. See Table 1-3 for an explanation of the choices.
- **Action** Specify whether you want to delete the items immediately or to move them to the user's deleted items folder.

Table 1-2. Message Sensitivity Levels

Sensitivity Level	Description
Normal	No special sensitivity is attached to the message.
Personal	Header is marked to denote the fact that the message is personal.
Private	Recipients cannot change the message when they reply to or forward it.
Confidential	Data is encrypted, using the security features applied to your Exchange Server system.

Table 1-3. Custom Message Removal Selection Options

Custom Message Option	Resulting Action
None	No custom messages are removed.
All	All custom messages that meet the other criteria are removed.
User Defined	The specific Inter-Personal Message (IPM) templates you define in the text box below the option are removed. Enter the message, and then enter the format IPM <*name*>.

Service Pack Changes on the Clean Mailbox Tool

If the dialog box in Figure 1-7 doesn't look like the dialog box you see, you probably haven't installed the Microsoft Exchange Server Service Pack. Service Pack 1 (SP1) provides additional options for the Clean Mailbox tool. The original Exchange Server 5.5 Clean Mailbox dialog box is shown in Figure 1-8.

Notice that there's a check box named Only Delete Mail Messages. If this check box is selected, that's what happens. If you deselect this option, Contacts, Calendar Items, and Tasks are removed. Notice also that the options for narrowing down the choices of items are missing from the dialog box. Administrators who faced hordes of angry users as a result of the limited options in the original Clean Mailbox dialog box were grateful for SP1.

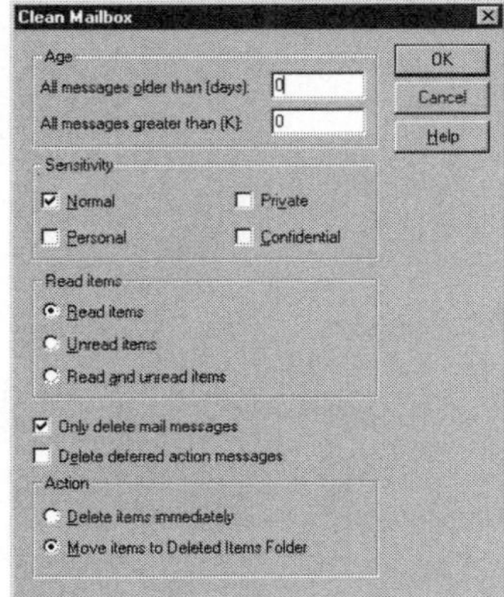

Figure 1-8. *The original Exchange Server 5.5 Clean Mailbox dialog box has fewer options than that of the Exchange Server Service Pack.*

Managing Spamming

You can establish some protection against spamming by getting rid of mail that is sent over the Internet from known spamming sites. Those sites can be named as a result of your own experience, or by using lists that are maintained by individuals and groups.

Spamming is the term used for the practice of flooding the Internet with multiple copies of a message, sent to recipients who did not request it. If your users are on the recipient end of this flood, so is your server and its disk space.

The solutions available to Exchange administrators for controlling spam attacks lie in the Internet Mail Service (IMS) connection. After all, it's unlikely that your internal mail service would be used for a spam attack.

You can filter out messages, or you can refuse connections from domains you want to exclude. Both methods are discussed in this section.

Using Message Filtering Against Spamming

You can prevent messages from known spamming sites from getting through to mailboxes by using the Message Filtering feature available in the IMS. Two approaches are available—you can either delete filtered messages, or you can save them for later examination (they're not delivered to the recipient's mailbox).

Enable Message Filtering

First you turn on the Message Filtering feature, which includes telling Exchange Server whose messages to filter. Here's how to enable the Message Filtering feature:

1. In the left pane of the Exchange Administrator window, expand the Site and select the Connections container.

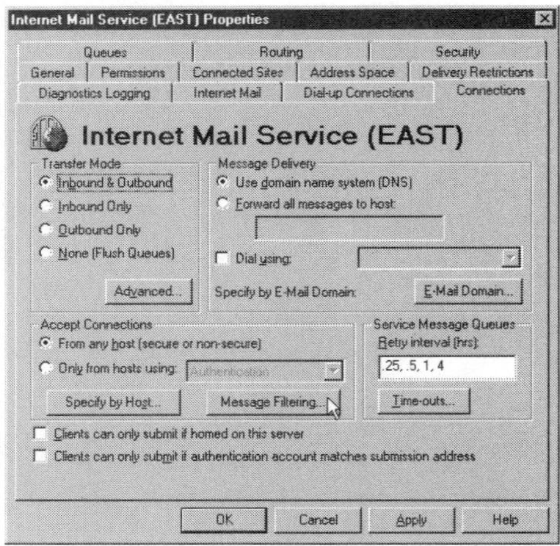

Figure 1-9. *The Connections tab of the Internet Mail Service dialog box provides a way to cut down on spamming.*

2. Double-click the IMS object in the right pane to open the Properties dialog box.
3. Move to the Connections tab (see Figure 1-9).
4. Click the Message Filtering button to open the Message Filtering dialog box shown in Figure 1-10.
5. Click Add to place a user or domain on your filter list.
6. In the Edit Domain/User dialog box, enter a domain name (for example, **spammer.com**) or a user/domain (for instance, **pest@spammer.com**). Click OK to add this entry to your filter list.

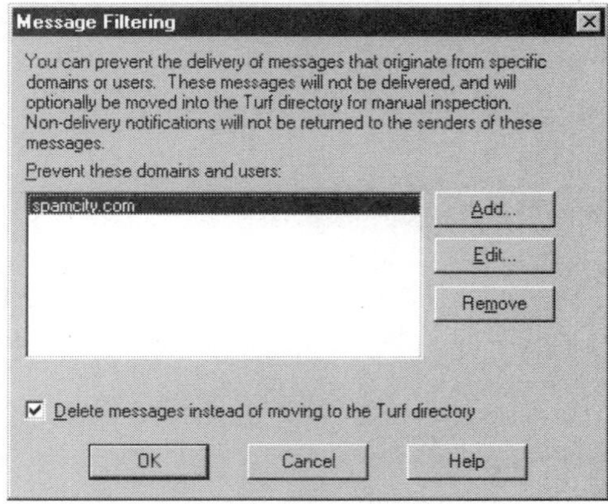

Figure 1-10. *Keep a list of spammers so that you can filter their messages out of your system.*

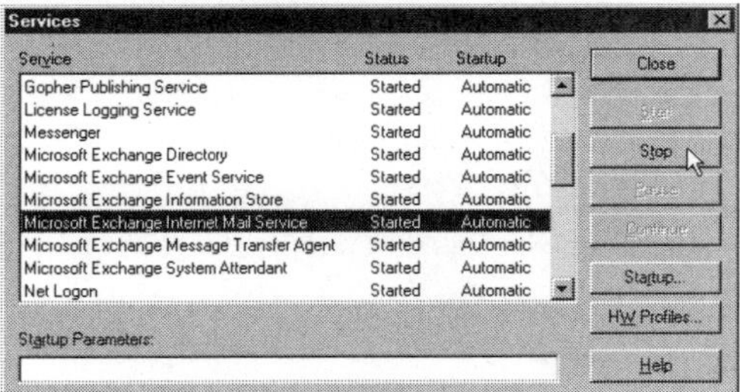

Figure 1-11. *Stop and restart the Internet Mail Service to begin filtering messages.*

7. Repeat for all the domains you want to apply your filter against.
8. If you want the filtered messages deleted automatically, select that option. If you want to examine the filtered mail, read the next section, "Saving Filtered Messages."

After you click OK twice to close the IMS Properties dialog box, you must stop and restart the IMS to have your changes take effect. To do this, open the Services utility in Control Panel and scroll to Microsoft Exchange Internet Mail Service (see Figure 1-11).

Select the IMS entry and click Stop. After the service is stopped, click Start.

Keeping Up with Spammer Lists The primary method by which administrators learn a spammer's domain name is that users are subjected to a spam attack. Having collected those names, you can also take preventive action against the spammers that haven't yet invaded your mail system. Several Web sites maintain a list of spammers you can add to your list of domains to filter. Try these sites, which I believe to be reliable:

http://www.rahul.net/falk/quickref.html

http://maps.vix.com/rbl/

http://www.webeasy.com:8080/spam/

Saving Filtered Messages

You may opt to save the filtered messages so you can examine them. One reason for doing this is to look at messages that are filtered for reasons other than keeping spammers out of your system. You may have some cogent and legal reason to keep mail from certain domains away from your users.

If you deselect the option to delete filtered messages when you're setting up the Filter Messages dialog box, Exchange Server uses a directory named TurfDir to hold the messages. Unfortunately, this doesn't work properly, so you have to take some steps to make it work.

The information about holding filtered messages in TurfDir is transferred to the registry. However, the TurfDir directory is not created on the root of the drive that Exchange Server is using. As a result, messages are not saved. No error message appears to tell you that the Save action failed (although you should see an item in the Application Log of the Event Viewer).

You have two choices to remedy the problem:

- Create \TurfDir manually.
- Create a different directory and change the registry to reflect the right location for saved filtered messages.

If you opt to use a directory other than \TurfDir, create the directory and then open a registry editor (in this example, I'm using Regedit) and make the following registry change:

1. Go to HKEY_LOCAL_MACHINE\System\CurrentControlSet\Services\MSExchangeIMC\Parameters\.
2. In the right pane, find the data item named TurfDir (see Figure 1-12).
3. Double-click the data item and enter the full path of the directory you created in the Value data text box. Then click OK to save the change.
4. Close the registry editor.

You must stop and restart the IMS in the Services utility in Control Panel to have the new registry settings take effect.

Caution Do not change the name of the item, it must be TurfDir. You are changing only the data value, which is a text string that names your directory.

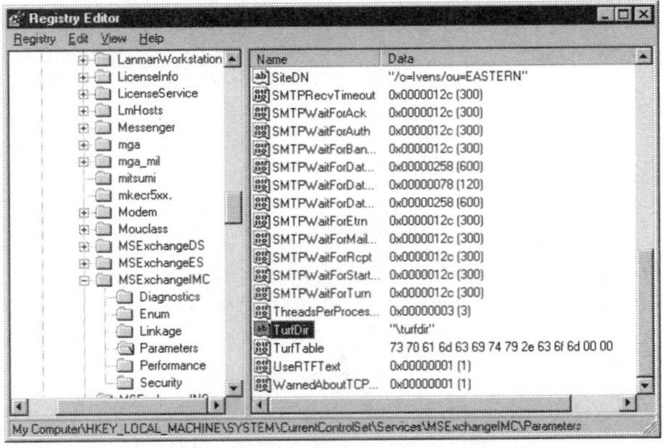

Figure 1-12. *The registry stores the location of saved filtered messages.*

Refusing Connections to Avoid Spamming

You can also tell Exchange Server to spurn connections from the domains of known spammers. When a domain connection is refused, mail from that domain is refused. In fact, nondelivery messages are sent back to the spamming domain (I love the thought of that; it seems so just).

Here's how to configure your Exchange Server system to refuse a connection:

1. In the left pane of the Exchange Server Administrator window, expand the site and select the Connections container.
2. From the right pane, double-click the IMS object you want to configure to refuse connections.
3. When the Properties dialog box appears, move to the Connections tab.
4. In the Accept Connections section of the dialog box, click Specify By Host to open the Specify Hosts dialog box (see Figure 1-13).
5. Click Add to add a domain to your list.
6. In the Add dialog box (see Figure 1-14, on the following page), enter the IP address and subnet mask of the domain for which you want to refuse a connection.
7. Select Reject Connection, then click OK.
8. Repeat for each domain you want to refuse a connection to. Then click OK twice to finish.

You must stop and restart the IMS in the Services utility of the Control Panel to put this new configuration into effect.

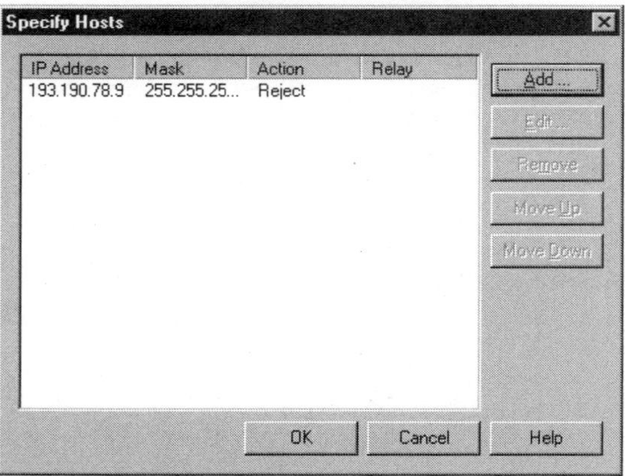

Figure 1-13. *Keep a list of Internet domains that you want to exclude from making a connection to your system.*

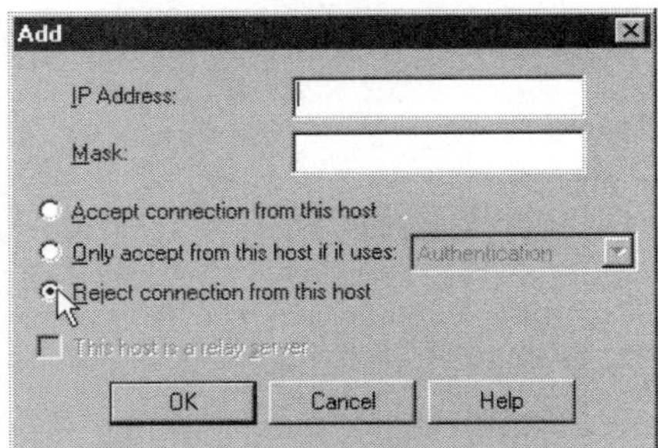

Figure 1-14. *You need to know the IP address and subnet mask of a domain if you want to refuse the connection.*

Tracking Messages

Messages get lost. Or perhaps it's more accurate to say that users report lost messages ("I sent it to Sam and he never received it"). Frequently the messages aren't really lost, and you can figure out what error occurred (frequently human). Reports of lost messages are high on the list of annoying Exchange maintenance chores. If you haven't been on the receiving end of a user "lost message" report (usually delivered in a whiney voice or an angry, self-righteous voice), that day is coming.

Sometimes, however, there really is a problem, and you need to track it down. In addition, sometimes you find that the troublesome message is causing a major blockage in your system.

In addition to looking for the problem when a message seems to be lost, tracking provides two other advantages. Turn on tracking to perform these maintenance chores, to see if you need to tweak your system:

- Analyze the routing of messages
- Analyze the time delay for messages

The trick to using tracking is that you have to plan ahead of time; you can't track a message if you haven't previously turned on the tracking feature. In this section I discuss the preparatory steps and the maneuvers involved in tracking messages.

Turning On Message Tracking

Message tracking is essentially log-keeping. However, Exchange Server does not track messages by default; you have to turn the feature on. And on, and on, and on. Exchange Server has a number of containers for which you might want to enable tracking, and you must perform this task for each container separately. There's no global command to turn on tracking everywhere. After message tracking is enabled, you can track messages. Do it now, quickly, before that first user shows up with a problem.

Here are the containers (along with their locations) you should configure for message tracking:

Note You may not have all of these containers; it depends on the services and connectors you installed in Exchange Server.

- **The Information Store** This is in the Configuration container under each site. The message tracking option is on the General tab.
- **The Message Transfer Agent** This is in the Configuration container under each site. The message tracking option is on the General tab.
- **The Internet Mail Connector** This is in the Configuration\Connections container under each site. The message tracking option is on the General tab. After you select the option, you must stop and restart the IMS in the Services utility of the Control Panel to have message tracking take effect. If you have multiple IMS connectors on the site, you must separately enable tracking for each of them.
- **The MS Mail Connector** This is in the Configuration\Connections container under each site. The message tracking option is on the Interchange tab. If you have multiple MS Mail connectors on the site, you must separately enable tracking for each one.
- **The cc:Mail Connector** This is in the Configuration\Connections container under each site. The message tracking option is on the Post Office tab.

The daily log files are held in the directory \Exchsrvr\Tracking.log. Each log file is named for its date, in the format <*Yyyymmdd*.log>, where <*yyyy*> is the year, <*mm*> is the month in two digits, and <*dd*> is the day in two digits. The \Tracking.log subdirectory is set up as a shared resource during the installation of Exchange Server, with the share name Tracking.log.

Configuring the Tracking Log Files

In addition to turning on message tracking, you need to configure a method for maintaining the log files. You can keep log files forever (or until you remove them manually), or configure your Exchange system to remove the files automatically after a specified number of days. This configuration task is performed in the Properties dialog box of the System Attendant.

To open the System Attendant Properties dialog box, expand the site and select the server you want to configure. Then double-click the System Container object in the right pane to open the Properties dialog box. As you can see in Figure 1-15, on the following page, the maintenance options for the tracking logs are on the General tab.

Either opt to retain all files (don't forget to do some housecleaning on a regular basis), or specify the number of days to keep old tracking logs.

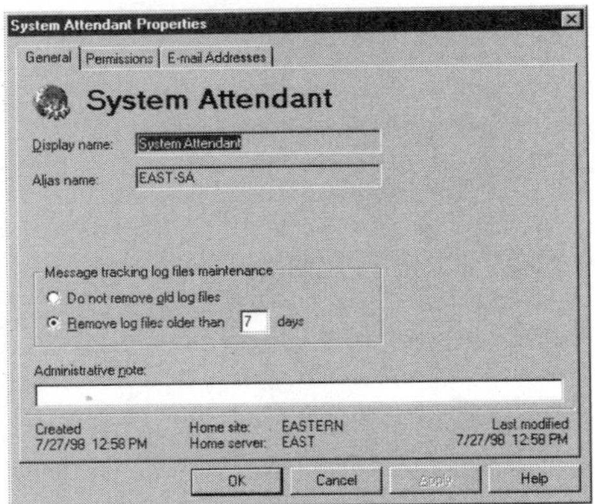

Figure 1-15. *You specify the way you want to maintain tracking logs for a server in the System Attendant object.*

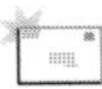

Note The containers that have the message tracking option are site containers. The System Attendant is a server container, so if you have multiple servers in the site, you need to configure the tracking log maintenance options for each server.

Moving the Tracking Log Files

If you have heavy mail traffic or you want to retain the log files for a while, the file sizes can grow quite large. It might be better to store them on another drive (if one is available). Here's how to reconfigure your Exchange system to write tracking information to log files that are in a new location:

1. Double-click the Services utility in the Control Panel, and stop the Exchange System Attendant service.
2. Copy the \Exchsrvr\Tracking.log directory to another drive. Be sure to create both the \Exchsrvr directory and the \Tracking.log subdirectory.
3. Open a registry editor and move to HKEY_LOCAL_MACHINE\System\CurrentControlSet\Services\MS ExchangeSA\Parameters. As you can see in Figure 1-16, the data item named LogDirectory displays the current location of the log files.
4. Open the LogDirectory data item and enter the new location in the dialog box in the format **newdrive:\Exchsrvr\Tracking.log.**

Tip If you use Regedit, the dialog box is named Edit String, and the text box into which you enter data is named Value Data. In Regedt32, the dialog box is named String Editor, and the entry text box is named String.

5. Click OK and close the registry editor.

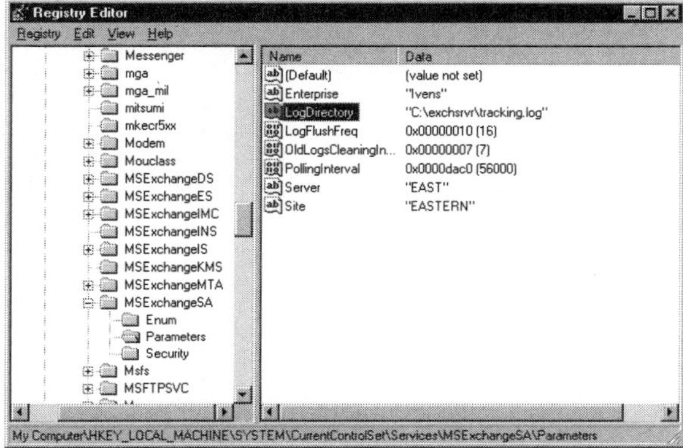

Figure 1-16. *The registry controls the location of the tracking logs.*

6. Restart the System Attendant service.
7. Delete the original \Tracking.log subdirectory.
8. Create a share on the new subdirectory (right-click the subdirectory and select Sharing), using the sharename Tracking.log.
9. Grant Administrators Full Control, Everyone Change, and the Exchange Server service account Full Control permissions to this share.

Tip If any administrator is in the middle of tracking messages, you see an error message when you attempt to delete the original subdirectory. When the administrator completes the task, you can remove the share. Don't forget to tell the other administrators about the new location, so that they don't think they're losing their minds.

Using the Tracking Tool

Exchange Server has a tracking tool available in the Administrator window, on the Tools menu. The tracking tool works by filtering criteria to identify the message you need to track, then tracing the message. The two parts are known as the Message Tracking Center.

Start by setting the criteria so you can locate the message:

1. From the Tools menu, choose Track Message.
2. In the Connect To Server dialog box, enter the name of the server you want to use.

Tip The server must be in your site, and the recipient or sender (depending on which of those elements you are using as search criteria) must be in the server's address list.

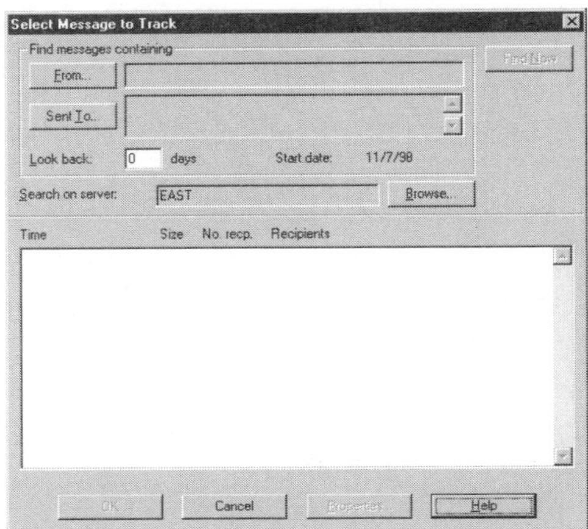

Figure 1-17. *Start your search by setting criteria for the message you need to track.*

3. In the Select Message To Track dialog box (see Figure 1-17), use the buttons to set the criteria for the message. You must select either a sender or a recipient.
4. If your criteria are based on the sender, click From to open a dialog box that displays all the addresses for the current server (see Figure 1-18). Select the sender you need, and click OK.
5. If your criteria are based on the recipient, click Sent To, which opens a dialog box that displays all the addresses for the server. Select the name you need and click Add, then click OK.

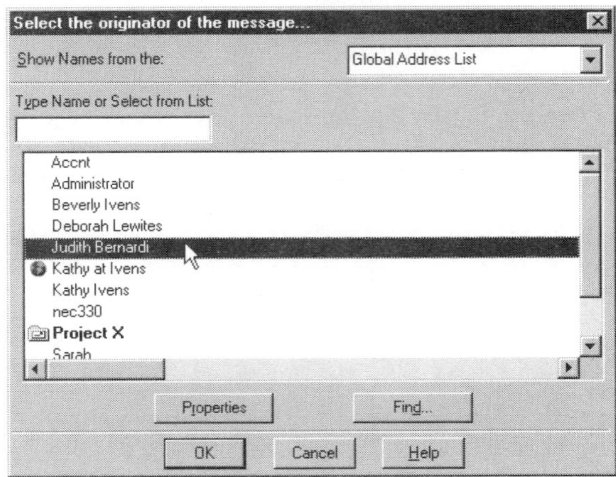

Figure 1-18. *Choose the user who sent the message you need to track.*

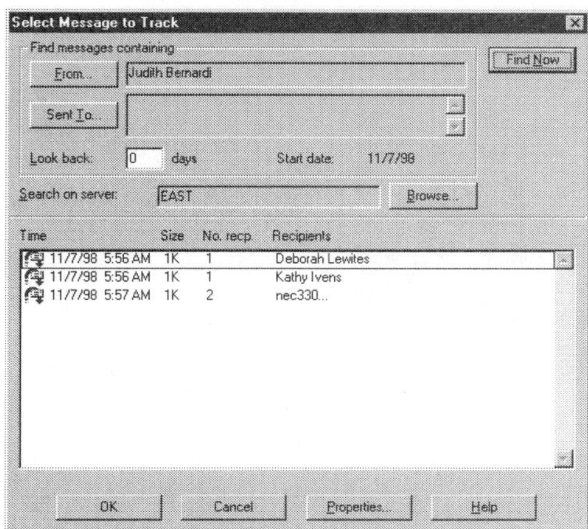

Figure 1-19. *The messages matching your criteria are displayed.*

6. Specify the number of days to look back, and then click Find Now.

The message(s) matching your criteria are displayed in the bottom of the dialog box (see Figure 1-19).

Select the appropriate message and click Properties to see the Message Properties shown in Figure 1-20.

Click Close to return to the Select Messages To Track dialog box, then click OK. This moves you to the next step, using the Exchange Server Message Tracking Center.

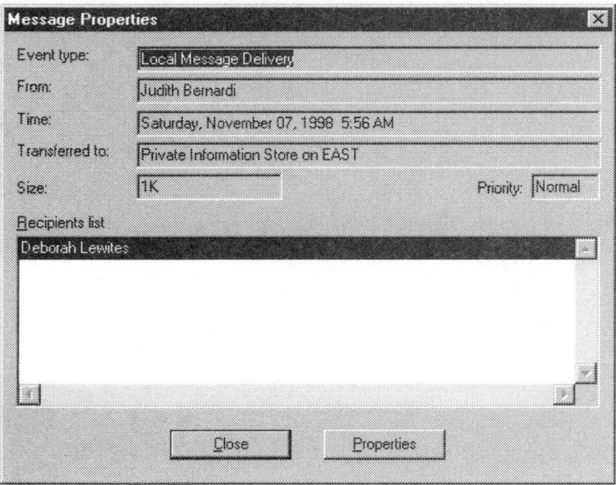

Figure 1-20. *This message was local, and it was transferred to the Private Information Store on the Server, so at least we know it didn't have a problem leaving the sender's Outbox.*

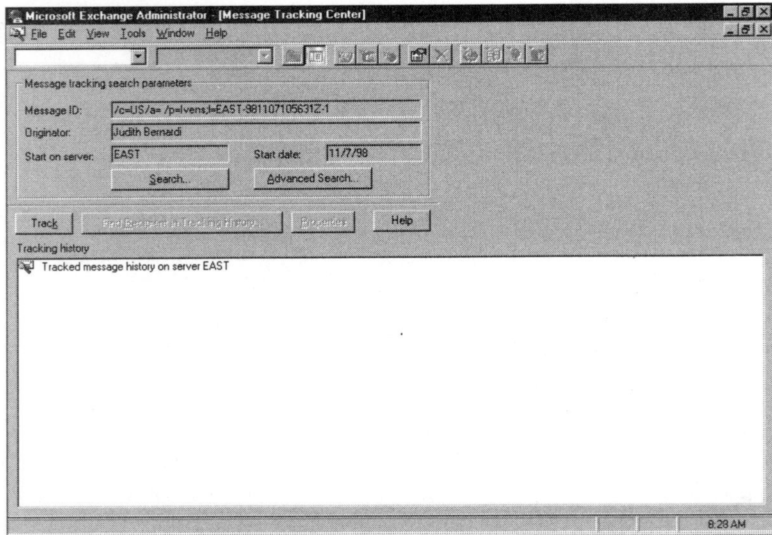

Figure 1-21. *Message properties, including the message ID, are displayed in the Message Tracking Center window.*

The Message Tracking Center

After you select the message, you're at the Exchange Server Message Tracking Center window, where you can track the message through your system (see Figure 1-21).

The Message Center can perform a trace that follows the selected message through the path it took in your system. You initiate the trace by clicking the Track button. Then, in the bottom of the dialog box, double-click the Tracking History object to expand it so you can see each step of the message's path through your system (see Figure 1-22).

Tracking with the Advanced Search Feature

You can use a different set of criteria by clicking Advanced Search. This function is required when the message you're tracking didn't have a sender or receiver on the current server's address list. Your search starts with the Advanced Search dialog box shown in Figure 1-23.

For each Advanced Search method (see the explanation that follows this section), establish your criteria and begin the search process (click Find Now).

Then perform the steps described in the preceding section to select a message and trace it.

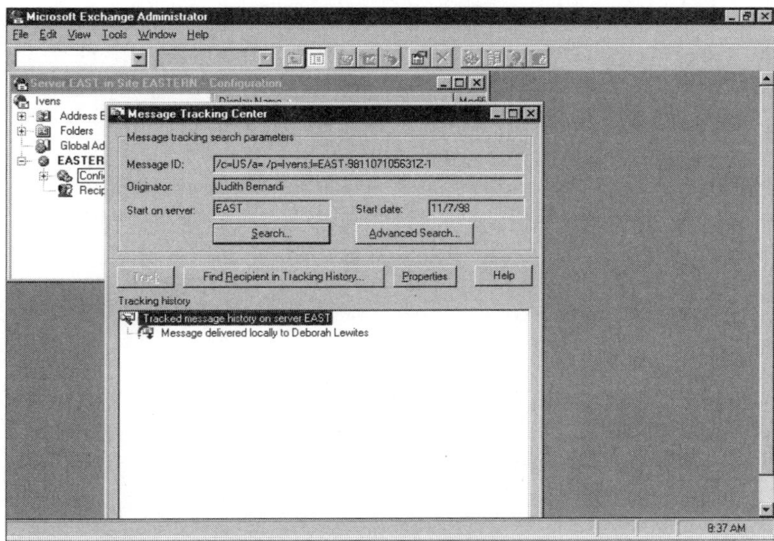

Figure 1-22. *The message's receiver is on the same server, so the trace shows one step.*

Tracking Messages Sent by Exchange Server

To locate any messages sent by the system, in the Advanced Search dialog box select Sent By Microsoft Exchange Server. Most of the time these items are status messages from one of the Exchange core components.

When you click OK, the Select System Message To Track dialog box opens. Complete the definition of your criteria with these actions:

1. Search a different server on the site by clicking the Browse button.
2. In the From text box, use the drop-down menu to select the core component you want to examine, as seen in Figure 1-24, on the following page.

Figure 1-23. *Start an Advanced Search operation by selecting the appropriate criteria.*

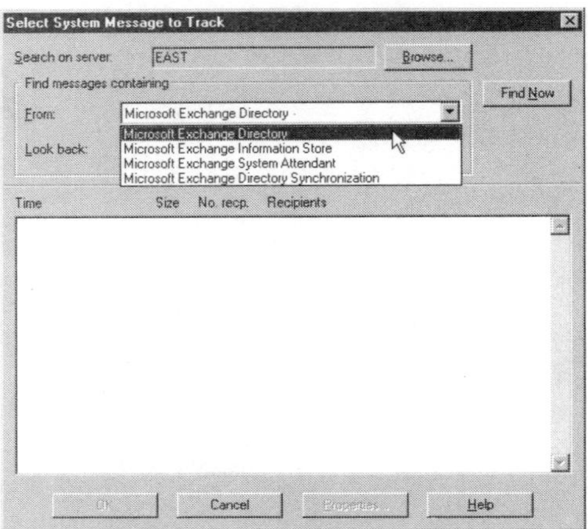

Figure 1-24. *Use the choices in the From text box to select the Exchange component you want to search.*

3. In the Look Back text box, specify the number of days you want to search through.
4. Click Find Now to begin the search.

Tracking Messages from Another Site

In the Advanced Search dialog box select Transferred Into This Site to locate messages that originated outside your Exchange Server site. The message may have arrived via a connector or a gateway. When the Select Inbound Message To Track dialog box opens (see Figure 1-25, on the following page), enter your criteria using these guidelines:

- If you want to search for a message from a particular sender, click From and select the name from the address list. The sender must be a custom recipient who has already been entered into the address list.
- If you want to search for a message that went to a specific recipient (or multiple recipients), click Sent To. The recipient(s) must be in the address list for your site.
- In the Transferred From text box, use the drop-down list to select the site connector that was used for the message.
- Specify the number of daily logs to search by entering a number in the Look Back box.
- Change the server you want to use for the search by clicking Browse.
- Click Find Now to begin the search.

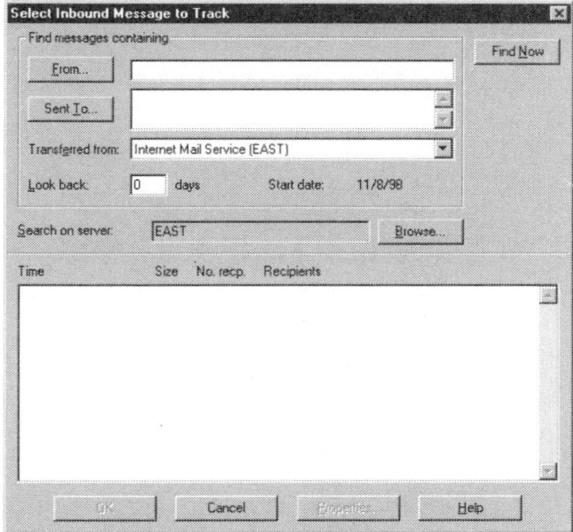

Figure 1-25. *You can track messages that arrived from an outside location.*

Tracking a Message by Using Its ID Number

If you know the message ID for the message you need to find, you can select the By Message ID option in the Advanced Search dialog box. This opens the Select Message To Track dialog box seen in Figure 1-26.

Obtaining a Message ID Number

There are two places to look for a message ID number: the daily log and the Outlook software on the client workstation.

You can open a daily log by double-clicking it from Microsoft Windows Explorer (it's a text file) and searching for a listing (use the sender or receiver, or just browse the file). As you can see in Figure 1-27, on the following page, the Message ID is preceded by the name of the server.

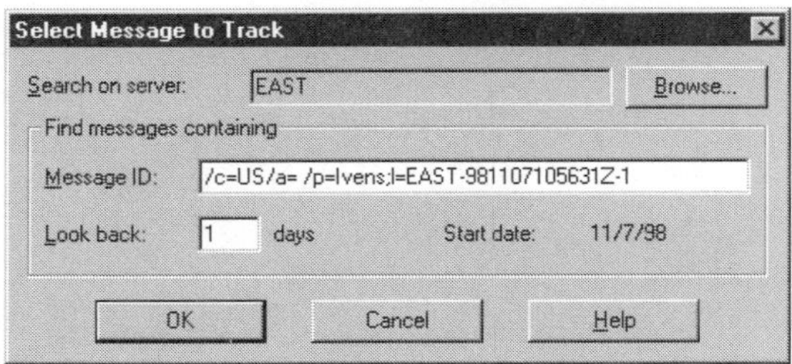

Figure 1-26. *If you know the message ID, you don't need any other criteria to begin the search.*

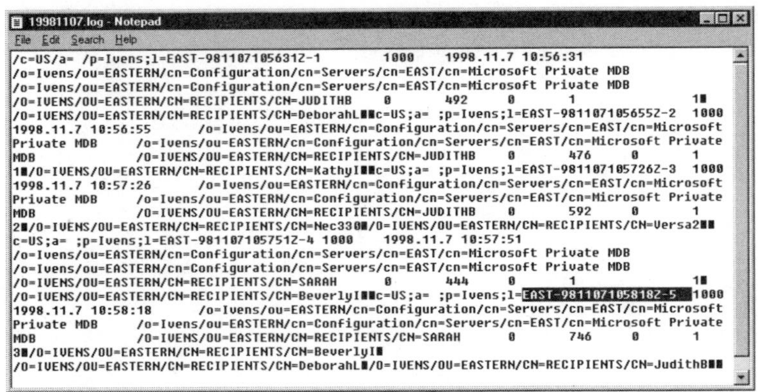

Figure 1-27. *Message IDs appear in the daily tracking log.*

You can also obtain the Message ID from the Outlook software of the user who is requesting the message tracking, by following these steps:

1. Open the message in question in the Outlook window.
2. Choose File from the menu bar, then choose Properties.
3. Move to the Message ID tab (see Figure 1-28).

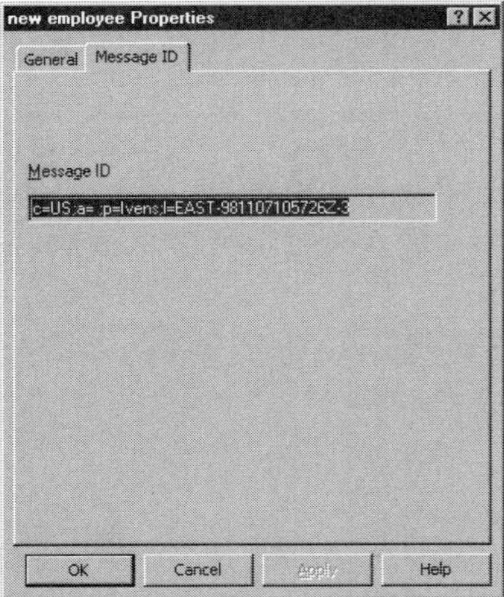

Figure 1-28. *Every message sent or received can have its properties examined for the information you need.*

Chapter 2

Managing the Private Information Store

Information Store Maintenance

Maintaining the Information Store (IS) is an important part of mailbox administration. Even though mailboxes are part of the Private Information Store, maintenance routines are performed on both the private and public stores.

Automatic IS Maintenance

Some maintenance routines are performed automatically on the IS, while your system is up and running. You can change the original configuration by selecting the server in the left pane of the Exchange Administrator's window and choosing Properties from the File menu. When the server's Properties dialog box appears (see Figure 2-1), move to the IS Maintenance tab to change the frequency and time that maintenance tasks are performed.

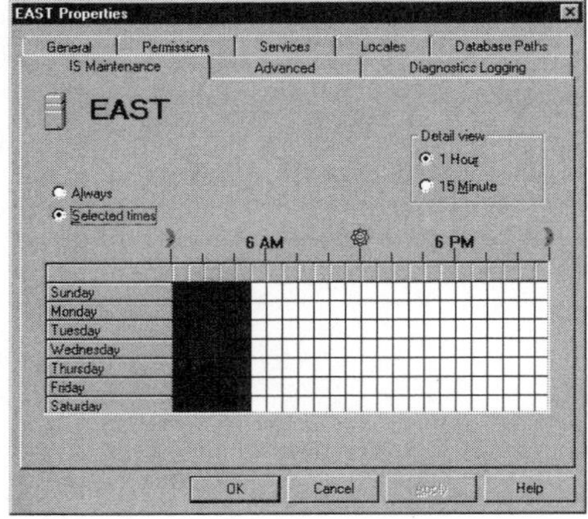

Figure 2-1. *Configure the Information Store maintenance schedule in the server's Properties dialog box.*

You should be careful to schedule maintenance at the time you expect your Exchange Server system to be the least busy. The server's response time for messaging activities is slower while maintenance tasks are being discharged.

Tip Never select Always as the schedule option because maintenance tasks will be performed every fifteen minutes. There is no way to meet that schedule and also handle messaging without bringing the server's response speed to "slower than an overweight snail."

Whether or not logging is enabled, the results of scheduled maintenance tasks are written to the Application events log.

One important element in regularly scheduled maintenance is an online defragmentation of the database. Sometimes the online defragmentation does not eliminate all the "air" in the database. You can check the results in the Application results log, as seen in Figure 2-2.

Offline IS Maintenance

Sometimes the online defragmentation does not work efficiently, and the Application event log shows a number of megabytes of free space, instead of the zero you see in Figure 2-2. (The most common time seems to be after a period of disk housecleaning, especially if old mailboxes are deleted.)

To keep your Exchange system running efficiently, the IS database needs to be as compact as possible. If the scheduled maintenance defrag doesn't empty all the air from the database, you can perform an offline defrag of the database. The procedure generally yields much better results than the regularly scheduled online procedure.

Before you begin, make sure you have free disk space equal to 110% of the database you're defragging. Priv.edb is the Private Information Store

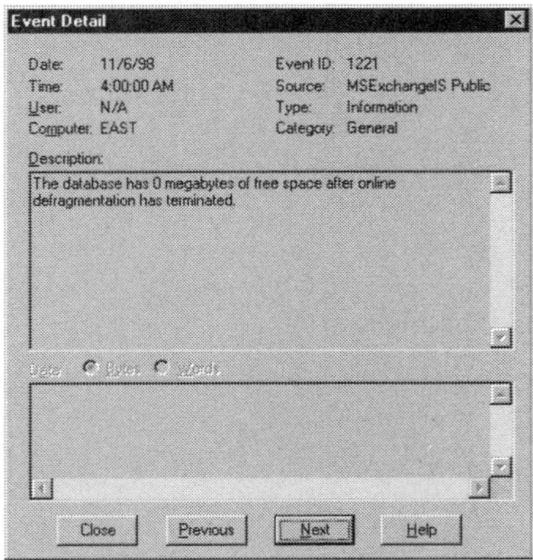

Figure 2-2. *This scheduled maintenance routine compacted the database properly.*

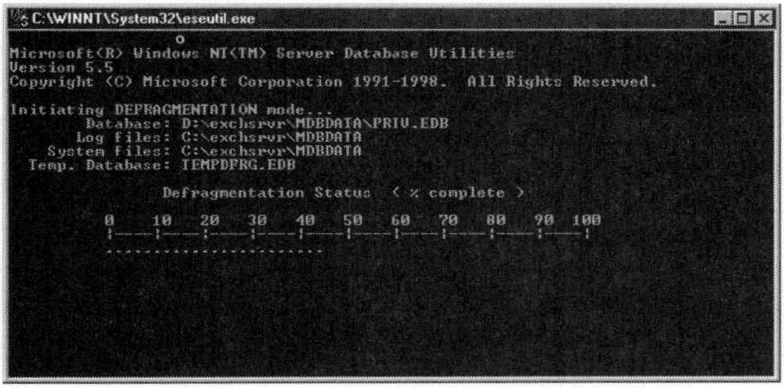

Figure 2-3. *Offline defragmentation of the database is accomplished from the command line.*

database, and Pub.edb is the Public Information Store database. You defrag them one at a time.

Here's how to defrag the IS database (which, of course, you will be doing late at night or very early in the morning).

1. Open the Services utility and stop the Microsoft Exchange Information Store service.
2. A dialog box may appear to tell you that other services must also be stopped. Write down the names of the other services (so you can start them again) and click OK.
3. From the Start menu, choose Run, and then enter **eseutil /d /ispriv** (to defrag the Private Information Store). A command window opens, and the defragmentation process runs (see Figure 2-3).
4. If you want to defrag the Public Information Store, enter the command **eseutil /d /ispub**.
5. Restart the Information Store Service in the Control Panel, along with any other services that were stopped.

It's a good idea to back up the Information Store immediately.

Moving Mailboxes

Balance the load! Load balancing keeps your system performance levels up (translate that as a synonym for "speedy") and therefore reduces the number of calls from users complaining that the system is slow (finding ways to reduce user complaint calls is the Exchange administrator's number-one priority).

One way to balance the load on your Exchange Server system is to split the mailboxes among multiple servers. You can relocate mailboxes rather easily, in either of two ways:

- Move mailboxes to another server on the site.
- Move mailboxes to another site.

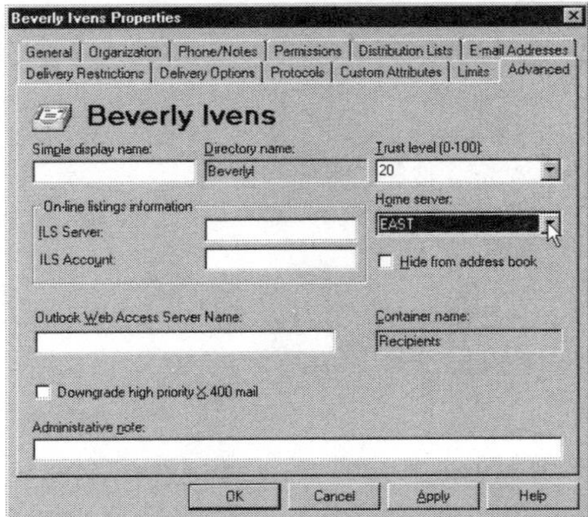

Figure 2-4. *The mailbox Properties dialog box has a field for relocating the mailbox.*

Moving Mailboxes to Another Server

A simple click of the mouse accomplishes the relocation of any mailbox to another server on the same site. Open the mailbox you want to move and move to the Advanced tab (see Figure 2-4).

Click the arrow to the right of the Home Server text box and select another server (all the servers on your site are displayed in the drop-down list). You're done (well, after you click OK).

If you are moving more than one mailbox (a highly probable action), you don't have to do so one mailbox at a time. Select multiple mailboxes using the Ctrl key. From the Tools menu, choose Move Mailbox. A small dialog box named Move Mailbox opens, displaying a list of all the servers on your site. Select the appropriate server and click OK.

Moving Mailboxes to Another Site

When an employee is transferred within the company, and that relocation means moving to another site, you need to move the employee's mailbox to that new site.

Using Exmerge.exe to Move Mailboxes Across Sites

The best, fastest, and most accurate way to move an employee's mailbox to a new site is to use Exmerge.exe, from the Microsoft BackOffice Resource Kit. It's a wizard, so all you have to do is supply information and answer questions. You also must be connected to the remote site.

Tip You can also use Exmerge.exe to transfer mailboxes between servers on the same site.

When you first launch the wizard, the opening window asks you to select the method you want to use to effect the transfer:

- One Step Merge copies the messages and folders from the mailbox(es) into a .pst file and then copies the file to the new mailbox. There's a check box available so that you can choose to delete the intermediate file as soon as the program ends. I advise you to deselect this option, because if it's enabled, the file is deleted even if the transfer fails.
- Two Step Merge separates the file's creation from the transfer of its contents to the new mailbox. This means you can create the file at one sitting, and then transfer the contents to the new mailbox at another time. This is useful if a one-step merge has failed, and you still have the .pst file.

Click Next after you make your choice, and follow these steps:

1. Enter the organization, site, and server of the current mailbox location (see Figure 2-5).
2. Click Options to display a dialog box that lets you limit the messages you're including in the transfer to a specific date range (based on message creation date). For instance, you may want to skip very old items.
3. In the next window, enter the information about the destination organization, site, and server. The organization and site are pre-entered (matching the previous window), so you can use the program to move a mailbox to another server in your site. Because you're changing sites, fill in the new site name in addition to the name of the target server.
4. The next window displays a list of all the mailboxes in the location you specified. Select the mailbox(es) you want to move.
5. The location of the .pst file that will be created is displayed in the next window. You can change the folder if you desire. The filename for each mailbox is *<useralias.pst>*.

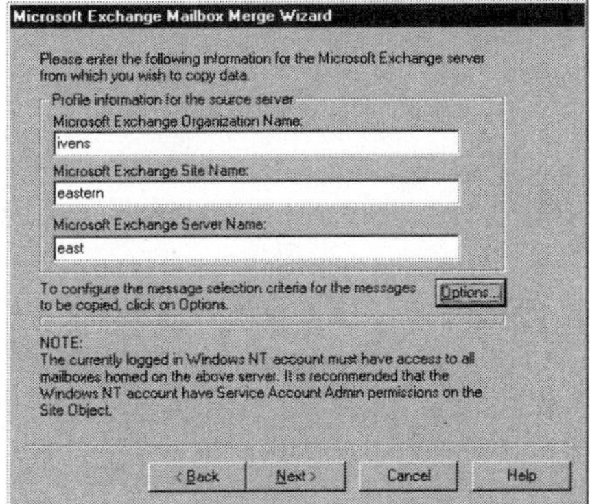

Figure 2-5. *Supply the information about the current site for the mailbox you want to move.*

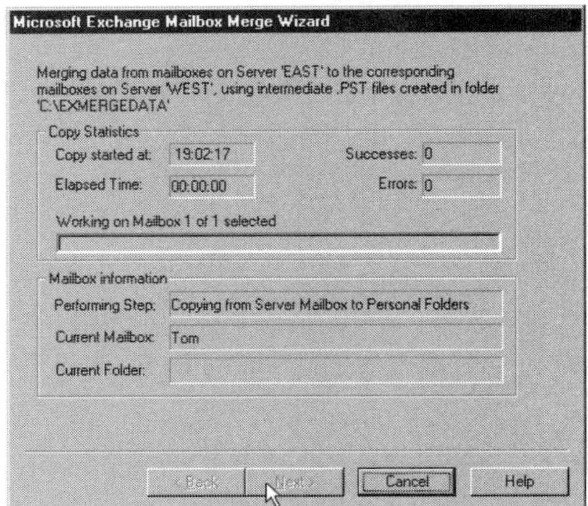

Figure 2-6. *The .pst file is imported into a new mailbox on the target server.*

6. Click Next to begin the transfer (see Figure 2-6). The new mailbox is created on the target server, and the contents of the .pst file are imported into the mailbox.

If you chose the two-step method, a window will ask you whether you want to create the file or transfer a file you've already created. The appropriate window is displayed.

If the operation fails, an error message announces that fact. If you want more information (and who wouldn't?), check the log file, c:\Exmerge.log. If you selected automatic deletion of the .pst file option, start all over again. If you opted to keep the file, select the two-step method and just effect the transfer.

If the operation is successful, delete the .pst file if you didn't opt to delete it automatically.

Moving Mailboxes Across Sites Manually

If you don't have Exmerge.exe, you must perform this task manually. This requires several procedures, some of which are performed in the Exchange Administrator window, and some of which are performed in the client software. In effect, you must replicate the work of Exmerge.exe by completing the following steps:

1. Create the new mailbox on the destination server.
2. In the client software, from the File menu, choose Import And Export.
3. In the Import And Export wizard, select Export To File and click Next.
4. In the next window, select Personal Folder File (.pst) as the target file type.
5. Select the Mailbox folder, and then select the option to include subfolders. (You can click Filter if you want to select certain item types for the export.)
6. The next window asks you to select from a number of options about handling duplicate items. The safest choice is to allow duplicate items to be created and then clean them up later (in the new site). The default filename is

displayed (Backup.pst), and you can change the location or filename or both by clicking Browse.

7. Click Finish to export the Mailbox data to the .pst file.
8. Copy the .pst file to the user's computer on the new site.
9. In the client software on the new site, activate the Import And Export wizard, choosing Import From Another Program Or File.
10. Select personal Folder File (.pst) as the file type.
11. Select the .pst file you created at the original site.
12. In the Global Address List, hide the mailbox on the original site until you know the new mailbox is working properly and the user is receiving mail there. Then you can delete the original mailbox.

Managing Address Books

One of your ongoing responsibilities as the Exchange Server administrator is the Global Address List (GAL), which includes every recipient in your organization: mailboxes, public folders, distribution lists, and custom recipients.

Another administrative chore is the maintenance of Offline Address Books (that's plural because Microsoft Exchange Server 5.5 can generate multiple versions of the OAB). These are downloaded by clients who work offline.

Maintaining the GAL

The GAL object is in the first level of objects in the Exchange Server hierarchy. By default, the entire list is available to every user in your organization. You can, however, create versions of the list, called Address Book Views (ABVs). These versions filter GAL recipients to match the needs of the users expected to avail themselves of a particular version. Notice that the object for these views is also on the first level under the organization. You can create subcontainers under the Address Book Views container to hold the views you build.

Adding and Removing Items from the GAL

The most common GAL maintenance tasks are adding and removing items. Mailboxes, distribution lists, and custom recipients can be created at the Exchange Server Administrator window. They are not, however, added directly to the GAL container. They're added at the site level, in the Recipients container. Then they're integrated into the GAL as replication occurs.

Use the various New commands on the File menu to create a new item for the GAL (New Mailbox, New Distribution List, and New Custom Recipient).

Tip If you haven't selected the Recipients container for the site when you use one of the New commands on the File menu, Exchange Server displays an error message that offers to take you there.

Hiding GAL Recipients

You can hide any of the four types of recipients in the address list. Hiding only prevents the recipient from being displayed in the GAL; it does not prevent the recipient from sending or receiving items. For instance, if a user knows the name of a hidden mailbox, he or she can enter the mailbox name in the To or Cc field of a message form, and the message will be delivered. The option for hiding a recipient is always on the Advanced tab of the Properties dialog box for the item you want to hide.

Maintaining Address Book Views

For a large organization, an Address Book View provides both efficiency and security. By creating multiple ABVs, you can prevent users from seeing any container other than their own home container (site or server). In effect, you're creating multiple virtual organizations within your company organization. The limited, smaller GAL that exists in an ABV is easier for clients to work with, and it also keeps users from seeing or accessing recipients in the other virtual organizations.

Tip If you permit customers or other outside organizations to communicate directly with your users through your Exchange Server system, the use of ABVs is an important security measure.

To create an ABV, specify the grouping attributes you want to use. Subcontainers are created automatically in a hierarchy under the Address Book Views container. Subcontainers for the first grouping are at the first level under the Address Book Views, subcontainers for the second grouping appear at the second level, and so on. You can have up to four grouping attributes and corresponding subcontainers. As part of the maintenance you perform, you can modify the existing groupings, or you can add additional ABVs and subcontainers.

Adding and Removing Recipients

After an ABV is defined, all the recipients that meet the criteria are automatically added to the view via the View Consistency Checker (VCC), which operates in the background (every five minutes). The Group By Attribute property (GBA) is used to generate the view. Changes made to the properties of a recipient (so as to include it in or exclude it from an ABV) must be made at the site where the recipient exists.

Deleting ABVs and Subcontainers

You can delete any empty subcontainer or any root-level ABV that has empty subcontainers. This step is common if you create ABVs for projects or for other nonpermanent reasons.

You can, however, run into a problem with ABVs that are filled with hidden recipients. You delete them, and five minutes later they're back. Hidden recipients aren't detected by the deletion process, and this can present a problem if the subcontainer contains only hidden recipients. What happens is that these recipients seem to be deleted (they disappear from the Administrator window). This is just a temporary illusion, because when VCC runs (within five minutes), the recipients are detected and the ABV subcontainer is re-created.

From the View menu, choose Hidden Recipients, and then change the properties so they no longer fit in the ABV.

Maintaining Offline Address Books

Offline Address Books are used by remote users. A remote user is a user who dials in from a remote site, or anyone on the network who chooses to work offline instead of maintaining a connection to the Exchange server. When these remote users connect to a Microsoft Exchange server computer, they can download OABs that list recipients who were specified when the OAB was created.

Remote users commonly exchange messages with a regular group of recipients and therefore can operate effectively with a subset of the GAL rather than the organization's entire GAL. In fact, most users have a limited number of recipients with whom they exchange messages, but it's not especially onerous for connected users to choose recipients from the GAL (they tend to transfer their oft-used entries to their personal address books). For remote users, the time involved in downloading the entire GAL is annoying, so the OAB is a welcome feature.

Note Two features new to Exchange Server 5.5 strengthen the OAB. One is that administrators can create subsets of the OAB, which effectively provides users with customized lists. The other is that downloading can be configured so that only the changes in the list since the last download are sent to the client, which saves connection time.

General Maintenance Tricks

In many organizations OAB problems abound with user calls tying up the help desk. These maintenance guidelines should help make it easier to keep OAB services running smoothly.

Specify a Separate OAB Server

The OAB is stored in a hidden folder, and you can change the default server for that folder (assuming you have a multiserver site). It's a good idea to specify a server that's not very busy with other tasks (especially the task of handling mailboxes and mail). The OAB files are both generated and stored in the server you designate. This is also the target server to which users are connected when they want to download. To change the server for OABs, follow these steps:

1. In the Exchange Server Administrator window, select the Configuration object for the site in the left pane.
2. In the right pane, double-click the DS Site Configuration object to open its Properties dialog box.
3. Move to the Offline Address Book tab.
4. In the Offline Address Book Server list box, select a server from the list.

Use an Effective Generation Schedule

You want to keep your OABs current, but generating a new list can be time-consuming if the list is large, and you change or add listings to the GAL frequently. To design a generation schedule that balances those needs, use the Offline Address Book Schedule tab of the DS Site Configuration Properties dialog box (see Figure 2-7).

Tip If you make a lot of changes to the GAL, click the Generate All button on the Offline Address Book tab of the DS Site Configuration Properties dialog box to force a manual generation immediately.

Don't Forget Your Legacy Exchange Client Users

Unless you enjoy hearing screaming complaints from users, make sure you generate your OABs so that any users who run Microsoft Exchange Client Versions 4.0 and 5.0 can download the list. If the list isn't compatible, those clients receive an error message when they choose the Download Address Book command from the Tools menu.

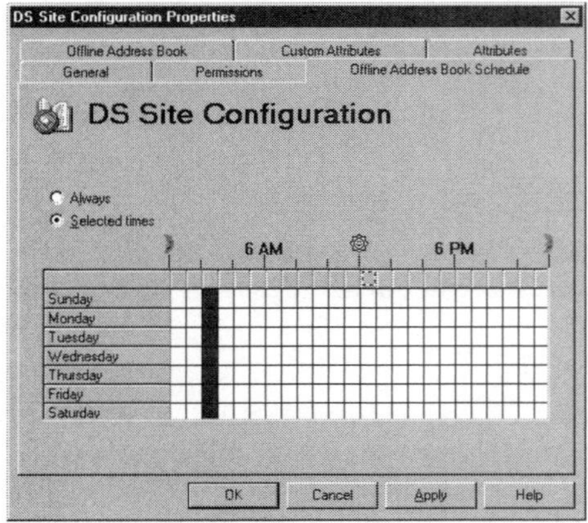

Figure 2-7. *Use the grid to specify when you want to generate updates to your Offline Address Books.*

By default, Exchange Server 5.5 does not produce OABs that are compatible with that legacy client software. Select the check box for compatibility that's on the Offline Address Book tab of the DS Site Configuration Properties dialog box. You must regenerate the OABs after you select the compatibility feature.

Explain the Options to Client Users

Because some users aren't sure which options to select when they download the OAB, it's a good idea to generate a publication that explains the choices (send it by e-mail). Of course, you'll still get calls and queries, but this action should reduce the number.

Exchange 5.5 offers far more options for the level of information available in an OAB, so there's now a choice named Full Details on the Outlook client.

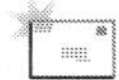

Note The information available with Full Details includes First Name, Middle Initial, Last Name, Display Name, Alias, Address, City, State, Postal Code, Country, Title, Company, Department, Office, Assistant, Phone, Manager and Direct Reports, Business Phone, Business Phone 2, Fax, Assistant, Home Phone, Home Phone 2, Mobile, Pager, Notes, Distribution List Membership, and E-mail Address.

In addition, individual names for distribution lists are not downloaded (although all or some of them may already be included in the local OAB).

Creating Organization-Wide OABs

The default list for the OAB contains the recipients at your site. You can, however, create organization-wide OABs by completing the following steps:

1. Select the Configuration container for your site.
2. In the right pane, double-click the DS Site Configuration object to display the Properties dialog box.
3. Move to the Offline Address Book tab.
4. Click Add.
5. In the Offline Address Book Container window, select the GAL container.

The GAL is added to the OAB list and is available for download.

Tip If you have a large organization with many recipients, it's only fair to caution your users that the download of an OAB that contains the GAL could take quite a bit of time. In fact, over a modem, the phrase "an excruciatingly long time" comes to mind. To shorten the download period, you can suggest that users download the entire OAB the next time they're in the office and can connect the PC to the Microsoft Exchange Server using the LAN. Thereafter, when working remotely, they can download the changes.

Chapter 3

Troubleshooting Mailboxes

I've found some common themes in the mailbox management problems Exchange administrators report. Because you're likely to encounter the same difficulties, I address them in this chapter.

Of course, mailbox problems are frequently associated with the Private Information Store, an area I also cover here.

Private Information Store Seems Too Large

After you've worked out all the mathematics and have configured mailbox sizes so as to keep your IS size at a reasonable level, you notice that the size of Priv.edb seems too large. Or perhaps backup or replication is taking longer than it should.

Frequently, the cause of these problems is the amount of disk space being used for the retention of deleted items. Even if you configured your system to remove deleted items after a short interval, deleted items can take up a lot of disk space. You can shorten the time you hold on to deleted items, but that's almost a guarantee that you'll face some user with a tale of woe about the need to recover an item.

Viewing Deleted Item Storage Size

Many administrators track deleted file usage for each recipient and then adjust the settings for those with large amounts of deleted files occupying disk space. I've seen users who seem to be on the Cc: list for every piece of mail generated within the organization, and even though messages are deleted after the contents are noted, each hour brings a fresh supply of mail that takes up too much disk storage space. You can shorten the number of days that deleted files are held for those users, and leave other users at the IS default setting.

You can keep an eye on the amount of disk space that deleted items are occupying on a mailbox-by-mailbox basis. To view this information, add a column for deleted items to the Mailbox Resources object:

1. In the Administrator window, expand the server with the Private Information Store for which you want to track deleted items.
2. Expand the Private Information Store object in the left pane.

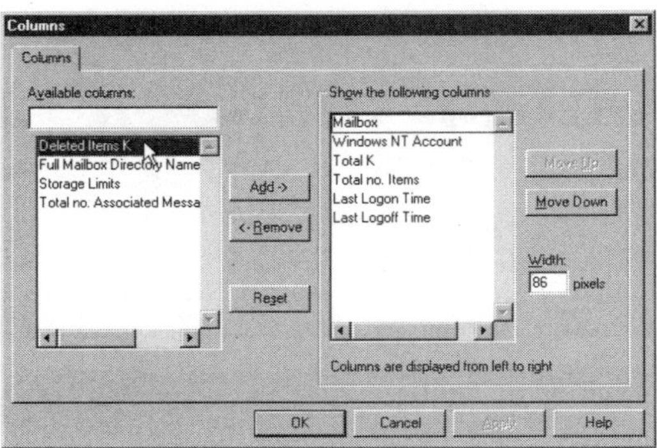

Figure 3-1. *You can decide what information you want to track in the Mailbox Resources object.*

3. Select the Mailbox Resources object.
4. From the View menu, choose Columns to see the Columns dialog box, shown in Figure 3-1.
5. Double-click Deleted Items K; this moves that column into the right pane, which contains the list of columns shown in the Mailbox Resources window.
6. Click OK.

When you're working in the Columns dialog box, you may want to consider performing two other tasks:

- **Eliminate any columns that display information you don't care about.** Double-click any column heading in the right pane (the columns that are displayed) to move it to the left pane (the columns that aren't displayed).
- **Change the order of the column display.** Select a column heading and click Move Up or Move Down to change the order of display (in the Mailbox Resources window, the top-to-bottom display order is changed to left-to-right).

Mailbox Resources Tab of the Private IS You can select the Private Information Store in the Administrator's window (expand the Server container) and open the Properties dialog box. When you look at the Mailbox Resources tab you see the same information displayed in the Mailbox Resources container. You can add columns to this tab, just as you can with the Mailbox Resources container.

These two windows don't communicate, however, and if you make changes in one place, those changes aren't updated in the other. To avoid confusion, select the Mailbox Resources window you want to work in, and do all your configuration changes and viewing from that window.

Mailbox Missing in Server Mailbox Resources List

Information about mailboxes on a particular server is located in the server container, in the object named Mailbox Resources (under the Private Information Store container). You can access a Mailbox Properties dialog box by selecting Mailbox Resources in the left pane of the Administrator window and then double-clicking the mailbox of interest in the right pane. This is commonly the location in which administrators who are responsible for a server do their work. (If the server is in a multiserver site, the complete list of mailboxes for all servers in the site is found in the site's Recipients container.)

When an administrator for a server creates a new mailbox, an object for that mailbox is created in the site's Recipients container. Note, however, that the mailbox does not appear in the server's Mailbox Resources list. Using logic, most administrators refresh the view, only to find that the refresh action doesn't help.

Tip In the Administrator window, the Refresh command is not located in the View menu (the common location for the command in Windows software). Instead, you can find it in the Window menu. Also, the standard Windows shortcut for Refresh, F5, works if you don't want to hunt for the command.

Don't worry; you're not losing your mind. You did create a mailbox; it does exist (check the Recipients container for the site). Exchange doesn't recognize what you created as a mailbox in the server's resources until there's been mailbox activity—either the user must log on to the mailbox, or the mailbox must receive a message.

There's a reason for this behavior: When you create a new mailbox, a directory object is created at the same time. The server's Mailbox Resources display, however, is obtained from the Information Store. No object is created in the Information Store until a mailbox is used, either by user logon to the mailbox or by the receipt of a message in the mailbox.

When you view the server's Mailbox Resources object, you see more information about a mailbox than you can get from the Recipients container. In addition to viewing the Properties dialog box, you can also see mailbox statistics (see Figure 3-2, on the following page).

To avoid that moment of panic, get into the habit of sending a message to a new mailbox as soon as you create it. A simple note welcoming the user to his or her mailbox does two things: it tests the new mailbox, and it forces the display of the mailbox in the server's Mailbox Resources.

Building Reports for Deleted Item Storage Size

If you have a substantial number of mailboxes, you may not want to scroll through the Mailbox Resources window to learn which ones you need to adjust. You can build reports that give you the necessary information, sorted the way you prefer.

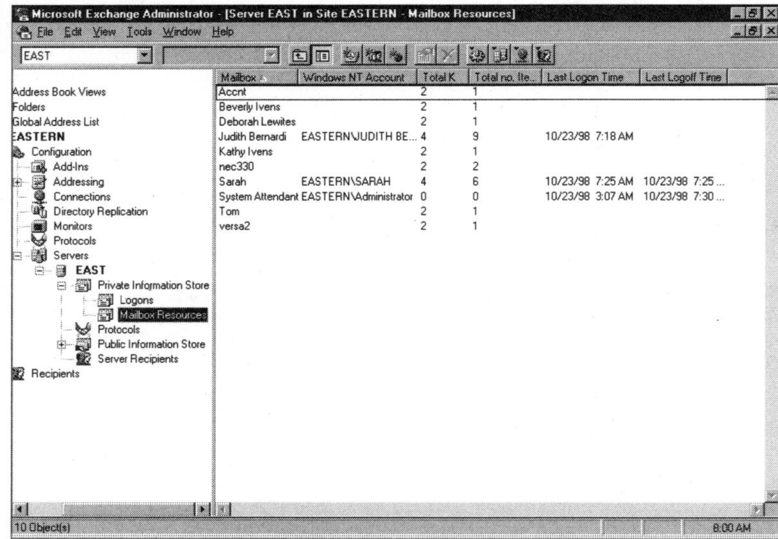

Figure 3-2. *Usage statistics for mailboxes can be viewed from the server's Mailbox Resources container.*

You can export the information in the Mailbox Resources window to a file, and then open that file in a spreadsheet application. You can sort the spreadsheet by the size of the deleted items to gain information about individual mailboxes, or you can track the total space occupied by deleted items against total disk size. To export data use the following steps:

1. In the left pane of the Administrator window, select the Mailbox Resources object.
2. Click anywhere in the right pane to activate the pane.
3. From the File menu, choose Save Window Contents to open the Save Window Contents dialog box.
4. Use the Save In text box to move to the folder you want to use.
5. Name the file.
6. Click Save.

By default the file is saved as a comma-delimited file (.csv). When you open the file in a spreadsheet application the column headings are automatically inserted as labels.

Tip Third-party tools providing powerful analysis capabilities are available. For example, Crystal Reports has developed a number of tools for developing reports from Exchange Server data.

Diagnostics Logging

Turning on diagnostic logging for Exchange Server components can help you in your troubleshooting efforts. When logging is turned on, the results are written to the Microsoft Windows NT Application Event Log. If you can't find the source of your problem (or you're not sure where to look), it's a good idea to turn on diagnostics logging. To turn on diagnostic logging on the Properties dialog box for each component, open the Properties dialog box and move to the Diagnostics Logging tab.

Here are the components that have a Diagnostics Logging tab in their Properties dialog box:

- Directory Service
- Directory Synchronization
- Internet Mail Connector
- Information Store (both Private and Public)
- cc:Mail Connector
- MS Mail Connector
- Message Transfer Agent
- Protocols IMAP4, NNTP, POP3

You can get an idea of the various levels of logging available by viewing the Logging tab in the Server Properties dialog box. Select the server and from the File menu, choose Properties, then move to the Diagnostics Logging tab (see Figure 3-3).

The higher the level of logging, the larger your log files are, so you must develop a plan to remove the files quickly (back them up first so that you can inspect them at your leisure). In addition, the flood of information that's delivered to the events

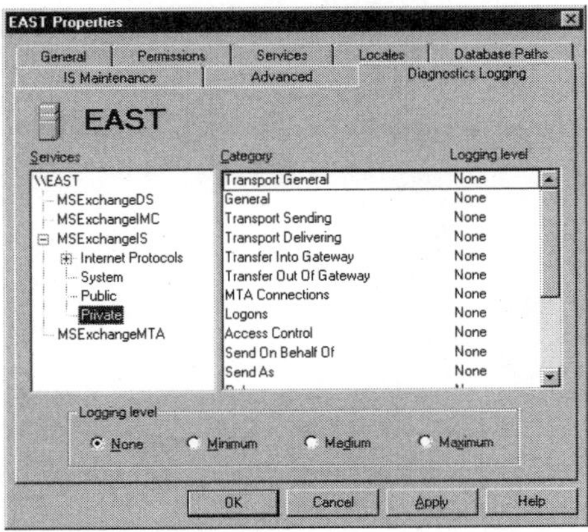

Figure 3-3. *Set diagnostic logging options to help solve problems.*

log will negatively affect performance. These tricks can help you diagnose problems and still keep a sane level of logging:

- Select high logging levels only for components that are giving you a problem.
- Where you have choices of events, select high logging levels for only one or two items at a time. Note which items you've tested so that you don't accidentally repeat yourself.

Tip The best way to use diagnostic logging in your troubleshooting efforts is to continually increase the logging level until you have enough information to determine the source of the problem.

Maintaining the Event Log

If you turn on diagnostics logging, you should complete the following steps to make sure the settings for the Application Log are configured for efficiency, and to avoid any problems:

1. Open the Event Viewer in the Administrative Tools section of the Programs menu.
2. Choose Log, then choose Log Settings.
3. In the Event Log Settings dialog box (see Figure 3-4), select the Applications log from the drop-down list.
4. Make any changes you feel are needed.

When making changes in the event log configuration, follow these guidelines:

- The size of the log is changed by 64k as you click the spin buttons. If you have plenty of disk space, and you've enabled a number of diagnostics logging options, it's not harmful to make the log file quite large.
- If you opt to maintain the log by any means other than Overwrite Events As Needed, you'll probably see messages telling you that the event log is full (unless you're a zealous administrator who checks and clears the log constantly). A full event log isn't a fatal error, but it does mean that your

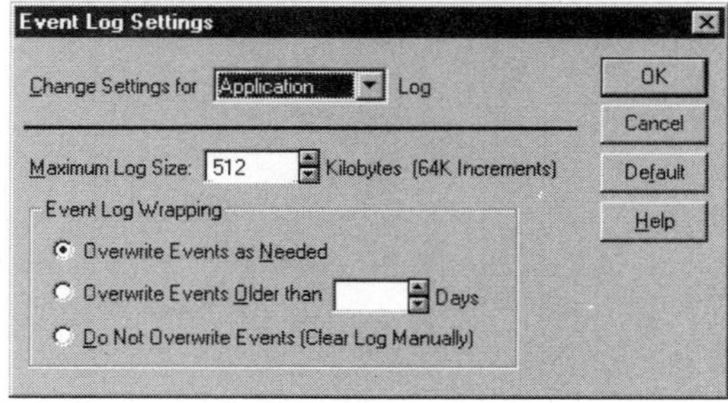

Figure 3-4. *In the Event Log Settings dialog box you can change the size of the log, change the way it adds items, or both.*

diagnostics logging stops until you clear out the log manually. Configuring the log to overwrite every *x* number of days (even if *x*=1) won't stop the log from filling up if you've turned on a lot of diagnostics logging.

Also remember that some events are written to the log in addition to the diagnostic logging criteria you set. For example, on my system I've given mailbox permissions to users who need to get into other users' mailboxes. Every time one user opens another user's mailbox, an event is written to the log. Because this occurs frequently in my office, the first-in-first-out nature of the log means I could miss important events if I don't check the log frequently. I've learned that yelling "So what? She has permission" at the monitor doesn't stop this activity; in fact, there's absolutely no way to disable it. I've increased the size of the log to accommodate this annoying practice. (I'm told that some administrators prefer to be notified of these actions; I just wish there were a configuration option for it.)

Diagnostics Logging for the IMS

There are some special considerations for diagnostics logging for the Internet Mail Service. To enable logging, expand the Site and select the Connections container. Double-click the Internet Mail Service connection you want to work with to display the Properties dialog box, and move to the Diagnostics Logging tab (see Figure 3-5).

Two of the choices—the SMTP Protocol Log (Simple Mail Transfer Protocol) and the Message Archival Log—work in a different way from standard diagnostics logging procedures.

Figure 3-5. *The Internet Mail Service provides a number of categories for diagnostic logging.*

SMTP Protocol Log

Enabling the SMTP Protocol Log does not write events to the event viewer. Instead, log files are kept in \Exchsrvr\IMSdata\log. Here are the salient facts:

- The SMTP Protocol Log is for incoming messages only.
- Each connection creates its own log.
- The logs are text files.

Table 3-1 shows the results of the available logging levels for the SMTP Protocol Log.

Table 3-1. Results of Selecting a Level for the SMTP Protocol Log

Level	Action
None	No text logs are created.
Minimum	Connection information is written to the log.
Medium	SMTP commands and headers are written to the log.
Maximum	Complete packets are written to the log.

If you opt for Maximum logging, every incoming message that is not sealed or encrypted is written in its entirety to the log. Anyone with access to the log file can read everyone's incoming messages (along with the diagnostic information you were searching for when you turned on the feature). In addition, the log files will grow inordinately large in a very short period of time. Think carefully about the ramifications of this action.

Message Archival Log

The Message Archival Log, like the SMTP Protocol Log, writes to its own log files instead of using the event log:

- Diagnostic logging for incoming messages is written to log files in \Exchsrvr\Imcdata\In\Archive.
- Diagnostic logging for outgoing messages is written to log files in \Exchsrvr\Imcdata\Out\Archive.

If you select either Medium or Maximum as the logging level, the text of every message is written to the log files. You can run out of disk space in a hurry if you choose this logging option and level.

Activating either the SMTP Protocol Log or the Message Archival Log requires some serious considerations, including legal questions. Your industry, your country, and your state may have laws or court precedents that your efforts can breach. Check with the company lawyer. You might also want to read the information available from the Electronic Messaging Association, which can be reached at *http://www.ema.org/*.

Using Performance Monitor

The Microsoft Windows NT Performance Monitor is a handy tool for troubleshooting. When you install Exchange Server, the following objects are added to the PerfMon configuration:

- MSExchangeDB
- MSExchangeDS
- MSExchangeIS
- MSExchangeIS Private
- MSExchangeIS Public
- MSExchangeMSMI
- MSExchangeMTA
- MSExchangeMTA Connections
- MSExchangePCMTA (added with Service Pack 2)

Each of these objects has a number of counters you can use to analyze performance as you troubleshoot problems.

In addition, the Exchange program group contains eight preconfigured PerfMon objects that are server-based.

Tip When you open a PerfMon window, there's no title bar and no menu bar. Double-click anywhere in the window to display those items.

Health Monitor

The Server Health Monitor measures memory and processor usage (see Figure 3-6). Here are some things to look for:

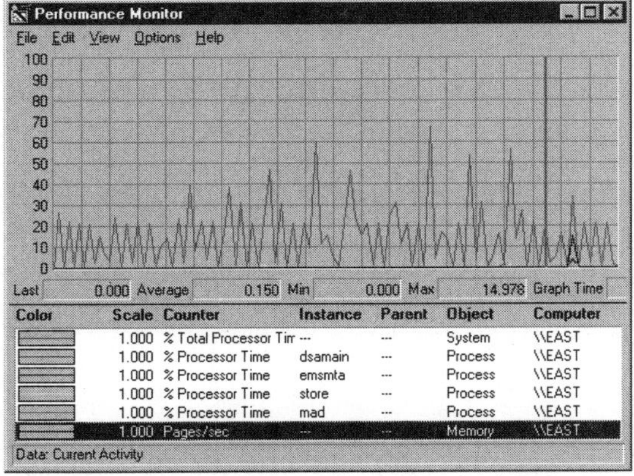

Figure 3-6. *Use the Server Health Monitor to keep an eye on the processor's workload to determine whether your server is performing efficiently.*

- If the % Processor Time measurement is in the teens, either your server is underutilized (probably not) or a service isn't running (more probable). Check the Services utility in the Control Panel.
- If the % Processor Time measurement is approaching 90% and remains at that level for some time, your server is overworked. Offload some functions or mailboxes to another server.
- The Pages/Sec counter is tracking the writes to the paging file. If the value is greater than 5 for an extended period, you should add RAM to the computer.

History Monitor

This monitor measures what its name implies—a history of the messaging work it's been doing since startup. The important measurement is the Work Queue Length, which tells you whether the server has been having a problem getting messages delivered. Problems could include a stuck message or a communication problem with other servers.

IMC Monitors

There are three monitors for the Internet Mail Connector (IMC):

- IMC Queues
- IMC Statistics
- IMC Traffic

Each IMC monitor displays the flow of traffic through the IMC, and each clearly explains what it's counting in the legend at the bottom of the window.

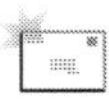

Note The name IMC was changed to IMS in Exchange 5.5, but the folks in charge of the Performance Monitors didn't get around to changing the name in the applications.

Load Monitor

The Load Monitor tracks several operations:

- The rate at which recipients submit and receive messages
- Client browse operations on the address book
- The number of associations with other Message Transfer Agents (MTAs)
- Replication updates

This monitor is most useful to ascertain the size of the load the server is handling.

Queues Monitor

You can use the Queues Monitor to keep an eye on the number of messages in the work queue. These are messages that have not yet been completely processed by the MTA. Both send and receive queues are shown (for both the Public and Private stores).

Users Monitor

The Users Monitor shows you the number of users connected to the IS. I guess it's a way to see how popular your e-mail system is with employees.

Using Event Viewer

Exchange writes significant events (and also writes not-very-significant events) to the Application Log of the Windows NT Event Viewer. Consult the section on Diagnostics Logging to learn how to set up event logging.

You can save log files to examine later, which is a good idea if you have an Error event (the error number is usually important if you have to call Microsoft for support).

Using the Performance Optimizer

There's a nifty tool called the Performance Optimizer. You saw it when you installed Exchange Server (it runs after the last step of installation). It's actually a wizard, and it examines your Exchange system and makes recommendations about your use of memory and disk space. Launch it from the Exchange Server program group.

Before you start, however, you should know that the Performance Optimizer stops all Exchange services, so it's not a good idea to run this on Monday at 9 A.M., when your entire user group is fetching e-mail. This is a middle-of-the-night process. You should also do a full backup first.

Like all wizards, the Performance Optimizer has numerous questions for you (see Figure 3-7). You start by reading the first page (it's informational); then click Next to get started.

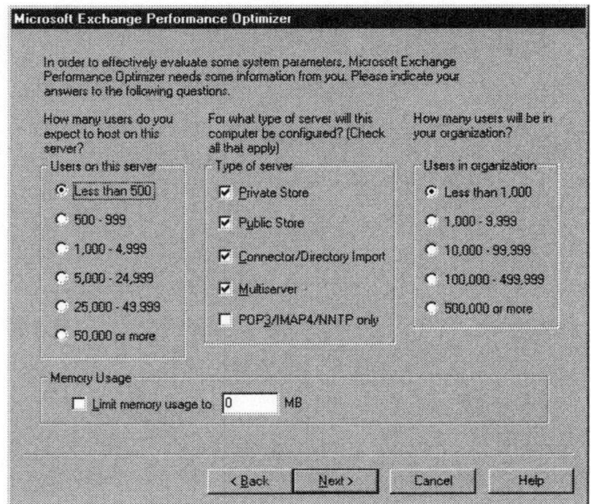

Figure 3-7. *The Performance Optimizer wants to know about the server and the organization.*

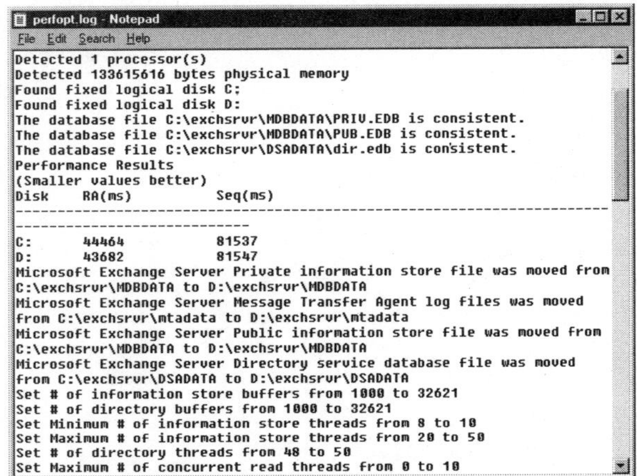

```
Detected 1 processor(s)
Detected 133615616 bytes physical memory
Found fixed logical disk C:
Found fixed logical disk D:
The database file C:\exchsrvr\MDBDATA\PRIV.EDB is consistent.
The database file C:\exchsrvr\MDBDATA\PUB.EDB is consistent.
The database file C:\exchsrvr\DSADATA\dir.edb is consistent.
Performance Results
(Smaller values better)
Disk    RA(ms)          Seq(ms)
--------------------------------------------------------------------------
----------------------------
C:      44464           81537
D:      43682           81547
Microsoft Exchange Server Private information store file was moved from
C:\exchsrvr\MDBDATA to D:\exchsrvr\MDBDATA
Microsoft Exchange Server Message Transfer Agent log files was moved
from C:\exchsrvr\mtadata to D:\exchsrvr\mtadata
Microsoft Exchange Server Public information store file was moved from
C:\exchsrvr\MDBDATA to D:\exchsrvr\MDBDATA
Microsoft Exchange Server Directory service database file was moved
from C:\exchsrvr\DSADATA to D:\exchsrvr\DSADATA
Set # of information store buffers from 1000 to 32621
Set # of directory buffers from 1000 to 32621
Set Minimum # of information store threads from 8 to 10
Set Maximum # of information store threads from 20 to 50
Set # of directory threads from 48 to 50
Set Maximum # of concurrent read threads from 0 to 10
```

Figure 3-8. *Details about the steps taken to optimize your system are available in the Perfopt.log file.*

After you click Next, the Performance Optimizer begins analyzing your system. This takes some time, so get a cup of coffee or do some work on another computer. When the analysis is complete, click Next.

Your current locations for all Exchange Server files are displayed, and there may be suggestions for moving some files to other drives. You can make changes if you disagree with a suggestion. Then click Next.

The Performance Optimizer offers to take care of moving the files for you. Unless you failed to make a backup, select the option to move the files automatically and click Next.

When the adjustments are complete, click the Finish button to restart all the services. If you want to see what happened, open \Winnt\System32\Perfopt.log (see Figure 3-8).

Part II

Client Software

Most Microsoft Exchange administrators spend more time working with client software than they spend working in the Exchange Administrator window.

Helping users configure and use client software is a time-consuming task. Additionally, consider all the time you spend helping users resolve problems and recover from mistakes.

The Exchange client software applications are robust and complicated. Users call on the Exchange administrator whenever they have a special need that requires tweaking or changing the configuration of their software. They call for help when a process doesn't perform as expected. They call in a panic when they see an error message.

The chapters in this section are designed to help you maintain and troubleshoot the client software that works with Microsoft Exchange Server.

Chapter 4

Maintaining Client Software

As a Microsoft Exchange Server administrator, you're going to spend quite a bit of time in front of workstations, working with client software. Whether you're holding training seminars, helping a user solve a particular need, or just configuring the software for a user who's unsure of the procedures, it's a safe bet that you'll have to know Microsoft Outlook extremely well.

E-Mail Delivery

Users can elect to have e-mail delivered to one of three locations, and this choice is frequently confusing. In addition, users occasionally want to change the location of their receiving mailbox. The three possible locations are

- Server mailbox
- Personal folder
- Offline folder

You can ascertain the current configuration for mail delivery by opening either the Mail utility in Control Panel or the Services dialog box available from the Tools menu of the client software. When the Services dialog box opens, move to the Delivery tab (see Figure 4-1, on the following page).

Tip If there are multiple profiles in the Mail utility, you can select the profile you want to work with. If, however, you use the Services command from the Tools menu on the client software, only the currently loaded profile is available for manipulation.

Delivering Mail to the Server

By default, when client software is configured for Exchange Server, the user's server-based mailbox is the delivery target for all e-mail. Mail can be viewed and sent by connecting to the server, which is normally just a matter of launching the client software (assuming a network logon has been completed).

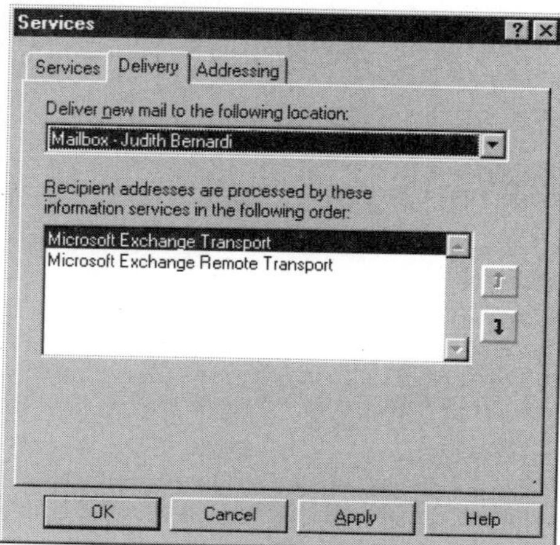

Figure 4-1. *Check the delivery location to make sure that mail is sent to the appropriate place.*

Sending Mail Through the Server

It's important to make sure that the order for outgoing address processing is appropriate. If Exchange Server is the only e-mail service (all of the user's e-mail is received and sent through this server), the Microsoft Exchange Transport is usually listed first. If the user has installed both Exchange Server and Internet Mail services, however, you may need to adjust the order in which outgoing mail is processed.

If Microsoft Exchange Transport is listed first, outgoing messages are processed and sent through the server. If your Exchange Server system is running Internet Mail Service, that's usually not a problem. If you want Internet mail processed by the Internet Mail Service installed on this client, move the Internet Mail Service to the top of the list by selecting it and clicking the Up arrow (see Figure 4-2).

If Exchange Server handles only company e-mail and users dial out for Internet mail, it's better to create separate profiles for users, one for each service. Perform this task in the Mail utility in Control Panel.

Receiving Mail in a Personal Folder

A personal folder file is located on the user's local drive and has the file extension .pst. This file is available for viewing existing mail and composing e-mail even when the server is down. However, the user cannot send mail or receive new messages until the server is available.

When the delivery point is changed to the user's Personal Folder, Inbox, Outbox, and Sent Items folders are automatically created in the .pst file. They can be accessed by opening the folders view in the client software (see Figure 4-3).

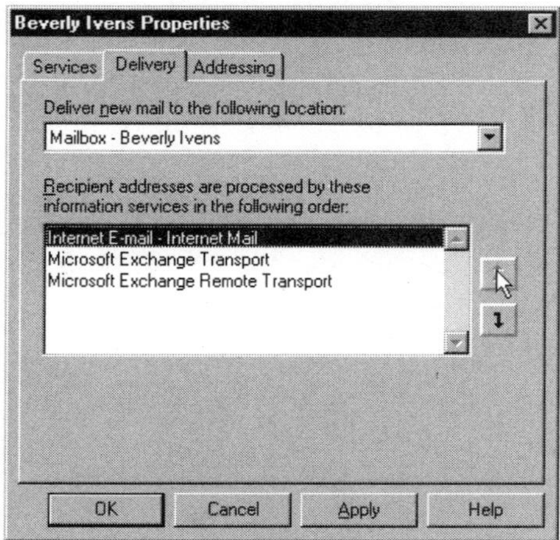

Figure 4-2. *Control the way outgoing mail is processed by changing the order of the installed services.*

If the delivery location is moved back to the server mailbox, those three items remain in the .pst file and can't be deleted (they just won't be used).

Note that in Outlook, the Inbox on the Outlook Bar is a shortcut to the server-based mailbox, not the Inbox in the personal folders. You can create an Outlook Bar shortcut to this Inbox by right-clicking on the Inbox folder and choosing Add To Outlook Bar. This puts two Inbox icons on the Outlook Bar, both in the Outlook Shortcuts section. Although you could remove the server-based Inbox shortcut from the Outlook Bar, it's a better idea to rename the new shortcut "Personal Inbox" or something similar.

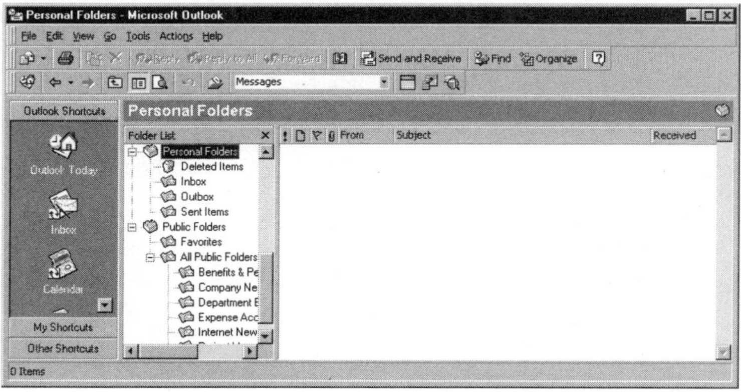

Figure 4-3. *You must open the folders to access mail folders in the Personal Folders container.*

If the user has a profile for Internet e-mail that is linked to a mail server other than Exchange Server (an Internet service provider [ISP] or CompuServe), the Inbox is automatically established in the Personal Folders container.

Using an Offline Folder

Offline folders are designed for users who dial in to a server instead of using a full-time network connection. An offline folder file is located on the user's local drive and has the file extension .ost. The most important feature of the offline folder file is that it's built to synchronize its contents with the user's server-based mailbox. When the user dials in, changes in either mailbox (or both) are synchronized so that both mailboxes have the same contents. In addition, tasks and calendar information are included in the synchronization between the folders.

The difference between an Offline Folder and a Personal Folder is that the Offline Folder is created as a mirror image of the user's folders on the Exchange Server. The synchronization feature keeps the mirror intact. On the other hand, the Personal Folder is just a storage location on the user's local disk (although personal folders can be configured for location on a server other than the Exchange Server).

Creating an Offline Folder is not the same as adding other services (choosing Add in the Services dialog box), because the Offline Folder is a subset of the Exchange service.

To add an Offline Folder for a user, follow these steps:

1. Connect the client software to the Exchange server.
2. Open the Services dialog box (from the Tools menu, choose Services) and select Microsoft Exchange Server in the Services list.
3. Click Properties and move to the Advanced tab of the Properties dialog box.
4. Select the Enable Offline Use check box, then click the Offline Folder File Settings button.
5. Accept the default path and name or click Browse to create a new path and/or filename.

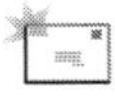

Note After you create an Offline Folder, the path and filename cannot be changed.

After you click OK, the server-based mailbox is mirrored to the .ost file. Hereafter, you can synchronize the folders by connecting to the Exchange Server, then, from the Tools menu, choosing Synchronize, then All Folders (or pressing F9).

Working with Public Folders

Public folders could be considered a client feature, even though they're stored on the server, because clients create public folders.

The most frequent user questions concern (1) giving other users permission to maintain a public folder and (2) changing the view of items in a public folder.

Configuring Public Folder Permissions

The owner (creator) of a public folder can manipulate the permissions of that folder by opening the folder's Properties dialog box and using the Permissions tab (see Figure 4-4).

The default permission level, for all users, is that of Author. Author rights include reading and creating items. The folder owner must specifically establish permissions that are different from the default. To accomplish this, click Add and then choose additional users and give them the desired level of permissions.

Permissions are usually assigned by associating a role with a user. Each role has a collection of rights that are granted automatically. If you want to select individual rights, and the collection doesn't match an existing role, the role is named "Custom."

If the folder owner wants help for folder administration tasks, it's easy to give owner permissions to someone else. There is no role named "Owner," but selecting Folder Owner in the Permissions section of the dialog box accomplishes this goal (the role becomes "Custom").

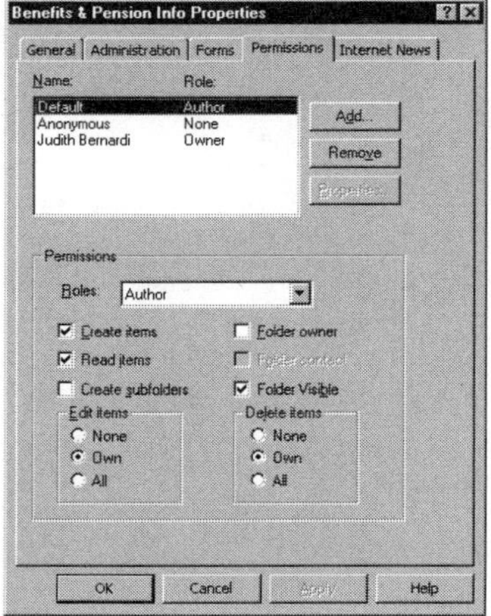

Figure 4-4. *Permissions for other users of a public folder can be set in the client software.*

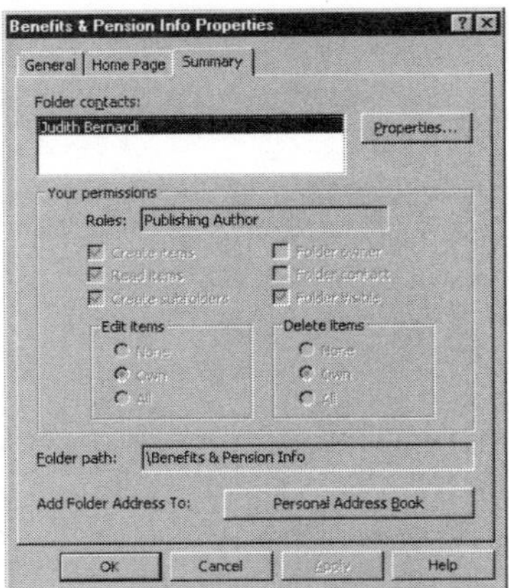

Figure 4-5. *Users can view their rights, but can't make any changes in a public folder Properties dialog box. This user has been given the role of Publishing Author.*

Users can see only their own permissions and the name of the owner in the Permissions tab of a public folder dialog box (see Figure 4-5).

If a user wants more rights, he or she should contact the owner of the public folder to request them. Clicking the Properties button next to the owner's name opens the Address Book properties for the owner, which probably has a telephone extension or address to help the user contact the owner.

You're likely to find that the owner of a public folder doesn't have the time or inclination to maintain the permissions and perform other maintenance tasks. So, of course, the Exchange Server administrator assumes these chores. Administrators can manipulate the permissions for a public folder in the Exchange Administrator window. Select the public folder and, from the File menu, choose Properties. Don't go to the Permissions tab of the dialog box; that's not where user permissions are set. Instead, click the Client Permissions button on the General Tab. The dialog box that is displayed is an exact replica of the Permissions tab of the folder's dialog box that the owner sees in the client software.

Tip Use the Exchange Administrator to propagate a folder's permissions to its subfolders. The client cannot do this.

Changing Public Folder Views

Views are the way in which items are displayed in a public folder. Public folder owners can change the default view that all users see. Users can change the view, but the changes are personal and don't change the default view for other users.

Changing the Default View of a Public Folder

To change the default view, you must have owner permissions for the public folder. Change the default view by doing the following:

1. Right-click the folder you want to change and, from the shortcut menu, choose Properties.
2. In the Properties dialog box, move to the Administration tab (if there isn't one, you don't have Owner permissions).
3. Click the arrow to the right of the Initial View On Folder text box and choose the view you want users to see when the folder is opened.

Changing Your Own View of a Public Folder

Nonowners can make whatever changes they wish to their view of the items in a public folder. To accomplish this, open the folder view and select the folder. Choose View and then select an action from the Current View menu (see Figure 4-6).

- Choose a predesigned view from the menu.
- Click Customize Current View to display the View Summary dialog box, where you can add and remove fields from the columns in your Outlook window, group and sort the display, and change the formatting and appearance.
- Choose Define Views to build the view from scratch.

When a user changes the sort order for a public folder or creates a brand new view, Exchange Server creates a new index for the folder. This means that if you create a view in a folder containing many items, the process can take quite a bit of time. It's a good idea to change the view of a public folder early in its lifetime, before the items pile up.

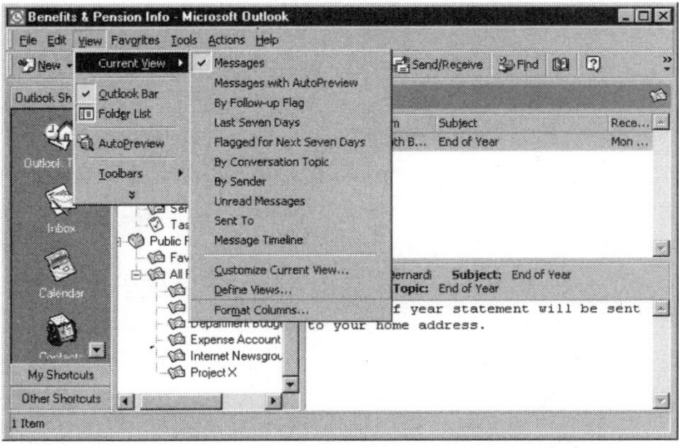

Figure 4-6. *You can make whatever changes you want to your view of the items in a public folder.*

As individual users create views and accompanying indexes, the number of indexes can get out of hand. As a result, Exchange Server doesn't save user view indexes permanently. A temporary cache of views and indexes is maintained, and the system deletes any that have not been used for eight days. If a user creates a view and then tries to use it again after more than eight days have elapsed, the index will have expired. The view has to be re-indexed when it's selected, which can take a lot of time. If your view is expired owing to lack of use, then the next time you open that view, you're going to have to wait while the system creates a new index.

Creating Rules for Public Folders

The owner of a public folder can create rules that govern the way items are handled when they're posted to the folder. To do this, open the Properties dialog box for the public folder and move to the Administration tab. Then click the Folder Assistant button.

When the Folder Assistant dialog box appears, click Add Rule to create the criteria for handling posts in the Edit Rule dialog box (see Figure 4-7).

- To specify multiple criteria, use a semicolon between each statement. The semi-colon is interpreted as OR.
- Click the Advanced button to set criteria that extend beyond the heading and message text of the posting (see Figure 4-8).
- After you've established the criteria, select an action. Any posting that meets the criteria initiates the action.
- A rule can have more than one action—for example, you can both forward an item and send an automatic reply to the user who posted the item.

If you're using an automatic reply, you must create the template for that reply. Select the Reply With check box and click the Template button. Fill out the message form and choose File, then choose Save & Close from the template menu

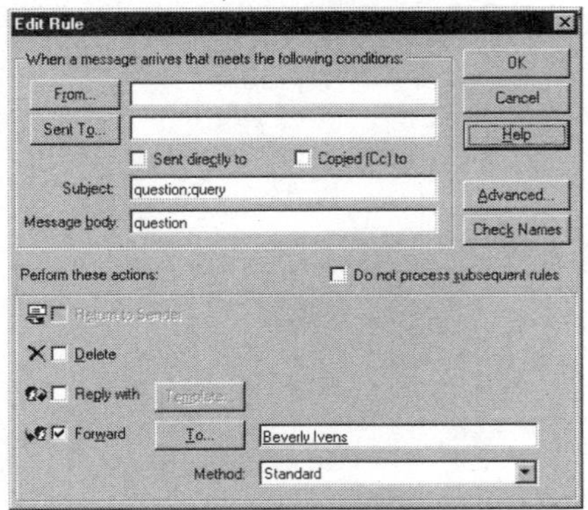

Figure 4-7. *You can automatically deal with postings that meet your criteria—in this case questions are forwarded to the company expert.*

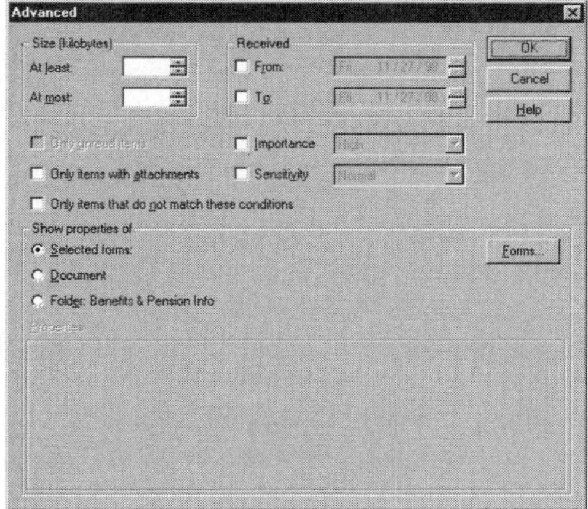

Figure 4-8. *You can flag a posting that matches, or fails to match, your criteria.*

bar. Your message should be related to the posting that kicked off this rule. For example, you might say, "Your query has been directed to the right department and you'll hear from somebody or other eventually." (Don't fill out the "To:" box, but you could send a "Cc:" to someone every time an automatic message is sent, as a backup protocol.)

If you establish multiple rules, all of them are implemented in the order in which they appear in the Folder Assistant dialog box. After you create multiple rules, you can select any rule and change its position by clicking the Move Up and Move Down buttons (see Figure 4-9).

Tip If you want a rule applied and the attendant action launched immediately, select the check box labeled Do Not Process Subsequent Rules when you create the rule in the Edit Rule dialog box.

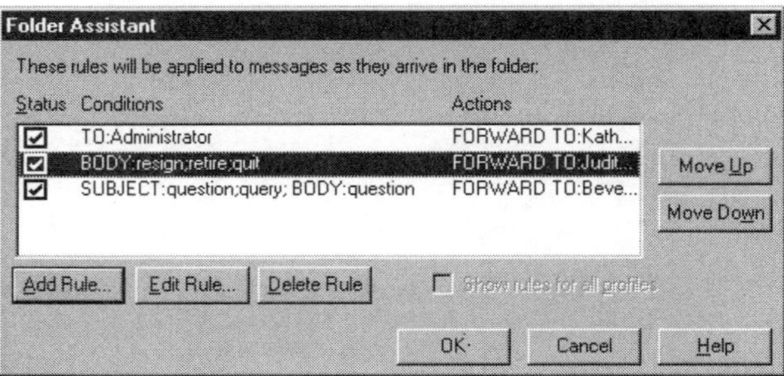

Figure 4-9. *Rules are applied in the order in which they're listed.*

Using Moderated Folders

A moderated folder is one in which every item posted to the folder is forwarded to a designated recipient for review (you can also forward items to another folder). If the item is deemed appropriate, it is sent back to the public folder for all to view. Moderated folders are usually employed for postings that might contain sensitive material. When you configure a folder as a moderated folder, you don't have to write rules to forward mail; it's all automatic. Here's how to create a moderated public folder:

1. Open the client software and create a public folder.
2. Right-click the new folder and choose Properties from the shortcut menu. (You can also turn an existing public folder into a moderated folder.)
3. In the Properties dialog box, go to the Administration tab and click the Moderated Folder button.
4. When the Moderated Folder dialog box appears (see Figure 4-10), select the option Set Folder Up As A Moderated Folder.
5. Click the To button to display the Global Address List and select the moderators (the persons to whom all postings are automatically sent). Click Add to move the name(s) to the right pane, then click OK to return to the Moderated Folder dialog box.
6. In the Moderators section, add the names of the moderators in order to give permission to post to the folder.
7. To send an explanatory e-mail message to every user who posts an item to the folder, select Reply To New Items With. Then choose whether you want to send a preconfigured Standard Response or a Custom Response that you can write yourself (a message window opens so that you can create the response).

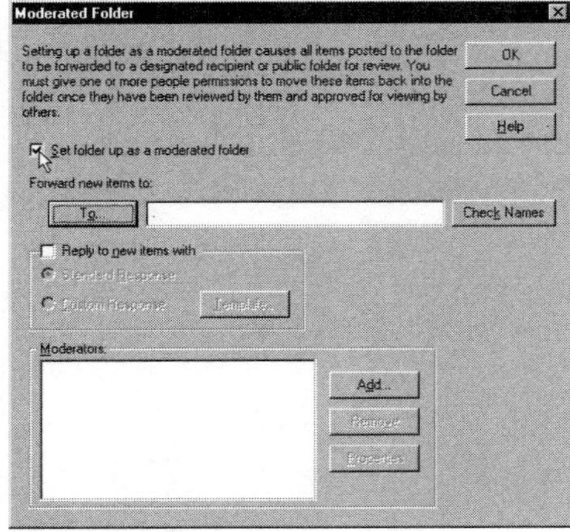

Figure 4-10. *Configure a moderated folder to automatically send postings to a moderator. You can optionally send a message to the user who posted the item.*

Note The Standard Response is "Thank you for your submission. Please note that submissions to some folders or discussion groups are reviewed to determine whether they should be made publicly available. In these cases, there will be a delay before approved submissions can be viewed by others."

Moderators receive the postings in the form of e-mail. They move appropriate items into the folder with the usual Move To Folder command available in the client software.

Owner-Only Public Folders

You can use public folders for sensitive, private, or other items that should be seen by a limited number of people. To make sure that only the appropriate people see the items, configure the folder for owners only.

In the client software, create a public folder and then open its Properties dialog box. In the Permissions tab, designate additional users and give them a role of Owner. Then go to the Administration tab and select Owners Only. The users you appoint are the only people who will be able to use the folder. Make sure the folder is hidden from the Address Book list.

Adding Public Folders to Your PAB

If the client software has a personal address book (PAB) installed, the user may be able to add public folders to it. This makes it easier to send items to the public folder. Here's how to make an e-mail address listing for a public folder:

1. Open the folder view in the client software and expand the public folder listing.
2. Right-click the public folder you want to add to the PAB and from the shortcut menu, choose Properties.
3. Move to the Summary tab and click the Personal Address Book button. If the Summary tab isn't available, this user doesn't have sufficient rights to perform this step.

Tip If the user is an owner of the public folder, the Administration tab has the Personal Address Book option—there is no Summary tab.

Working with Public Folders Offline

Users can work with public folders offline, which is handy for everyone and important for dial-in users. If you use public folders for shared documents, your users will find it very convenient to work with those folders offline. They can update changes when they connect to the server.

An offline file must be created for a user if he or she wants to work with public folders offline. To create this file, from the Tools menu choose Services, and then select Microsoft Exchange Server. Click the Advanced tab to set up the offline file (the filename extension must be .ost).

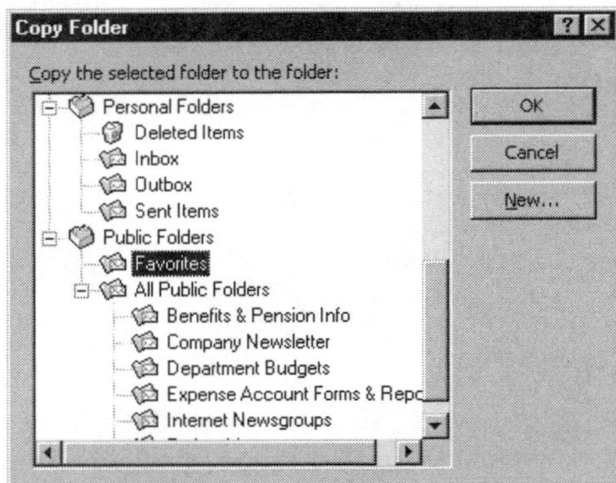

Figure 4-11. *Copy all the public folders you want to use offline to your Favorites folder.*

You begin using the offline folder file while you're attached to the Exchange server. A mirror image of your folders on the Exchange server is sent to the offline file. All the basic Outlook folders (Inbox, Outbox, Deleted Items, Sent Items, Calendar, Contacts, Journal, Notes, and Tasks) on the Exchange server are immediately ready for offline use. You cannot pick and choose any of the basic folders; they are all made available for offline use.

You have total freedom of choice, however, about which public folders you want to use with offline files. To work with public folders offline, follow these steps:

1. Right-click the public folder that you want to use offline.
2. From the shortcut menu, choose Copy *<folder name>*.
3. In the Copy Folder dialog box (see Figure 4-11), select the Favorites folder and click OK.

After you've copied all the public folders you want to use offline to the Favorites folder, you must configure the folders for synchronization:

1. Right-click the copied folder (in the Favorites container) and from the shortcut menu, choose Properties.
2. Move to the Synchronization tab and, in the dialog box section named This Folder Is Available, select the option When Offline Or Online (see Figure 4-12).

When you're preparing to work offline, or coming back online, you can synchronize individual public folders or all the public folders in the Favorites container:

- Select the individual folder you want to synchronize. Choose Tools, then choose Synchronize. From the submenu, choose This Folder.
- Synchronize all your offline folders from the Tools menu by choosing Synchronize, and then selecting All Folders from the submenu. Every folder is synchronized, not just the public folders.

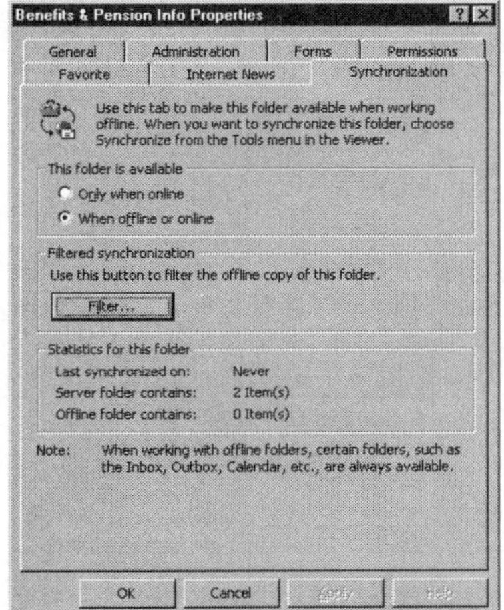

Figure 4-12. *Configure the public folder so it's available offline.*

You can automate Synchronization by selecting Tools on the Mail Services tab and using the choices in the Options dialog box.

Delegate Access

Giving delegate access to a mailbox can be an extremely productive procedure, but I've found that many users don't understand either the concept or the implementation. In fact, I've encountered many Exchange Server systems in which users don't even know that the feature is available.

Delegate access is an efficient way to assist an employee who receives a lot of messages that don't need personal attention. This usually applies to executives who want to give mailbox access to an assistant.

Delegate access is also a method of handling mailboxes that are connected to resources instead of users. For example, you can give a mailbox to a conference room, an equipment room, a library, or any other element of your company that employees use. Requests for use, questions about resources, and so on can be sent to the mailbox.

Setting Up Delegate Access

The Delegate Access feature is an add-in for all versions of the Outlook client. To make sure the add-in is loaded, from the Tools menu, choose Options to open the Options dialog box. Move to the Other tab and click the Advanced Options button. When the Advanced Options dialog box appears, click Add-In Manager. In the displayed list of add-ins, those that are installed have a check mark (see Figure 4-13, on the following page).

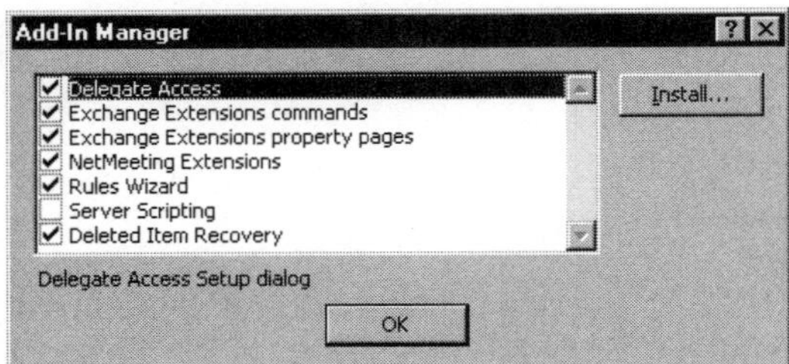

Figure 4-13. *Be sure Delegate Access is running on this Outlook client.*

If an item in the Delegate Access add-in check box does not have a check mark, you must install that item. Click Install to open a window that lists all the add-in files available for Outlook and then select Dlgsetp.ecf.

If there's no listing for Delegate Access in the add-in list, you must return to the Outlook Setup program and run a Custom installation to install the Delegate Access add-in.

Naming and Configuring a Delegate

The Delegate Access feature is implemented by the mailbox owner, who gives permissions to a delegate. The owner determines the level of access a delegate is granted. You must be connected to the Exchange server to perform this task.

To name a delegate, from the Tools menu choose Options, and go to the Delegates tab of the Options dialog box (see Figure 4-14).

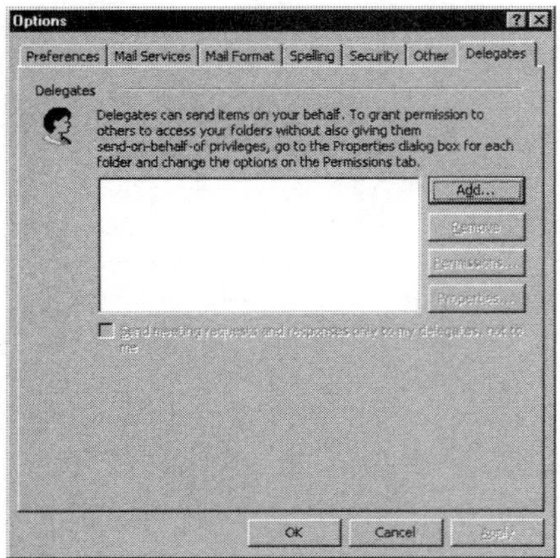

Figure 4-14. *Start in the Delegates tab when you want to give another user delegate access to a mailbox.*

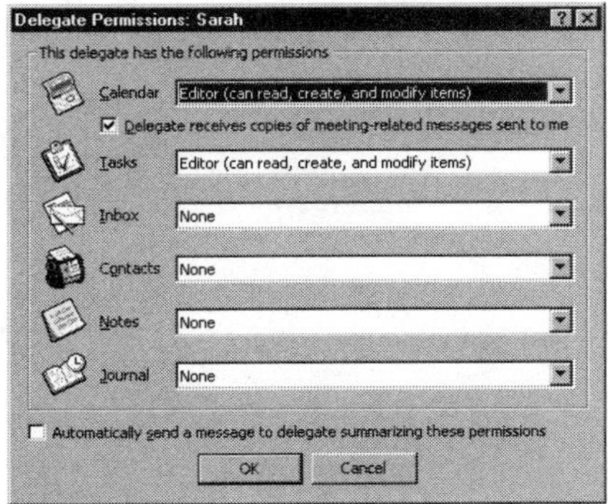

Figure 4-15. *Set delegate permission levels for each folder in the client software.*

Click Add to see the Global Address List and select the user to whom you want to give delegate access permissions. When you click OK, the permissions for this delegate are displayed so you can configure this delegate's rights (see Figure 4-15).

For each folder listed on the dialog box, you can choose any of the following permissions:

- **Editor** Reads and creates items. Deletes and modifies any item in the folder.
- **Author** Reads and creates items. Deletes and modifies any items you create.
- **Reviewer** Reads items.
- **None** Has no rights.

At the bottom of the dialog box there's a selection for sending this delegate an e-mail message that summarizes the permissions. It's a good idea to do so.

When you finish configuring the permissions, click OK to return to the Delegates tab. There's an option to have meeting requests and responses sent only to the delegate on that tab. If you select this option, any meeting notice meant for you is automatically sent to the delegate's mailbox. Also, if you're having a meeting, all responses (RSVPs) are sent directly to the delegate's mailbox. This is handy if your delegate is an assistant who normally takes care of your calendar. (Just don't forget to ask your delegate, "What am I doing today?" because your own mailbox won't receive the meeting notices.) If you want to take advantage of this option, return to the Permissions page (select the delegate and click Permissions to get there) and give your delegate Editor permissions for your calendar. Also, remember to select the option to have your delegate receive copies of meeting-related messages.

Configuring Delegates for Resources

If someone in your company is responsible for booking conference rooms, audiovisual equipment, or other company resources, you can make his or her job easier by handling requests via e-mail.

Create a mailbox for the resource. When you create the mailbox, use one of these options to attach it to a Microsoft Windows NT account:

- Select the option to use an existing Windows NT account and use your own account or another supervisor-level account (the person in charge of all company resources of this type is a good choice). Then create a delegate for the administration of the mailbox.
- Select the option to use an existing Windows NT account and use the employee who is responsible for the day-to-day administration of the resource.

There is a potential problem with the latter option: the employee might quit, change jobs within the company, retire, or otherwise be disconnected from the mailbox. You probably won't remember that you attached the mailbox to that employee, and when you delete the employee from the user database, the mailbox disappears. Assigning a delegate is a better idea.

Set up a profile for the resource mailbox in Outlook and log on to Outlook using that profile. Use the steps described in the previous section to establish delegate access for the employee who is responsible for the resource.

You can set up as many resources as you wish, using the same delegate for each resource, or assigning groups of resources to certain delegates.

You can further automate the use of a resource by agreeing to all requests for the resource on a first-come-first-served basis. Log on to Outlook to open the resource mailbox and use these procedures:

Tip The first-come-first-served automation isn't etched in cement. The delegate can, of course, make any desired changes to scheduling.

1. From the Tools menu, choose Options and click the E-mail Options button on the Preferences tab to open the E-mail options dialog box.
2. Click the Advanced E-mail Options button and check the Settings for the Automatic Processing Of Mail section of the dialog box. Make sure that the option to process requests and responses on arrival is selected.
3. Click OK twice to return to the Options dialog box and click the Calendar Options button to open the Calendar Options dialog box.
4. Click the Resource Scheduling button to open the Resource Scheduling dialog box (see Figure 4-16).

Tip Some of my clients found that selecting Automatically Decline Recurring Meeting Requests makes automated scheduling easier. If you don't have a lot of requests for a resource, however, you may want to try operating the resource with recurring requests. If this approach doesn't work, come back to the dialog box and select the option to decline them.

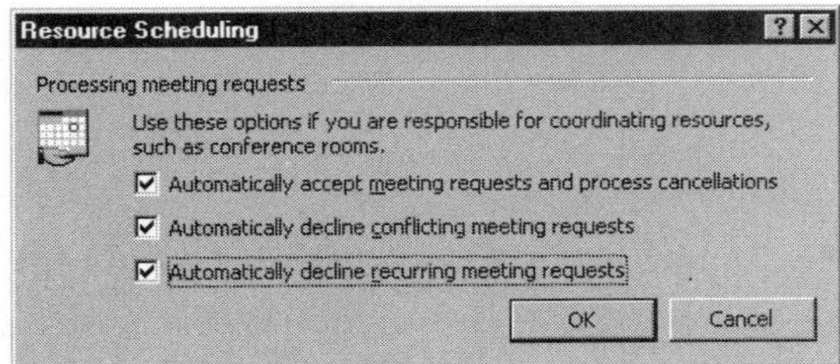

Figure 4-16. *Decide how you want to handle resource requests.*

Acting as a Delegate

The best way to notify a person about his or her new status as a mailbox delegate is to automatically send an e-mail message when the delegate is named (see the earlier section on naming a delegate). The delegate receives a message that announces the delegate rights and gives instructions for implementing delegate access (see Figure 4-17).

If an automatic message wasn't sent, the delegate needs to receive a phone call or an e-mail message with the necessary information.

Implementing Delegate Access for Another User

A user who's been named a delegate for another user's mailbox has rights in that other user's mailbox. The delegate can open the mailbox and manipulate its contents to match the permissions levels.

In the client software, from the File menu, choose Open, and then choose Other User's Folder from the submenu. The Open Other User's Folder dialog box appears, as seen in Figure 4-18, on the following page.

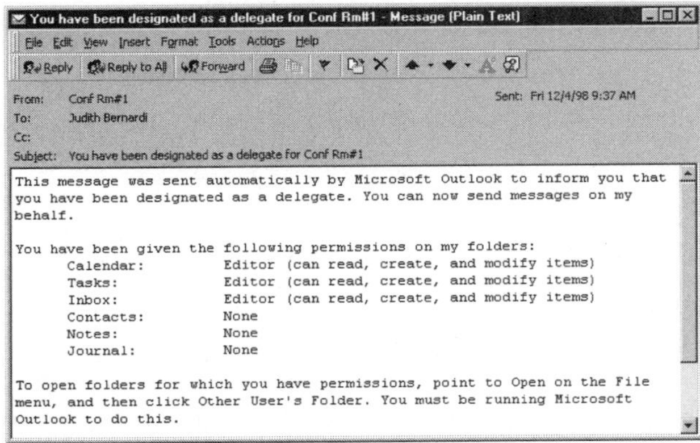

Figure 4-17. *The automatic delegate message is chock-full of information that a delegate needs.*

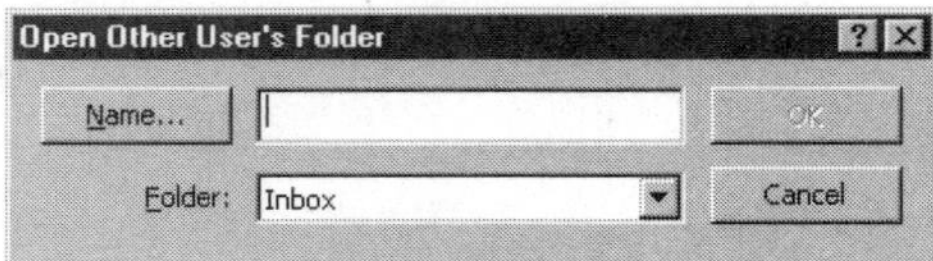

Figure 4-18. *Delegates need to open the folder to which they've been given access.*

Enter the folder name or click Name to see the Global Address List and select the appropriate mailbox. The mailbox opens in a separate window, and the delegate can read, respond, send, or do whatever needs to be done (depending on the level of rights).

If the delegate access configuration includes redirection of meeting requests, those messages are delivered directly into the delegate's mailbox.

Implementing Delegate Access for a Resource

Delegate access for a resource means tracking the use of the resource rather than dealing with e-mail for a user. The messages for the resource are sent directly to the delegate's mailbox.

Automatic Resource Scheduling with Scripts

If you have numerous resources to schedule—for example, conference rooms, equipment, or limousines—it might be more efficient to automate resource scheduling. You can use scripts to accomplish this; you won't need delegates. The resource itself accepts or rejects requests based on availability. Also, the resource account doesn't have to be logged on to Exchange Server.

Note Scripting doesn't really fit the premise of this book, which is designed to assist you with those tasks you perform frequently. If you need the ability to maintain resource scheduling automatically, however, you should know about scripting. Incidentally, it means users won't be asking you for help in acting as a delegate for a resource.

Setting up scripting is a two-part task—you start on the Exchange server and finish in Outlook.

Installing the Scripting Agent

You may have included the scripting agent when you installed Microsoft Exchange Server 5.5, so you should first check your system to see if it's there. To accomplish that, open the Control Panel on the server that runs Exchange Server 5.5. Open the Services utility and check for the existence of Microsoft Exchange Event Service. If it's there, terrific! If it's not, you must install it:

1. Run Setup from the Exchange Server CD-ROM (it should start in Maintenance Mode Setup).
2. Chose Add/Remove Components.

3. Select Microsoft Exchange Server, then click Change Options.
4. Select Microsoft Exchange Event Service.
5. Click OK twice to start the installation of the Event Service.

Configuring the Resource Account

The resource account must have sufficient permissions to install and manage scripts, and those rights are configured in an EventConfig object in the Events_Root container. This container is installed on your Exchange system when you install Microsoft Exchange Event Service.

There is an EventConfig object for each Exchange server in the site, and the naming convention is EventConfig_*<servername>*. You must select the server that contains the resource account. The path to the EventConfig_*<server>* object is \Organization\Folders\System Folders\Events Root (see Figure 4-19).

1. Select the EventConfig_*<server>* object, and from the File menu choose Properties to display the Properties dialog box for this object.
2. On the General tab of the dialog box, click the Client Permissions button; don't use the Permissions tab (you're setting up permissions that will be implemented in client software).
3. Give the resource account sufficient rights so that scripts can be installed and configured from the client software. (I usually give Owner rights, which ensures that anything that needs to be accomplished will be accomplished.)

Setting Up the Resource Client

At the client computer, log on to the Exchange server as the resource account. Then check to make sure that the Server Scripting add-in is installed. From the Tools menu, choose Options, and go to the Other tab. Then click the Advanced Options button to display the Advanced Options dialog box, where you click the Add-In Manager button.

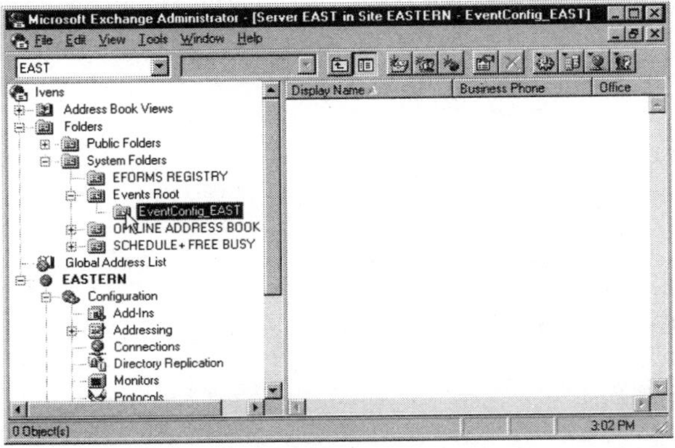

Figure 4-19. *The EventConfig containers are in the organization's folders hierarchy.*

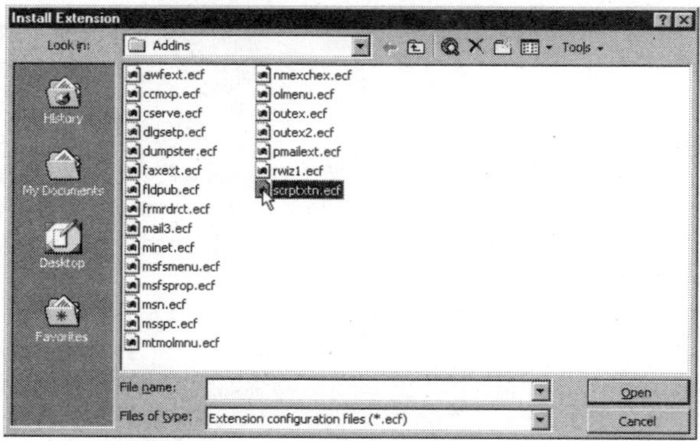

Figure 4-20. *It's easy to install add-ins for Outlook client software.*

Now you can see the list of add-ins for this Outlook installation. If Server Scripting has a check mark in the check box, you're all set. If there's no check mark, select the check box and then click the Install button to open the Install Extension window (see Figure 4-20).

Select Scrptxtn.ecf and click Open. Server Scripting is now available.

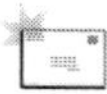

Note If the Scrptxtn.ecf file is not available, it means that your original installation of Outlook did not include this add-in (the Typical installation does include add-ins). You'll have to run Setup for Outlook to install add-ins.

Choosing a Script

Install the script you want to use at the client computer, where the resource account logs on. Use Microsoft Explorer or My Computer to locate the script.

You can choose from a variety of places to obtain a script, but remember that all these scripts are sample scripts. You may have to customize them for your own situation. Here are some sources for a sample script:

- The Exchange Server CD-ROM has a sample script named Autoaccept.txt in \Server\Support\Collab\Sampler\Scripts. There's also a Readme.txt file in that folder.
- Microsoft Knowledge Base Article Q184271 has a more advanced sample script. (If the Article number has changed, search on scripting agent.)
- Various Web sites that are dedicated to Exchange Server and Outlook have sample scripts. One of the most popular sites is *http://www.slipstick.com*, which always has at least one advanced sample script for this purpose.

Note The sample script on the Exchange Server CD-ROM has some severe limitations. For instance, it won't process a request if the meeting duration is greater than thirty minutes.

To use a sample script, follow these steps:

1. Open the script you want to use by double-clicking it. Notepad opens (the script is a text file), and you can customize it if necessary.
2. Select all the text and copy it to the clipboard.
3. Close Notepad.

Installing the Script

Now you're ready to install the script in Outlook (logged on to Exchange Server as the resource account).

1. Right-click the Inbox for the resource account, and from the shortcut menu choose Properties.
2. Move to the Agents tab.
3. Click New to open the New Agent dialog box (see Figure 4-21).
4. Name the script.
5. Select A New Item Is Posted In This Folder.
6. Click the Script radio button and then choose Edit Script.
7. When Notepad opens, it displays boilerplate text that you must clear (from the Edit menu choose Select All, and then press the Delete key).
8. From the Edit menu, choose Paste to insert the text you placed on the clipboard.
9. From the File menu, select Save. Close Notepad.

Your script is installed. You can eliminate the delegates for this resource mailbox.

Testing the Script

You can log off the resource account; it does not have to be logged on for automated scheduling to work.

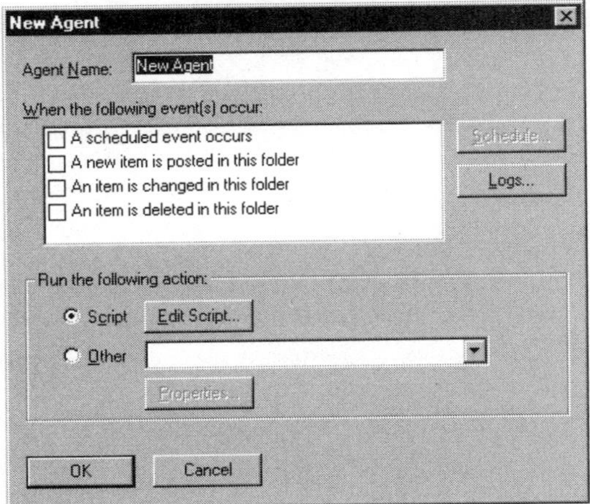

Figure 4-21. *Add a new script to process meeting requests automatically.*

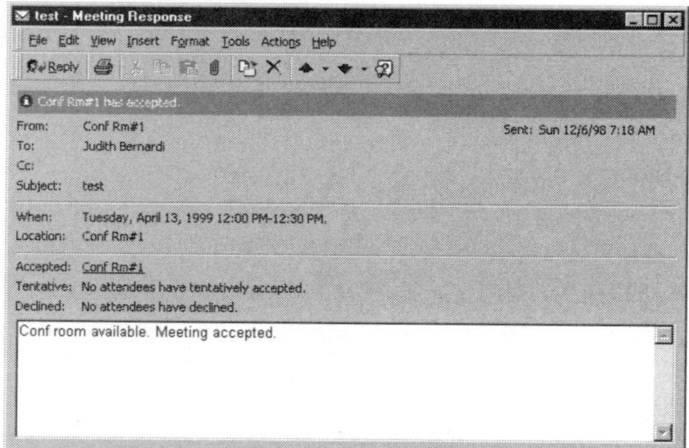

Figure 4-22. *The automated reply arrives in the Inbox of the person who initiated the meeting request (or that of any delegated user).*

Use any Exchange Server account to create a meeting request. Make sure you include the resource in the invitations. You should receive a message from the resource, as seen in Figure 4-22.

Using Mailbox Rules

Outlook has some powerful features for handling e-mail automatically, based on criteria set by the user. Many users have difficulty understanding the concepts and implementation.

Using the Out Of Office Assistant

The Out Of Office Assistant is aptly named because it's used to generate automatic replies to messages received by somebody who is not working and therefore not checking e-mail. This is not the same as being out of the office and checking in from a remote location, because in that case messages are read and answered.

The Out Of Office Assistant is implemented in two steps:

1. Create the autoreply text.
2. Tell the Assistant whether you're out of the office. If you are, the rules are implemented. If you're not, the rules are ignored. The notification is a toggle.

You can also enhance the way the Out Of Office Assistant works by creating specific rules for specific circumstances instead of using the basic autoreply system.

Configuring Automatic Replies

Start from the Tools menu, and choose Out Of Office Assistant in the client software window. The Out Of Office Assistant dialog box is displayed, as seen in Figure 4-23.

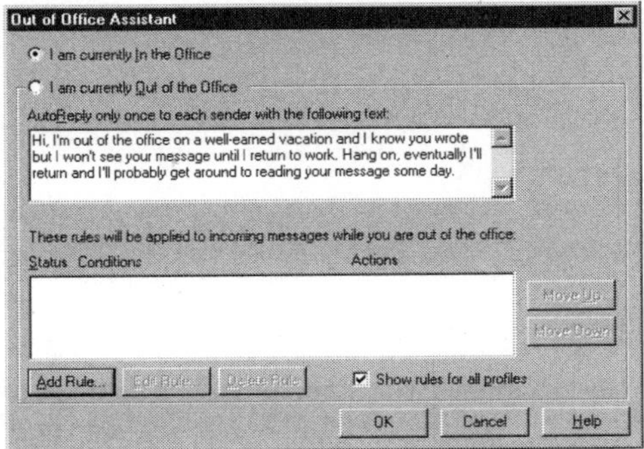

Figure 4-23. *You can merely insert text for an autoreply, or get fancy with specific rules to cover all sorts of circumstances.*

The easiest way to implement the Out Of Office Assistant is to enter message text that will be sent to each person who writes you. The Assistant tracks the senders so that each person receives your response to the first message, and subsequent messages from that person do not generate an automatic response. Meanwhile, of course, the messages themselves are sent to the Inbox.

Also, just as a matter of interest, note these facts:

- The AutoReply message has the following in the Subject field: Out Of Office AutoReply: *<original subject text>*.
- The AutoReply message does not appear in the recipient's preview pane (if message preview is turned on).

The return message is not sent until you open this dialog box and select I Am Currently Out Of The Office. This means you can create the AutoReply text at any time and then implement it later.

Tip A number of clients have told me that it's a good idea to "fudge" any information about a return date in the AutoReply text. Either omit it or state a date that's later than the actual return date. People start chasing you on that date, and you might need several days before you can catch up on all your e-mail.

Configuring Out Of Office Rules

Suppose, however, that you have work that can't wait until you return from your cruise. Perhaps there's a project you're running that has to keep going even in your absence. Or perhaps you've given the telephone number of your vacation chalet to a co-worker, along with instructions to telephone you if something major occurs. After all, if your company has been sold to a major competitor, you'd probably want someone to e-mail you about this even if you were on vacation. To cover all contingencies, you can create rules for handling mail that arrives in your absence, in addition to sending an AutoReply.

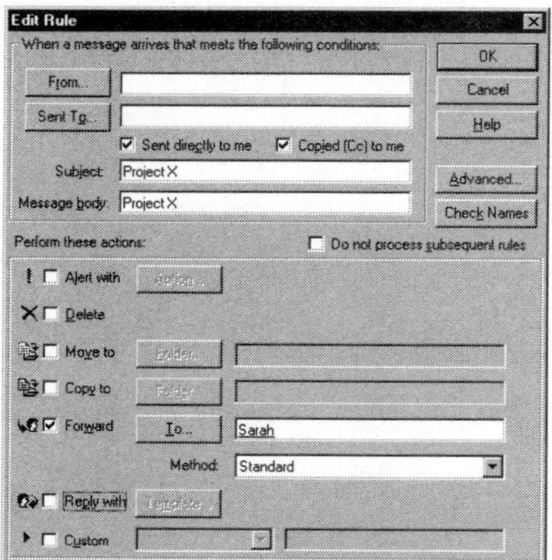

Figure 4-24. *This rule is designed to make sure any message about Project X is handled by another employee.*

In the Out Of Office Assistant dialog box, click the Add Rule button to start creating a rule. The Edit Rule dialog box appears. As you can see in Figure 4-24, the top half of the dialog box is for setting conditions, and the bottom half is for designing actions that take place when those conditions are met.

Here are the concepts that some users have a problem understanding:

- You can have multiple conditions in a single rule.
- You can have multiple actions in a single rule.
- You can have multiple rules.
- Multiple rules are applied in the order in which they're listed.

The last concept in particular is not well understood, and therefore it causes problems. If you don't put the rules in the correct order, it's possible to create problems, such as conflicting actions. All the rules are applied (even if the message meets the criteria for the first rule) except the following:

- Any rule that has a delete action. The action deletes the message at that point, and subsequent rules are not applied to the message.
- A rule that is created with the option Do Not Process Subsequent Rules.

Another potential problem with multiple rules is that messages can pass a variety of criteria and generate an action each time. Senders receive two automatic replies, or the message is moved to multiple folders.

Using Out Of Office Assistant for Internet Mail

The rules feature in version 5.5 of Exchange Server contains a significant change. Previously, rules such as those you create in the Out Of Office Assistant launched

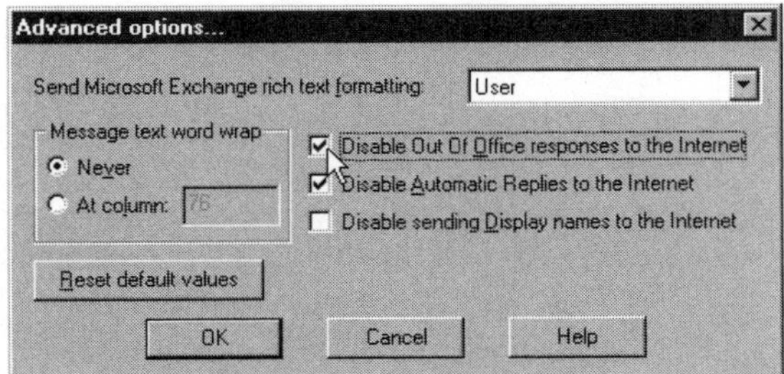

Figure 4-25. *Change the default if you want Out Of Office Assistant to work with Internet mail.*

regardless of the source of the message. In Exchange Server 5.5, however, the default configuration is to launch the actions for rules for organization mail and to ignore Internet mail.

You can change the configuration if you want rules to launch actions when mail is received from Internet addresses. This change is made at the server, not in the client software:

1. Open the Exchange Administrator window and expand the Site and Configuration containers.
2. Select the \Configuration\Connections container in the left pane.
3. Select the Internet Mail Service in the right pane.
4. From the File menu, choose Properties to display the Internet Mail Service Properties dialog box.
5. Move to the Internet Mail tab, and click the Advanced Options button.
6. In the Advanced Options dialog box (see Figure 4-25), deselect the option that disables Out Of Office responses to the Internet.

While you're there, you might also want to deselect the option that disables automatic replies to the Internet. This option covers the Rules Wizard (or the Inbox Assistant in earlier versions of client software), which lets users filter and manipulate all e-mail (covered later in this chapter).

Out Of Office Assistant Tricks and Tips

Here are some helpful guidelines for getting the most out of the Out Of Office Assistant.

Create Counterbalancing Rules to Respond to All Messages

Frequently you'll find that a user needs to create a rule for one specific circumstance. Perhaps if a message arrives from a certain user (usually the boss), the message should be forwarded to another employee. Every other message, however, should get an automatic reply. Or perhaps messages with a specific subject need attention, but all other messages can generate an automatic reply. The easiest way to accomplish this is to create balancing rules. Begin by setting up the first rule (for this example, I'm using a message from the boss):

1. In the Edit Rule dialog box, enter the name of the sender (your boss) in the From field. If there are several people on your list of "people you need to take care of," put a semicolon between each name.
2. Select Forward and name the person who is going to handle messages from the boss.

That takes care of those important messages. But suppose you want everybody else who sends a message to get an automatic reply saying, "I'm out of the office; I'll call you when I'm back"? Don't worry; you don't have to create a rule that inserts the names of the immediate world in the From field. Here's what you do:

1. Create a new rule, and in the From field enter the same names you used for the previous rule.
2. Choose an action for saving the message somewhere (move or copy it to a folder).
3. Select Reply With and click the Template button to open a blank message form.
4. Enter **Out of the Office** or something similar in the subject field.
5. Enter the appropriate text in the message section.
6. Choose File, then choose Save & Close to return to the Edit Rule dialog box.
7. Click the Advanced button.
8. In the Advanced dialog box, select Only Items That Do Not Match These Conditions.
9. Click OK twice to return to the Out Of Office Assistant dialog box, where both rules are listed.

You can do the same thing with the Subject field and Message body field, entering text that launches an action for a rule to forward your mail to someone, or even

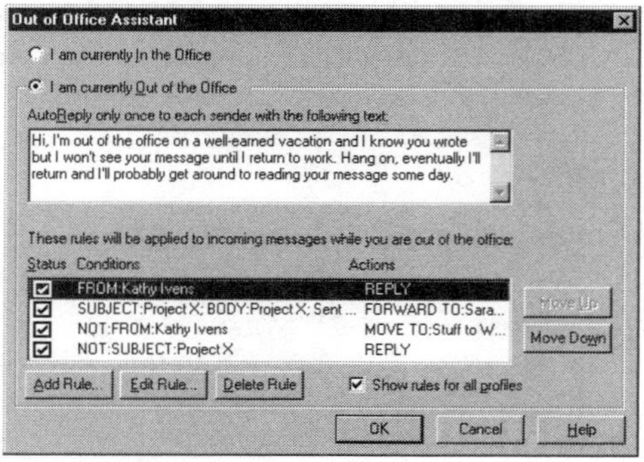

Figure 4-26. *Take care of special situations, as well as ordinary situations, by creating counterbalancing rules.*

automatically replying with special text. Then use the same criteria for another rule, specifying a nonmatch of conditions to take care of all your other e-mail.

In fact, you can set up multiple rules for handling specified criteria, and create a counterbalancing rule for each set of criteria, as seen in Figure 4-26.

Using Folders in Actions is Tricky If you choose an action that moves or copies messages to a folder, the action won't take place until you return and connect to Exchange Server. This is because an action involving folders is a client-based rule, and only server-based rules are implemented while you're not connected to Exchange Server. Server-based rules include those that have actions that can be performed within the Private Information Store (mailboxes).

What does work is *forwarding* messages to a public folder, because that is a server-based action. For this to work, the public folder must accept postings (instead of forms) and must be listed in the Global Address List (GAL).

To list a public folder in the GAL, you must clear the default setting of hiding public folders. In the Exchange Administrator window, select the Public Folders container under the server that holds the public folder you want to change:

1. Select the folder (in the right pane) and from the File menu, choose Properties.
2. Move to the Advanced tab of the Properties dialog box.
3. Clear the Hide From Address Book option.

Incidentally, the public folder has to be in the GAL only while the rule is being created. Afterwards you can hide it again, and the rule will still work.

If you consider the ramifications of this, there are some interesting procedures you can design. You can create a public folder for each user who requires it (translate that as users who receive mail that might be important for the company). Be sure that at least one other user has permissions for that folder. Out Of Office rules that don't specifically forward mail based on From or Subject criteria, instead forward mail to the public folder. The second user can examine the folder at any convenient time and take care of important messages. When the user who is out of the office returns, those messages are forwarded back to the Inbox or any other folder of choice. This empties the folder so that it's ready for the next time the user is absent from the office.

Limitations of Template Responses

An automatic response using a template that's generated by a rule is missing two of the elements that are part of the built-in AutoReply feature:

- The subject field does not include the original subject.

- The reply is sent each time a message is received instead of just once to each sender.

Controlling Which Messages Are Saved

Here's a clever way to handle the massive amount of e-mail you could face when you return after time away from the office. Create a rule that moves all messages with "urgent" in the Subject field to a folder. Then, in the balancing rule (messages that do not have "urgent" in the Subject field), launch a response and delete the message. In the text of your response template, explain what's going on. For instance, you might say, "If it's very important that I see this message upon my return, please resend it with the word "urgent" in the Subject field. Otherwise, please wait until after my return because I'm zapping the message."

Delaying the Sending of a Message

It might be a real service to include instructions in your template text for delaying the message until you return. In case you're not aware of this feature, here's how to use it (and explain it in your reply template):

After the message is composed, from the message form menu bar, choose View, and then choose Options. When the Message Options dialog box appears, select Do Not Deliver Before, then enter a date and time (see Figure 4-27).

Turning Rules On and Off

When you return to the office, from Out Of Office Assistant, select I Am Currently In The Office. This turns off all the rules.

Don't delete the rules, however; save them for the next time you're out of the office. You can clear the rules you don't want to use the next time by clicking the box in the Status column. This ability to toggle rules on and off is a great time saver, because it means you can just let the rules you create pile up, then choose those you need.

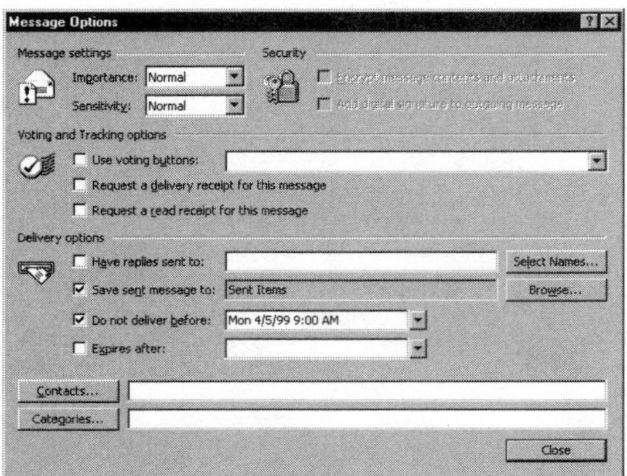

Figure 4-27. *Click the arrow to the right of the date field to display a calendar so you can point and click to insert a date.*

Another reason to save old rules is that it's frequently easier to edit a rule than to re-create a rule. For example, suppose your last vacation came in the middle of the company's work on the yearly budget. You created a rule that launched an action if the word "budget" appeared in the subject or text, perhaps forwarding the message to an assistant. Now you're going on vacation again, but the important project is the annual employee reviews. Edit your "budget" rule by changing the text to "review." Don't forget to make the same change to any counterbalancing rule.

Using the Rules Wizard

The Rules Wizard works on the same general principle as the Out Of Office Assistant, but there are two major differences:

- The rules you create are being applied continuously (not just when you're out of the office).
- The rules cover more than incoming mail.

The Rules Wizard is available in Microsoft Outlook 98, but earlier versions of Exchange clients (Outlook 97 and Exchange) use the Inbox Assistant (covered later in this chapter). If the Outlook 98 client is an upgrade from a previous version of Outlook or Exchange Client, you can upgrade existing Inbox Assistant rules. The first time you open the Rules Wizard, an offer to convert the rules is displayed. Rules that involve custom forms cannot be converted to the Rules Wizard; they need to be created again.

Creating a New Rule with the Wizard

Open the Rules Wizard by choosing Tools from the menu bar, and then choosing Rules Wizard to display the Rules Wizard dialog box. Click New to create a new rule. The first Wizard window opens (see Figure 4-28); and you select the point at which you want to apply the rule.

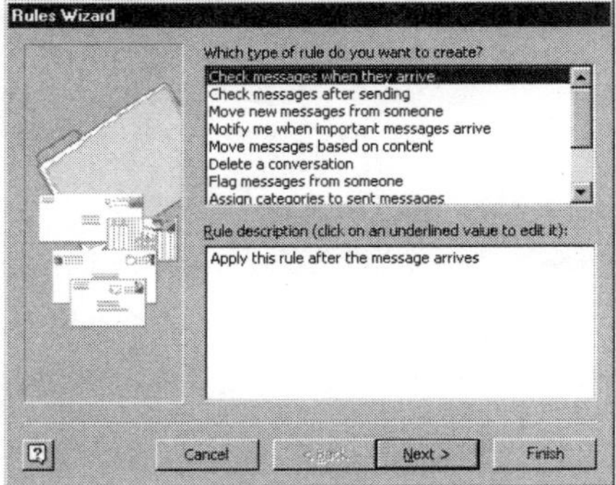

Figure 4-28. *You can create rules for incoming or outgoing mail.*

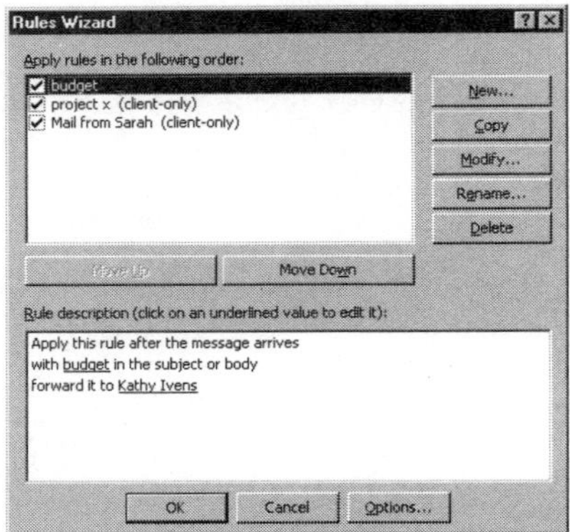

Figure 4-29. *Move rules up and down to affect the order of processing.*

As you do with all wizards, click Next to move through all the Wizard windows. Here are some guidelines for using the Wizard:

- If you select an option that contains underlined text, there's additional data entry required. You must make a selection (such as a name or a folder) or enter text. Click the underlined text after the description is moved into the bottom box to display the appropriate dialog box; then make a selection or enter text.
- You can choose multiple criteria and multiple actions from any Wizard window (make sure they don't conflict).
- The Wizard has an exception list, so you don't have to create counterbalancing rules.
- If you want to move or copy messages to a folder, you're creating a client-based rule, which won't take effect until you're logged on. (The Wizard notifies you whenever you create a client-based rule.)
- You can create a rule that assigns a category to a message (assuming you're using categories in Outlook). Note, however, that the Wizard doesn't check to make sure you've created the category you specify. (Incidentally, categories are client-based rules.)

You can create multiple rules, and they're processed in the order in which they display in the Rules Wizard dialog box (see Figure 4-29). You can turn rules off and on by selecting and clearing the check box.

Creating a New Rule with a Message

You can also create a rule based on a message, which gives you a head start on the criteria. As a shortcut for creating a rule, you can use the message's sender, subject, body text, or any other element you want to use as criteria.

Open the message and, from the message form menu bar, choose Actions, and then choose Create A Rule. The Rules Wizard opens with criteria specifications

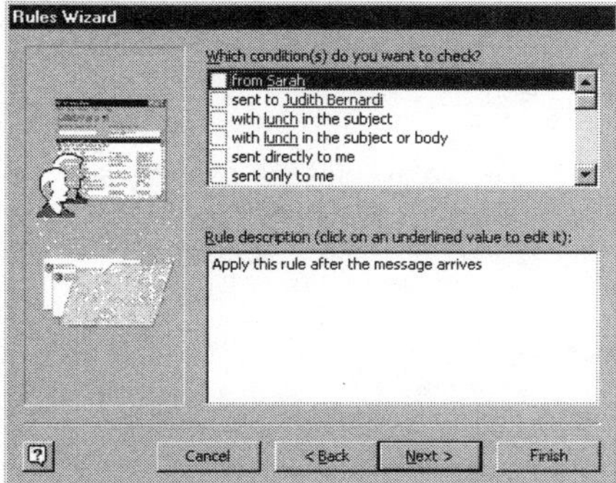

Figure 4-30. *The Rules Wizard leaped to the second Wizard window because some information was already available.*

already filled in (see Figure 4-30). Choose the conditions you want to use for the new rule by selecting the appropriate check box(es).

Click Next to move through the Wizard and finish configuring the new rule.

Using the Inbox Assistant

The Inbox Assistant, for clients with versions of Outlook and Exchange earlier than Outlook 98, looks and acts like the Out Of Office Assistant. From the Tools menu, choose Inbox Assistant, and then click Add Rule to create a new rule (see Figure 4-31).

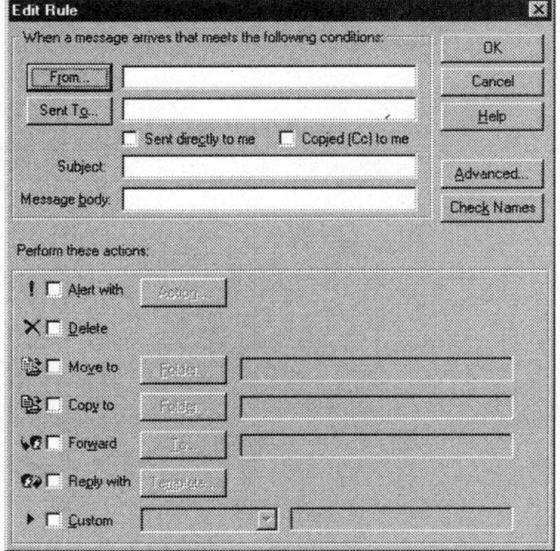

Figure 4-31. *The criteria and actions available in the Inbox Assistant are the same as the Out Of Office Assistant.*

The Inbox Assistant applies rules and actions regardless of whether you're logged on. Like the Rules Wizard, however, actions that involve copying or moving items to a folder don't take effect until you log on.

Tip If you use the Rules Wizard or Inbox Assistant from a remote location, rules launch their associated actions when you log on and synchronize.

Macintosh Client Issues

Until recently, the Macintosh client wasn't anything you'd rush to install. It was barely functional and difficult to administer, because little helpful information was available. However, that original software has been replaced by the Outlook Macintosh client, which brought the feature setup from "barely functional" to "functional." It operates with a feature set that will remind you of the older, 16-bit Exchange clients.

The Macintosh Outlook client upgrade included in Exchange Server 5.5 Service Pack 2 brought some additional functionality. It's named Macintosh Outlook version 8.1. I discuss it in this section in case you're considering the product for your Macintosh users.

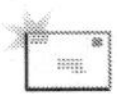

Note Macintosh Outlook version 8.1 supports Mac OS 8.5.

Macintosh Outlook User Interface

The user interface of version 8.1 is closer to the look and feel of the Windows version, which should make user training easier (for you, although not necessarily for the Macintosh users, unless they've previously spent a lot of time using Windows).

Some customization of the Outlook Bar is available, and there's a folder banner that resembles the one on Outlook for Windows. The menu bar and toolbar commands are arranged similarly to the Windows Outlook client.

Macintosh Outlook E-Mail Functions

Outlook for Macintosh version 8.1, like previous versions, works only with Exchange Server. The software does not support Internet mail (POP3 or [IMAP4]), so it cannot connect to an ISP. Version 8.1 includes several new (to the Mac version) e-mail features:

Note Outlook Express for Macintosh does support Internet mail.

- Message flags (both sending and receiving)
- Recall message

- Respond to voting messages (Mac users still cannot create and send voting messages)
- Support for Secure/Multipurpose Internet Mail Extensions (S/MIME)-based message security for the Power Mac

Macintosh Outlook Calendar Functions

The interface for Calendar remains as it was for previous versions of Outlook for Macintosh clients, which means that the Calendar is still displayed in a separate window (which can be accessed from the Outlook Bar).

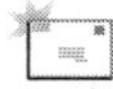

Note Separate windows are also used for Contacts and Tasks information.

Version 8.1 has been updated to include these features:

- Users can view Calendar details of Windows Outlook users.
- Full interoperability of Calendar features with all other Outlook for Macintosh versions.
- Interoperability with Schedule+ users on all platforms.

Macintosh Outlook Forms Support

There is some support for forms in version 8.1. The software is able to display custom forms that are implemented with HTML and Microsoft Exchange Server Collaboration Data Object (CDO) scripts (the forms open in the user's browser). Macintosh users cannot display any custom forms that were created with an Outlook 32-bit client, nor can they create forms.

Outlook Web Access Clients

Users can connect to Exchange Server through their browsers. This feature, named Outlook Web Access, is useful for clients who do not have traditional client software such as Outlook. The most obvious beneficiaries of this feature are the UNIX users in your enterprise.

Support for OWA is provided by Exchange Server, Internet Information Server (IIS), and the Active Server Pages component of IIS. This combination of server-side components provides the active messaging required for browser-based clients.

Client-Side Functions

The client reaches Exchange Server with the standard HTTP, using your server's URL. The browser displays the output generated by the active messaging features on the server. The browser must support JavaScript and frames (to be sure, supply your users with either Microsoft Internet Explorer 4.0 or later, or Netscape Navigator 3.0 or later).

The connection begins with a choice to enter the site as an anonymous user, or to connect to a mailbox. Anonymous users can see only those public folders you've made available (which may be none). A request to connect to a mailbox is accompanied by a user logon (the Microsoft Windows NT account attached to the mailbox and the password for the Windows NT account).

Tip If the user connects to the Internet through an ISP and he or she wants to use the OWA to connect to the Microsoft Exchange Server, the user has to log on using the domain/mailbox_alias format. For example, if your domain name is XYZ and your mailbox alias is johnd, you should enter **XYZ/johnd** in the OWA logon box.

Even though there's a requirement for JavaScript support for the browser, the server is actually supplying VBScript along with Active Pages to process client requests to find or create messages. Frames create a user interface that divides the window in a manner that resembles mail client software windows.

Server-Side Functions

On the server side, multiple applications and features are working to provide the client side with services. To support these client connections, the server must be running IIS 3.0 or later, Microsoft Windows NT 4 with SP3, Active Pages, and Active Messaging. HTTP and Lightweight Directory Access Protocol (LDAP) must also be installed.

Communication between the client and Exchange Server involves MAPI. Requests from the client are translated to equivalent MAPI functions, as if they were coming from an Outlook client. Exchange sends MAPI output, which Active Messaging translates to HTML for the browser.

All the work and processing take place on the server. In fact, there's an enormous load on the server for browser connections—far more than the standard software client creates.

Tip IIS 3.0 or later does not have to run on the same Microsoft Exchange server. If IIS is running on another server, you need to install the OWA component of Microsoft Exchange Server on the IIS server and specify the Microsoft Exchange server name during installation of this component.

OWA Limitations

There are some functions that OWA clients cannot perform, and it's a good idea to let your OWA users know about them. Otherwise users will call you asking, "How do I do such and such?" Here's what's missing:

- Automatic archiving
- Creating and using automatic signatures
- Accessing Personal Address Book

- Changing permissions in folders
- Creating folder views

Controlling the Use of OWA

Because of the strain on the Exchange server, it behooves administrators to put some controls on the number of users who access the server via OWA. You need to consider the appropriate use of OWA as you set guidelines for the users in your enterprise.

If you have a mixed environment, providing OWA services for UNIX users is a necessity. This is one of the few instances in which Microsoft provides integrated services for UNIX. Here's an opportunity to be a hero and a true geek—you're one of the few IT professionals who can provide an enterprise solution.

I've talked to several administrators who were in the middle of upgrades for departments or divisions that used OWA to stem the tide of user complaints. During the upgrade, users were angry because they couldn't get their mail. The tales I heard involved upgrades to hardware, the client operating system, and migration from another mail application. Incidentally, hardware upgrades almost always include operating system upgrades; it's a two-fer for client users and usually involves twice as many problems, as users face a learning curve in addition to potential glitches and problems.

During the rollout of an operating system or of Exchange Server, the Exchange administrator can establish and configure mailboxes for every user in the organization rather quickly. Installing and configuring the client operating system, however, takes more time. It's much easier to get a browser up and running than it is to install and set up all the workstation elements. For the short period needed, browser access to mailboxes may prevent user revolts.

Dial-in users can sometimes get to their mailboxes via a browser more easily than they can connect with client software. Exchange Server is occasionally overly fussy about handling remote procedure call (RPC) communications over telephone connections and just refuses to participate in any communication with a dialed-in Outlook client. In fact, I've experienced this even when I can ping successfully, so I know the server is available.

Tip Microsoft Windows NT users who connect to the LAN via Remote Access Server (RAS) often experience delays and finally receive a message indicating that the server is not available but that they can work offline. To get around this problem, configure the client's Hosts file, which is located in the <*%systemroot%*>\system32\ drivers\etc folder, with the host name and the IP address of the Microsoft Exchange Server.

OWA and Public Folders

Providing public folders for OWA clients is not trivial, but if you're committed to providing OWA services, you probably have to provide some public folder

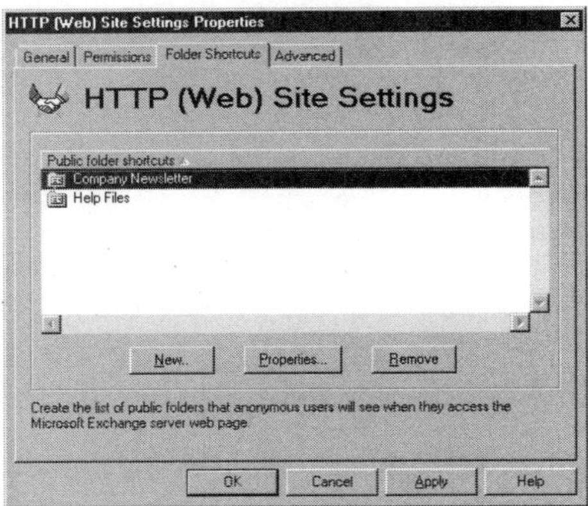

Figure 4-32. *Create shortcuts to public folders for browser clients.*

access. Otherwise you've made second-class citizens of your OWA users (you may have noticed that UNIX fans tend to get upset at such a notion). Administrators who send messages that say, "Be sure to check this month's award winners in the Awards folder," will hear from frustrated users if the folder isn't accessible to the OWA message recipients.

To make a public folder available, create a shortcut that can be displayed for OWA clients. The shortcut is configured on the Folder Shortcuts tab of the HTTP Properties dialog box (see Figure 4-32), which is a site object (Site\Configuration\Protocols). Click New to see a list of folders and select those you want to use.

Shortcuts are site-specific, so OWA users who connect to one site won't see shortcuts to folders on other sites. You can solve this problem by creating a shortcut to a public folder that's replicated to the site.

Managing Outlook Express Clients

Outlook Express is employed by users who dial out to a server, more so than with corporate users who have Exchange Server available on the corporate network. The server could be an ISP, or it could be an Exchange server that mobile users dial into.

There's no option to add Exchange Server as a service in Outlook Express, but there is a way to configure the software to connect to Exchange Server in order to send and retrieve e-mail. Administrators use this trick to enable mobile clients to log on to the server with their laptops when they're in the office and thus to link to the network. The network needs to be running TCP/IP to accomplish this, because you're using the TCP/IP stack to achieve the connection. Your Exchange Server configuration must include IMS and either IMAP4 or POP3.

To configure Outlook Express to let a user connect to your Exchange server, that user must have an existing Windows NT account and an existing Exchange mailbox.

Connecting Outlook Express Directly to Exchange Server

Creating an account that connects to an Exchange server using POP3 or IMAP4 requires the same steps you take to create any new account in Outlook Express. The difference is in the settings:

1. From the Outlook Express menu bar, choose Tools, and then choose Accounts.
2. Go to the Mail tab in the Internet Accounts dialog box.
3. Click Add, and then choose Mail to start the Internet Connection Wizard.
4. Enter the user name that will appear in the From field for outgoing mail (see Figure 4-33). This should be the same name that's currently configured if this user has been using Outlook Express to dial in for mail. Then click Next.
5. In the E-mail Address text box of the next Wizard screen, enter the user's Simple Mail Transfer Protocol (SMTP) address for your Exchange Server. If you're not sure what to enter, double-click the user's mailbox in the Exchange Administrator window and go to the E-mail Address tab (see Figure 4-34, on the following page). Click Next in the Wizard to move on.
6. In the next Wizard window (see Figure 4-35, on the following page), select a protocol for the incoming mail server (POP3 or IMAP).
7. In the Incoming Mail Server text box, enter the name of the Exchange server on which the user's mailbox resides (and that is running the protocol you selected).
8. In the Outgoing Mail Server text box, enter the name of the Exchange Server that's running Internet Mail Service. (This isn't necessarily the same server on which the mailbox resides.) Then click Next.

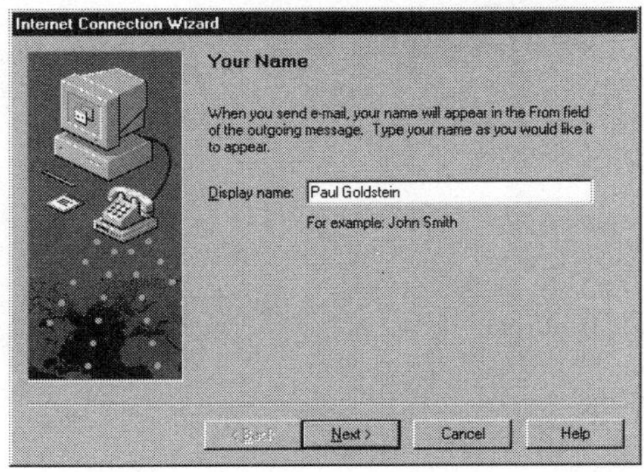

Figure 4-33. *Enter the name that will appear in the From field of messages.*

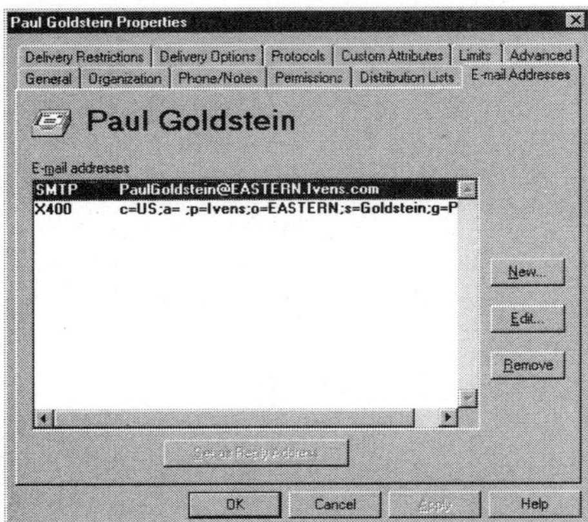

Figure 4-34. *The e-mail address is the SMTP address displayed in the user's mailbox.*

Tip Use the fully qualified domain name of your Microsoft Exchange Server instead of its NetBIOS name to make sure that you can connect to your mail server from the Internet. For example, instead of **East** enter **east.mydomain.com.**

9. For POP3, enter the POP account name in the form **domain\nt_id\mailbox_alias**. For IMAP4, use the form **domain/nt_id/mailbox_alias**. In the Password text box, enter the user's Windows NT account password. Then click Next.
10. Enter a friendly name—this is the name that appears in the Account list in Outlook Express.

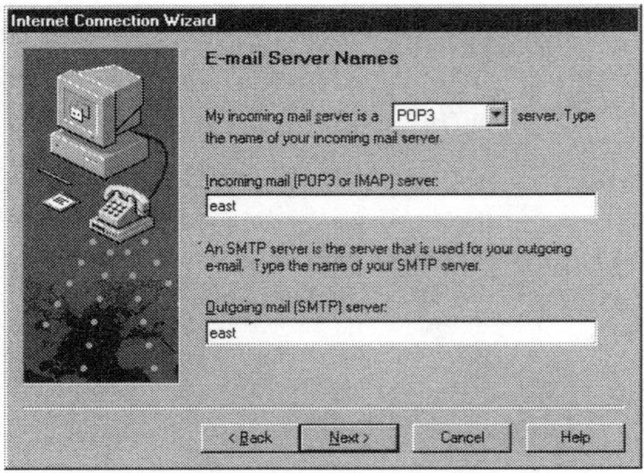

Figure 4-35. *The server information refers to your Exchange server.*

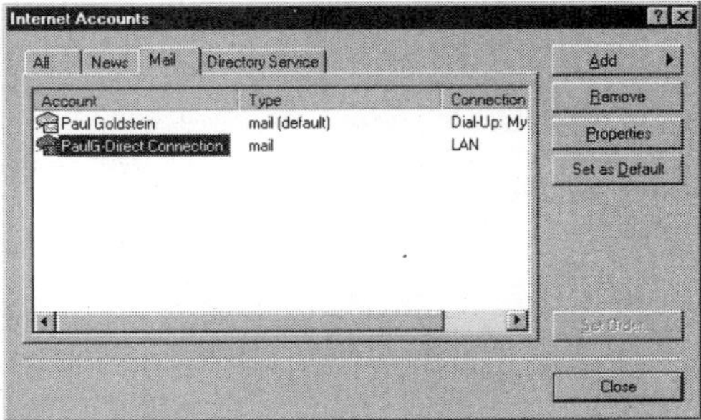

Figure 4-36. *The Exchange Server connection appears in the Account list.*

Note The friendly name must differ from any existing Outlook Express account name.

11. Select the LAN as the connection type and click Next.
12. Click Finish to complete the configuration.

The new connection appears in the Mail Account list for Outlook Express (see Figure 4-36). The user can select the appropriate account when it's time to retrieve or send e-mail.

You can also configure advanced options for this account by selecting the account and choosing Properties. The option you may want to change is on the Advanced tab, where you can configure Outlook to leave a copy of the message on the server (see Figure 4-37). If this is not checked, all the mail in the user's Inbox is downloaded and deleted from the server. (Note that you can also configure the way in which server mail is removed.)

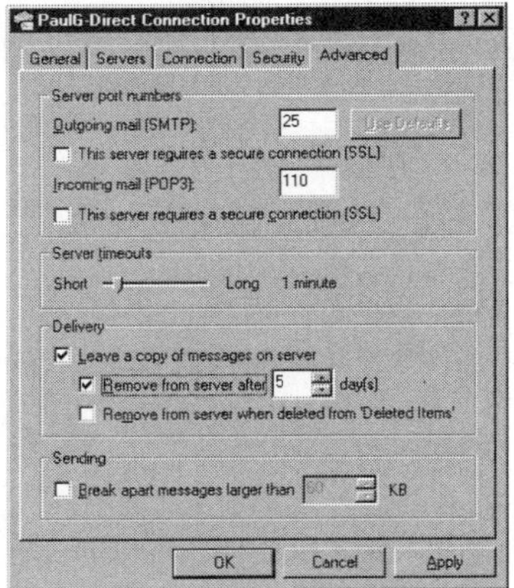

Figure 4-37. *You can keep user mail on the server to match the way Outlook works.*

Testing the Outlook Express Connection

After you install and configure a mail account in Outlook Express, you can test it by sending a mail message to the user's Internet address. Because POP3 has no send feature, the ability to send a message and successfully retrieve it ensures that both your SMTP and POP3 server settings have been configured correctly in the client.

Managing Multiple Users and Profiles

Exchange administrators face a wide variety of challenges when it comes to the word "multiple." There are users with multiple mailboxes on the Exchange server, users who want your help with multiple Internet mail accounts for external ISPs, and multiple users on the same workstation who each need to reach the Exchange server to collect mail.

The tasks you need to perform vary according to the problem you're trying to solve. However, it's safe to assume you'll be working in client software. In fact, it's safe to assume that you'll be working at the user's workstation because of the link between the logged-on user and the Exchange mailbox.

Tip The first step in maintaining, configuring, or troubleshooting multiple elements is to make sure there's a mailbox on the Exchange server for the user profile you're working with.

Multiple Mail Profiles

You can create as many mail profiles as you need for any computer, using the Mail utility in the Control Panel. Because mail profiles (and access to an Exchange Server mailbox) are connected to the computer logon name, log on to the computer with the name of the user for whom the new profile is being created.

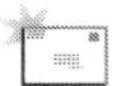

Note The Mail Settings utility in the Control Panel might be named Mail And Fax.

I'm assuming there's already one profile existing as a result of installing and configuring client software. When the Properties dialog box appears, click Show Profiles to display a list of current mail profiles (see Figure 4-38).

To create a new mail profile, click Add to open the Setup Wizard, seen in Figure 4-39.

The first Wizard window lists the available (installed) mail services, and you can select and deselect services, depending on what you need for this profile.

Note The name of the Setup Wizard varies, depending on the operating system and existing client software. You may see the Microsoft Outlook Setup Wizard or the Inbox Setup Wizard.

Figure 4-38. *Start a new profile by displaying the list of existing profiles.*

If your Exchange Server system handles Internet mail, don't select the Internal mail service for the profile. The Internet mail service listed in the Setup Wizard is a discrete service that is meant to be installed for those who use a dedicated Internet mail server (an ISP).

You can select both Microsoft Exchange server and Internet Mail as services. Some companies (usually small or medium-sized businesses) run Exchange Server only for local e-mail (internal e-mail among the employee group). There is no IMS connection on the Exchange server, and users who send and receive mail across the Internet must dial out to an ISP to do so. Some companies even set up and pay for those ISP accounts.

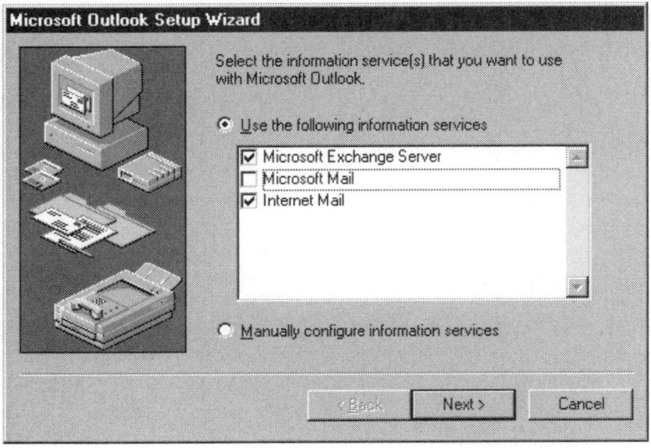

Figure 4-39. *Start by selecting the services you need for this profile.*

Figure 4-40. *All the mail profiles on a computer are displayed, and you can see or change the properties for any of them.*

Follow the steps provided by the Wizard, filling out information as required. Remember that if you're setting up the Exchange Server service, you must be connected to the Exchange server because the presence of the appropriate mailbox is checked during setup.

Tip Don't accept default filenames for profiles, .pab files, or .pst files. Always change the name to the profile/user name. This eliminates any danger of overwriting existing files when you create new profiles, and it makes it much easier to find the files if you have to work with them.

When you finish creating the new profile, it's listed in the display of profiles when you click the Show Profiles button (see Figure 4-40).

There's no option on the Mail (or Mail And Fax) Properties dialog box to choose a profile when the client software is launched. You can, however, make this option available from within the client software.

Launch the software, which opens with the predetermined default profile. Don't worry if an error message appears (because the profile and the logged-on user don't match). Even if you cannot connect to the Exchange server, the software window appears. Then follow these steps:

1. From the menu bar choose Tools, and then choose Options to display the Options dialog box.
2. Move to the Mail Services tab (see Figure 4-41).
3. Select the option Prompt For A Profile To Be Used.
4. Click OK.

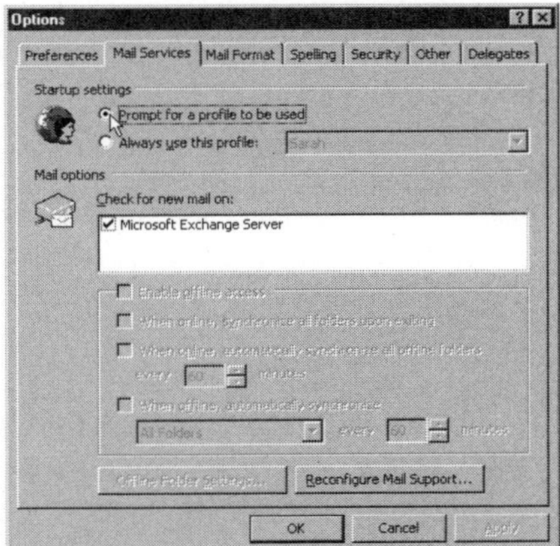

Figure 4-41. *Configure the software startup options to offer a choice of profiles.*

Hereafter, when you launch the client software you can choose the profile you want to use, as seen in Figure 4-42.

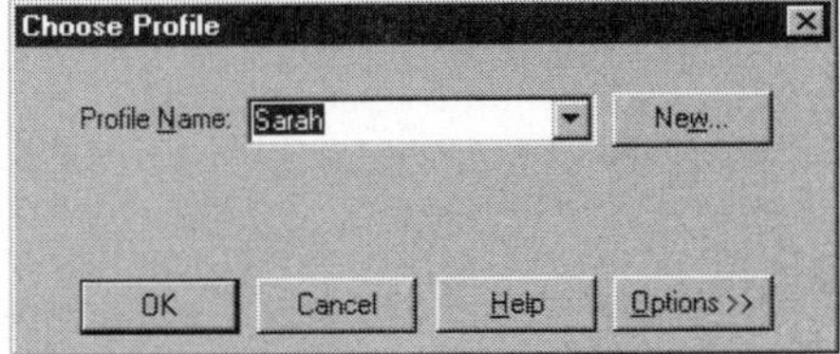

Figure 4-42. *Pick the profile you need.*

Tip You can also create a new profile from the Choose Profile dialog box. 

Multiple Internet E-Mail Addresses

If your Exchange Server installation is for internal mail, and users dial out for Internet mail, you'll probably get a call for help from any user who has multiple e-mail addresses (the user has more than one mailbox at an ISP or has multiple ISP accounts). Here's how to set up Outlook to collect Internet mail from multiple mail accounts (I'm assuming that Outlook was configured for one Internet e-mail account when it was first launched—this section is concerned with setting up additional Internet e-mail accounts):

1. Open the client software (using the appropriate profile if there are multiple profiles).
2. Choose Tools, then choose Services to display the Services Properties dialog box. The Services list includes Internet E-Mail.

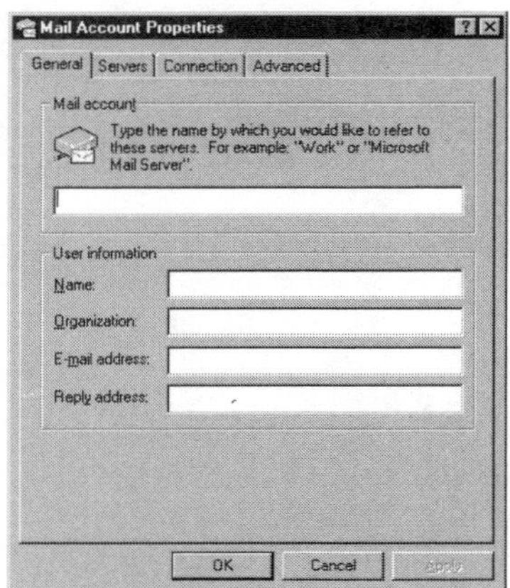

Figure 4-43. *Configure new e-mail accounts in the Mail Account Properties dialog box.*

3. Click Add to display the Add Service To Profile dialog box.
4. Choose Internet E-mail, and then click OK to open the Mail Account Properties dialog box seen in Figure 4-43.

Enter a friendly name for this account in the Mail Account text box. This is the name that Outlook uses. Make sure you use a name that's unique to Outlook and describes the account. For example, enter **kathy-getmail** for the user Kathy who needs to access a different ISP named Getmail (the original ISP is named MyISP), or **Kate-MyISP** for the user Kathy who has established a separate mailbox for "kate" on MyISP.

Fill out the other fields, including the other tabs, with the information provided by the ISP, noting these guidelines:

- You can connect to one ISP and retrieve e-mail from other ISPs.
- The SMTP server (outgoing mail) is always the server at the ISP into which you've dialed. This is true even if you're setting up an Outlook e-mail account to retrieve mail from a different ISP.

Within Outlook, choose Tools, then choose Send And Receive, and then select the account for which you want to retrieve mail. The Send command on the Tools menu doesn't list multiple accounts because mail is only sent through the account used to log on to the ISP.

Multiple Mailboxes on the Exchange Server

A user might need multiple mailboxes on the Exchange server for numerous reasons. Some users are responsible for resource mailboxes, or for long-term projects that have mailboxes. Perhaps a user in the Human Resources Department needs a personal mailbox in addition to a mailbox for employee inquiries about benefits.

The Exchange clients permit only one instance of the Exchange Server service, and the configuration includes the mailbox name. There is, however, a way to work around this—you can configure your system so that a user can access additional mailboxes beyond his or her own (the one that's linked to the user Windows NT logon ID).

For such a configuration, the following circumstances must be true:

- Both mailboxes must be set up on the server.
- Both mail profiles must be configured.
- The user must be able to log on to the workstation under both logon names (the names attached to the mailboxes). After the configuration for opening multiple mailboxes is complete, the user will not have to log on separately.

Note I'm assuming that you set up the second user on the network and on the workstation.

Let's walk through the steps, using some real users from my system (which is usually easier to follow than reading about User 1 and User 2).

Sarah writes the "Dear Richard" column for the company newsletter and wants to keep her identity and the messages separate. Both Sarah and Richard exist in the domain user list, and Sarah's workstation has logon profiles for both users. A mail profile has been set up for both (Richard's profile has only the Exchange Server service; there's no need to set up personal folders or any other service).

In order for Sarah to open Richard's mailbox when she opens Outlook as Sarah, she must follow these steps:

1. Log on to the workstation as Richard and open Outlook, using Richard's profile. This opens Richard's Inbox (see Figure 4-44).

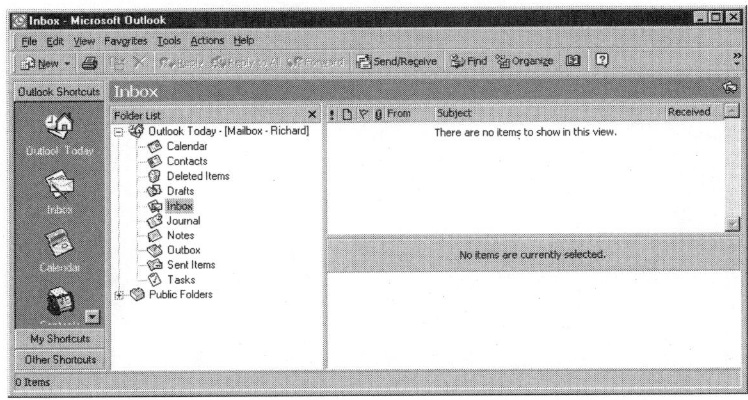

Figure 4-44. *Richard (really Sarah) is logged on, and his Exchange Server mailbox is open.*

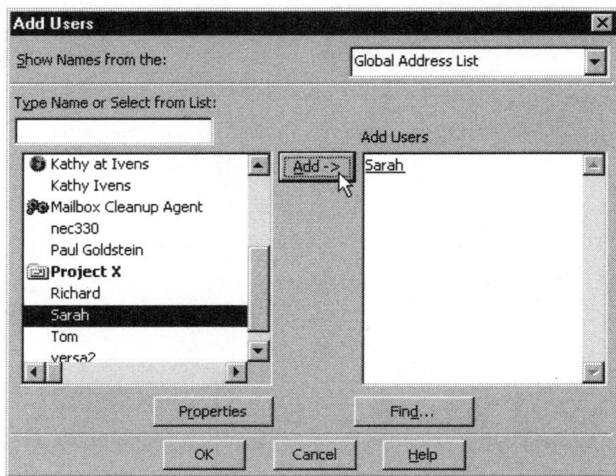

Figure 4-45. *Sarah, pretending to be Richard, is adding her own name to the user list for Richard's account.*

2. From the Tools menu, choose Options to display the Options dialog box.
3. Go to the Delegates tab, and click Add.
4. In the Add Users dialog box, select the name of the user who wants to open this mailbox (in this case it's Sarah). Click Add to put the name in the Add Users list (see Figure 4-45) and then click OK.
5. In the Delegate Permissions dialog box, select Editor for all boxes (see Figure 4-46). Also select the option to see any private items that arrive in the mailbox.
6. Click OK twice to return to the Outlook software window.

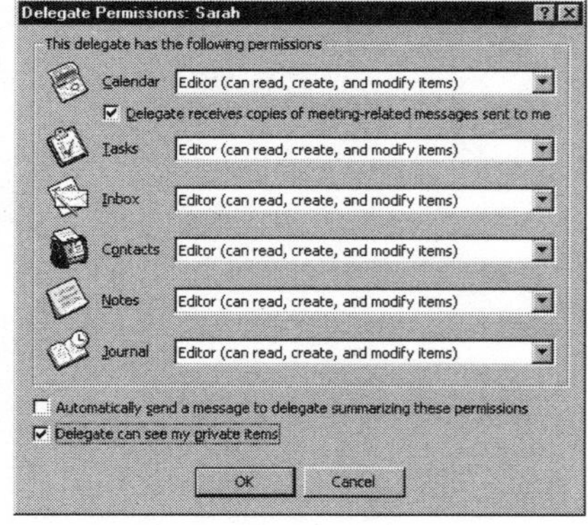

Figure 4-46. *Richard is giving Sarah total access to his mailbox.*

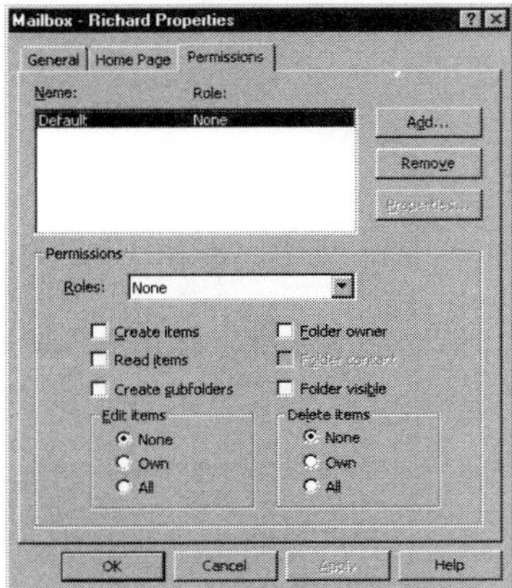

Figure 4-47. *Sarah needs to give herself the permissions she needs to manipulate Richard's mailbox at will.*

7. Make sure the Folder List is displayed in the Outlook window.
8. In the Folder pane, right-click the container for the Mailbox, and choose Properties from the shortcut menu.

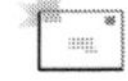

Note Depending on the client software, the mailbox container has the label Mailbox-<*user name*> or Outlook Today (Mailbox-<*user name*>). In this case, of course, the user name is Richard.

9. In the Mailbox Properties dialog box, go to the Permissions tab (see Figure 4-47).
10. Click Add to display the Add Users dialog box.
11. Select the real user (in this case Sarah) and add that user name to the Add Users list in the right pane. Then click OK.
12. Back on the Permissions tab, select the name you just added to the Permissions list. Then select Owner in the Roles box (see Figure 4-48, on the following page).
13. Repeat the same steps for all the other folders in the Folders List. Then exit Outlook.

Richard logs off the workstation, and Sarah logs on. She launches Outlook, using her own profile. Outlook opens in its normal fashion, with her mailbox in the window. Richard is nowhere in sight, and neither are any of his folders. All that's left for Sarah to do is configure Outlook to show her Richard's mailbox in addition to her own whenever she opens Outlook. Here's how she does that:

1. From the menu bar, choose Tools, and then choose Services.
2. In the list of services, select Microsoft Exchange Server, and click the Properties button.

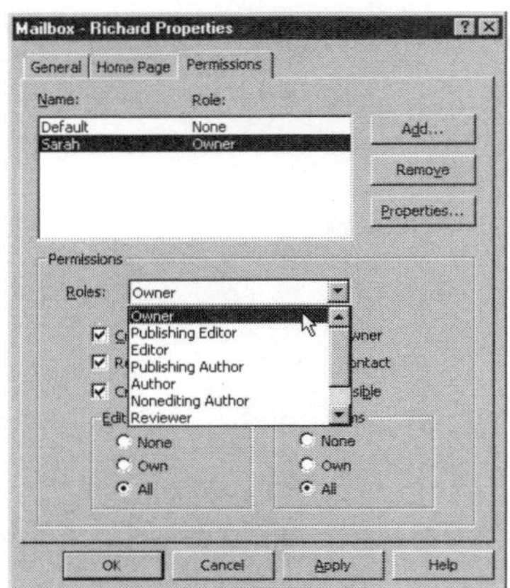

Figure 4-48. *Sarah is now a co-owner of Richard's mailbox.*

3. In the Microsoft Exchange Server Properties dialog box, go to the Advanced tab (see Figure 4-49).
4. Click Add, and enter the name of the additional mailbox in the Add Mailbox dialog box. Then click OK three times to return to the Outlook window.

Caution There is no user list available in the Add Mailbox dialog box, so you must know the exact name of the mailbox you want to add.

Figure 4-49. *Use the Advanced tab for the Exchange Server service to add mailboxes to your Outlook window.*

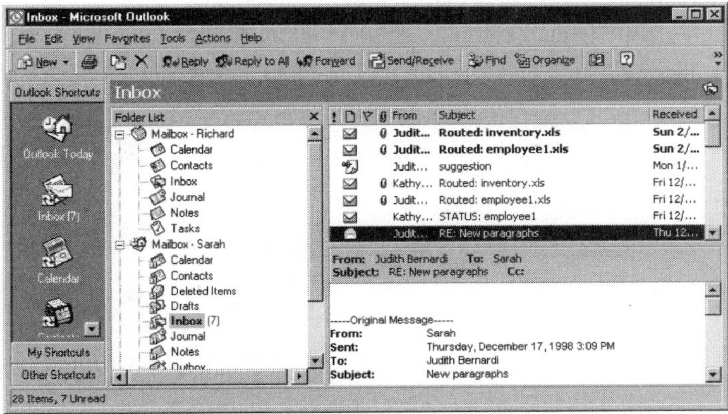

Figure 4-50. *Sarah has two mailboxes to work with now.*

Voilà! Sarah's Outlook window has both mailboxes, including the Inbox and all the folders for Richard (see Figure 4-50).

Chapter 5

Troubleshooting Client Software

For most Microsoft Exchange Server administrators, troubleshooting client software is a daily chore. Users ask for help in a steady barrage of phone calls and e-mail.

Most of the information in this chapter concerns Microsoft Outlook, because that's the most widely used client program in Exchange Server environments. Additionally, there isn't a lot of information about troubleshooting the problems that users encounter as they compose e-mail. That's because there aren't a lot of frantic user calls on the subject. General troubleshooting tips for sent mail are found in Chapter 2, as the problems are usually on the Exchange server. This chapter does cover nondelivery receipt problems.

Missing Components in Outlook

As an administrator, you're going to receive calls from users looking for a feature. You'll hear, "It's not on my menu." The default installation omits some features, so there's going to be additional work for you if your users need those features. In addition, some client workstations are going to have the wrong Outlook installation package, and you may have to reinstall Outlook.

Understanding the Differences Between Outlook Programs

There's a difference between deciding on which Outlook components to install and which Outlook software to install. If you deployed Outlook from a server or had total control over the installation, you probably haven't had a problem with the wrong "flavor" of Outlook being installed. If the users in your organization handled their own installations, however, you probably ran into the "I installed the wrong one" problem. Many administrators have faced this.

There are three Microsoft Outlook software program modes available during installation: Outlook Internet Mail Only (IMO), Outlook Corporate or Workgroup (CW), and Outlook No E-mail. They are very different in their feature sets, and only Outlook CW works with Exchange Server.

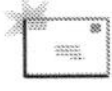

Note I don't know of any Exchange administrators who found that a client had installed the No E-mail mode by mistake. This installation option is used when there's a need for a personal information manager without any e-mail services.

Many administrators who have found the wrong software on client systems told me that users exclaimed, "But I only use it for e-mail, so it seemed like the right one to install." Other users apparently thought that the words "Corporate" and "Workgroup" meant "for servers only."

Unfortunately, Microsoft doesn't package, sell, or distribute these Outlook modes separately. The decision is made during installation. And, in all fairness to those users who installed the wrong mode, it's important to point out that the Setup program makes some decisions for users. Setup inspects the computer on which the installation is taking place and then presents limited choices to users.

If the computer has Microsoft Outlook 97, the user is asked if this is an upgrade from a previous version of Outlook. If the user answers Yes, the Setup program looks at the Outlook profile and decides which mode to install (frequently the decision is to install Outlook IMO).

If the user answers No, that still doesn't solve the problem. The answer triggers a search of the computer, during which the installation utility looks for any other e-mail programs. If it finds Eudora, Microsoft Outlook Express, or Netscape Communicator it asks which of those programs you want to update from. If the user selects one, the setup program installs Outlook IMO. The user has to know that the answer should be None Of The Above. Having answered No, followed by None Of The Above, the user finally has a chance to make his or her own decision. Users who want to install Outlook CW in order to connect to Exchange Server have to know about refusing all offers, which is not an instinctive action.

The modes are mutually exclusive; they cannot work together. If Outlook IMO is installed, install Outlook CW. For the rest of this chapter, any references to Outlook are to Outlook CW.

Tip Here's how to tell which mode is installed. Open the Help menu and choose About Microsoft Outlook. When the dialog box opens, check the second line of text (the first line is the version number). The second line indicates either CW or IMO. If there is no second line, and all the copyright information begins immediately under the version information on the first line, the No E-mail version is installed.

Adding Outlook Components

The setup program doesn't install all the available components for Outlook, so if users need one of these missing components, some postinstallation work must be done.

Installing Basic Components

For the components available during setup, you may find that some users have some services installed while other users don't. For example, Personal Folder services may not be installed automatically. This is not always a result of user choice during installation; it's because the Outlook setup program made its own decisions after inspecting the computer.

To add a component to an Outlook installation, you must have already installed the files for that component. It's a simple matter to add the feature, because the files are in the system. From the Tools menu, choose Services to display the Services dialog box. Click Add, then select the service you want to install.

Note You can install multiple instances of some services. For instance, you can have more than one Personal Folder (remember to name each .pst file with a unique filename). You could even have multiple Internet E-Mail Services (for different accounts that dial into different hosts). You cannot, however, have duplicate instances of the exact same service, such as MSN.

Creating Offline Folders After Installation

Offline folders are created during the first configuration of the client software. The Configuration Wizard asks if you travel with this computer, and an affirmative answer results in the creation of an offline folder.

If a user discovers a need for offline folders after he or she has been using the client software, you don't have to create a new profile; you can create offline folders from the client software. The client must be connected to Exchange Server while you perform this task:

1. From the Tools menu, choose Services.
2. On the Services tab, select Microsoft Exchange Server and click Properties.
3. Move to the Advanced tab.
4. In Outlook 98, select Enable Offline Use, and then click Offline Folder File Settings. Outlook 97 contains no check box option; just click Offline Folder File Settings.
5. A default path and filename are displayed, and it's a good idea to change the filename to match the user instead of using the generically named file. Outlook will ask you for permission to create the new file.

After the offline file is created, synchronize the client to the server. From the Tools menu, choose Synchronize, and then choose All Folders.

Installing Optional Components

Some files are not installed during a normal installation and must be specifically installed later. In addition to the basic Outlook features, these components are available:

- **Development Tools** These include tools for designing forms, a script debugger, and Visual Basic Help.

- **PIM Converters** These include converters for ACT, Ecco, Sidekick, and Schedule+.
- **Lotus Organizer Converter** This imports data from Lotus Organizer.
- **Integrated File Management** This enhances Outlook to give you access to system folders in addition to Outlook folders.
- **Spelling Dictionary**
- **News Reader**

The Integrated File Management component and the News Reader are the commonly installed optional features.

The Integrated File Management component is usually added to Outlook installations because it's so useful. Once it's installed, Outlook can access any folder on the local system or on the network. In fact, an icon for the local system (in the form of My Computer) can be placed on the Outlook Bar.

The News Reader isn't actually an Outlook component. Outlook doesn't have news reader capabilities, but Outlook Express does. When you install the optional News Reader, you're really installing the News Reader component of Outlook Express. When users launch the News Reader, an Outlook Express window opens.

Here's how to install optional components:

1. Close Outlook if it's running. In fact, it's a good idea to reboot the machine to make sure no mail services or .dlls are running (which can interfere with the installation).
2. From the Control Panel, open the Add/Remove Programs utility.
3. Select Microsoft Outlook 98, and then click Add/Remove.
4. In the Outlook 98 Active Setup dialog box (the title says Maintenance Wizard), click the Add New Components button.
5. Select Install From CD or Install From Web, depending on the source of the original installation.
6. The Active Setup program offers to search your system to see which Outlook components are already installed. Click Yes.
7. The list of available optional components is displayed, indicating whether a specific component is installed (see Figure 5-1).
8. Select the check box next to each component you want to add.
9. Click Next, and then wait a couple of moments while the Setup program does some behind-the-scenes work.
10. Click to select a Download Site (even the CD is considered a download site).
11. Click Install Now.
12. If you're installing from an Internet site, your Dial-Up Networking or RAS connection opens, and your browser travels to that site.
13. When the file installation is complete, a notification of success displays. Click OK.
14. You're instructed that you must restart Windows. Click Yes to let the setup program shut down the computer.

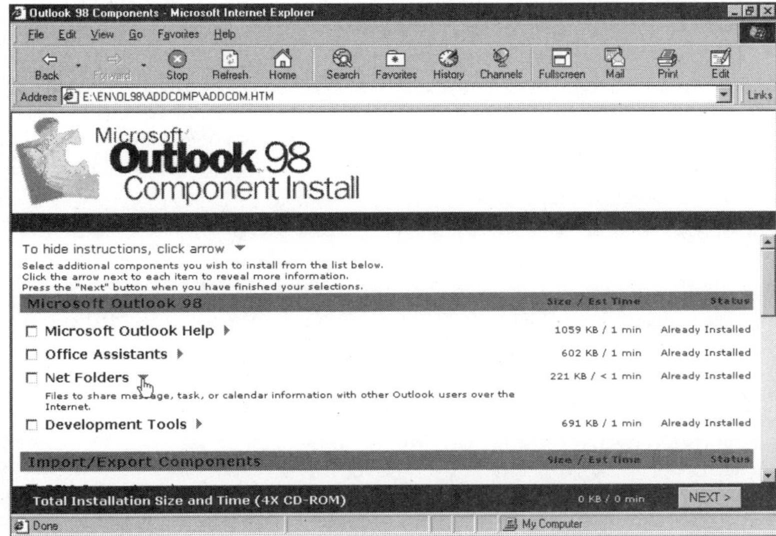

Figure 5-1. *Click the arrow to the right of the component name to display information about that feature.*

Troubleshooting NDR Messages

Nondelivery reports are annoying, and users get them frequently. Not every NDR is a result of a bad address, although most of them are. Sometimes users receive NDRs for which the solution lies at your end, either in the client software or the Exchange Server system.

Internet Gateway Failures

When a user attempts to send a message to an Internet/SMTP address and receives an NDR from the Exchange Server system administrator with the message No Gateway Installed, it's probably an error on the client software. This problem is frequently encountered on systems that are supporting Microsoft Mail.

It's most likely that the processing order of outbound mail is configured incorrectly. In the client software, from the Tools menu, open the Services dialog box and go to the Delivery tab. Make sure Microsoft Exchange Remote Transport is listed before Microsoft Mail Transport (or any other non-Exchange transport). Select Microsoft Exchange Remote Transport and click the Up arrow to position it before the other transport mode (or do it the other way around).

Note that this problem doesn't prevent the user from receiving Internet mail, just sending it. The problem does occur, however, when the user replies to a message received from the Internet.

Secondary Connector Errors

When a message with multiple recipients travels through a connector on the Exchange server to reach one recipient and travels through another connector to reach another recipient, the sender may receive an NDR. For example, a user may send a message to three recipients—one on the Exchange system, one with an Internet address (uses the Internet connector), and one that requires a different connector (perhaps PROFS, Notes, or cc:Mail).

An NDR, if received, is for the foreign connector. What's strange is that the recipient on the Exchange server can reply and include all the recipients, and no NDR will show up.

This is a known problem. If you encounter it, contact Microsoft to find out if a fix is available.

NDR During Outbox Replication

If a user sends a message to his or her Outbox at the same time that Outbox is in the process of replication, Exchange Server returns an NDR.

This is a known problem. If you encounter it, contact Microsoft to find out if a fix is available.

NDR During Synchronization

If a mobile user logs on, and the client software begins synchronization and also sends a message to the Outbox, the user may receive an NDR.

This is a known problem. If you encounter it, contact Microsoft to find out if a fix is available.

Recipient Not in Address Book

This problem occurs for mobile users who send a message to an Internet recipient who is not listed in the Global Address List (GAL) or the user's Personal Address Book (PAB). When the user connects to the server, the message is sent, and an NDR follows in a short time (in fact, frequently within a moment or two).

If the mobile user types an e-mail address directly into the To: field while he or she is connected to the Exchange server, the problem doesn't occur.

The easy solution, of course, is to make sure that users add an Internet recipient to their PAB before composing a message to that recipient. You might want to try another solution, however. You can reconfigure the client software so that it must be online to work, and then configure it back to offline work. There are reports that toggling the offline feature off and on again often solves this problem.

1. From the Control Panel, click the Mail utility. (If there are multiple profiles, select the appropriate profile and click Properties.)
2. Select the Microsoft Exchange Server service and click Properties.

3. Configure the service so that the client software automatically connects to the network. (In Outlook 98, you may have to select Manually Control Connection State to make this option available.)
4. Start the client software, which will connect to the server, either through the LAN or by using a Dial-Up Networking connection or RAS connection. (I guess it's obvious that you can't do any of this if the user isn't in a position to connect to the server automatically—it won't work from an offsite location.)
5. Send a message to an Internet recipient who is not listed in an address book (just enter the e-mail address in the To: field). Then hang around a couple of minutes to make sure that no NDR shows up (if it does, something else is causing the problem).
6. Disconnect from the server. Then return to the Mail utility and reset the Exchange Server Properties to work offline.

If this doesn't solve the problem, then the user must add Internet recipients to the PAB before trying to send mail. In fact, even if it does solve the problem, it's not a bad idea to tell users to add Internet recipients to the PAB before attempting to send a message.

Messages Sent by Rules

Are users who employ rules (from Inbox Assistant, Rules Wizard, or Out of Office Assistant) to forward messages to Internet recipients receiving NDRs? The solution is easy, but it's not in the client software; it's on the Exchange server.

Unlike previous versions, Microsoft Exchange 5.5 disallows automatic replies and automatic forwarding to the Internet by default. You must deselect that default prohibition to permit client software the use of this feature:

1. In the Exchange Administrator window, select the Connections icon for the site in the left pane.
2. Select the IMS object in the right pane and, on the File menu, click Properties.
3. On the Internet Mail tab, click Advanced Options.
4. Deselect the default options (see Figure 5-2).

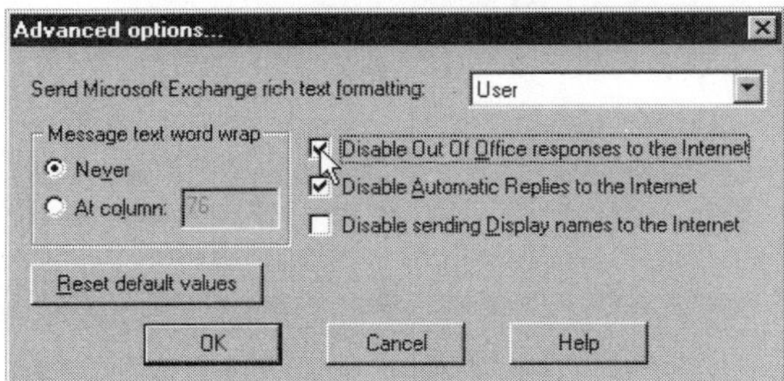

Figure 5-2. *Get rid of the prohibitions on Internet messages sent by rules.*

Mail Stuck in the Outbox

Client software sometimes refuses to ship a message out of the Outbox. There are several causes for this problem, so you'll have to do some homework before attempting a solution. The problem occurs most frequently (but not exclusively) with users who work offline—the Outbox isn't cleared after connecting to the server.

Tip I once received a call from a panicked user who had sent a message that went to the Outbox and was still there an hour later. The user, who was working offline, hadn't connected yet to the server (and it took me far too long to ascertain that fact). Make sure the first question you ask is "Are you working offline?," followed by "Have you connected to the server yet?" Take nothing for granted!

Opening a Message Keeps It in the Outbox

If a user opens a message that's in the Outbox and closes it again, it won't be sent. Instead it stays in the Outbox. This happens most often to offline users, because connected users don't usually have enough time to open the message—it's sent to the server quickly. I suppose that a user who is really fast with a mouse could duplicate this error, however.

Essentially, the rule of thumb is that Exchange Server only picks up messages that have an italicized listing in the Outbox (see Figure 5-3).

If you open a message that's in the Outbox, when you close it the listing is no longer displayed in italics. This is a notice from the software that the message is not going to be sent. It doesn't matter whether you made changes to the message or not. It will sit in the Outbox forever. The only way to send the message is to choose Send from the message form again.

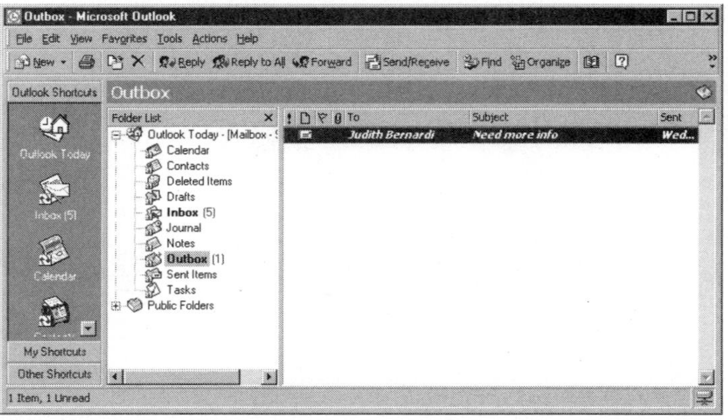

Figure 5-3. *Outbox listings in italics are ready to go to the server.*

Stuck Message Caused by Corrupt .pst File

Personal folder files wreak havoc on message sending if they are damaged. Unfortunately, corrupt .pst files aren't incredibly rare, so you should consider this as a possible cause of such problems as stuck messages.

Try repairing the personal folder file (see the section "Using the Inbox Repair Tool," below). If that doesn't work, create a new personal folder file via the Mail utility in the Control Panel. If that doesn't work, create a new mail profile for the user.

Multiple User Files Can Confuse the Software

Sometimes mail doesn't leave the Outbox because the client software isn't quite sure about the validity of the sender or the recipient. If the user has created additional personal folder files, that may be the source of the problem. Even though it's possible, and permissible, to have multiple personal folder services, this situation can sometimes cause confusion.

The solution is to rename the existing .pst files and create a new profile (use a new .pst filename). If everything works fine, make a backup of the new .pst file and try importing the old files. If the old files do not contain much important data, however, skip the import to avoid bringing back any problems.

Check the Outbox with Another Client

You can search for the file Exchng32.exe (the built-in Exchange client software) on your computer, and if you find it, run it. Launching the file starts a configuration process, and you should configure the settings you use for Outlook. If this works, and mail is delivered and sent, uninstall Outlook and then reinstall it from scratch.

Using the Inbox Repair Tool

Windows supplies an Inbox Repair tool, but you must know the full path of the .pst file to use it. You can find the path from the Tools menu, in the Mail utility in the Control Panel, or in the Services dialog box in the software window (under the Tools menu). Click Properties for the Personal Folders service.

On machines running Microsoft Windows 9X, the Inbox Repair Tool is on the Programs\Accessories\System Tools submenu of your Start menu. If it's not there, use Find to search for the file Scanpst.exe and run it. The Inbox Repair Tool is located in the Administrative Tools group if you are running Microsoft Windows NT 4.0.

When the Inbox Repair Tool window opens (see Figure 5-4, on the following page), enter the full path and filename of the personal folder file. Click Browse

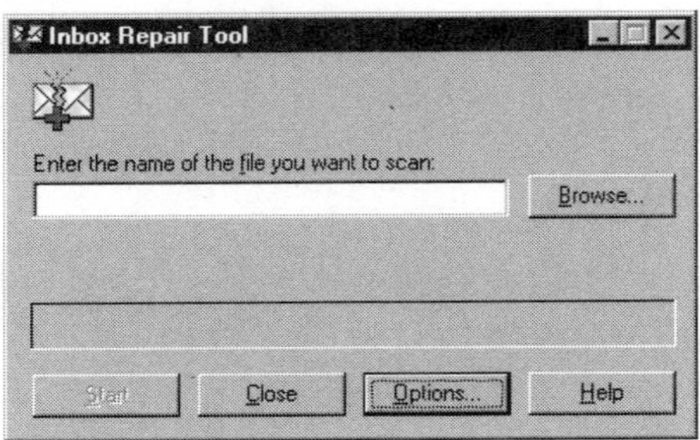

Figure 5-4. *Locate the .pst file for the repair tool.*

if you find that faster than typing a long path (the browse starts in the Windows folder, which is quite logical).

Click Options to configure a log file for the repair. You can replace any existing log, append information to an existing log, or choose to omit a log file.

When the .pst file is in the text box of the window, and your log options are selected, click Start. The software scans the .pst file, and when it's finished it reports on the file's condition. If there are errors, you can back up the original file before beginning the repair process (see Figure 5-5). A message appears when the repair is complete.

If you want to check the log, the filename is the same as the .pst file, but it has the extension .log. You can use Notepad to view the log entries (see Figure 5-6).

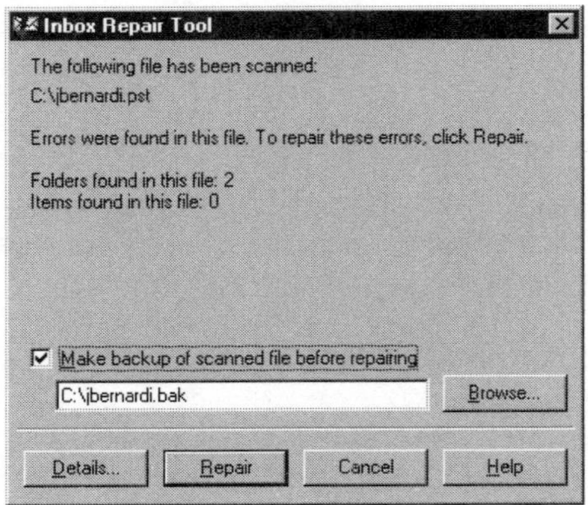

Figure 5-5. *Repairing this file cleared up the problem of mail stuck in the Outbox.*

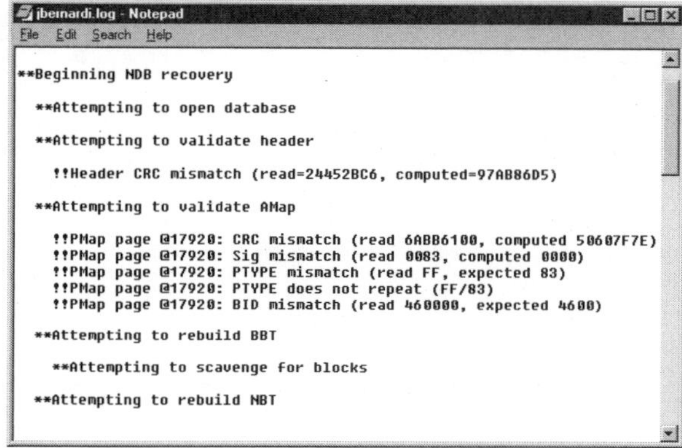

Figure 5-6. *The repair tool log is a text file, which you can examine.*

Troubleshooting Replies and Forwards

Unfortunately, sending a reply to a message isn't always a "click and do it" function. There can be problems with the format of the reply, or with some of the functions available for replying to messages. By default, Outlook uses the message format type of the original message when you reply.

Tip The information in this section also applies to forwarding messages.

Original Message Isn't Indented

Outlook provides an option to include and indent the original text when you reply to a message. In fact, that's the default option. Sometimes, however, you click the Reply button and the original message text is not indented. Some users find this extremely annoying; they like the indentation because it clearly delineates the original message (especially if they insert replies between paragraphs of the original message).

The Include And Indent Original Text option does not work if the original message is plain text. The recipient can do nothing except write the sender a message requesting another text format.

Prefix Characters Don't Appear for Original Message

If you configure Outlook to use a prefix at the beginning of each line of the original message (instead of indenting it), that option will not work properly in some situations. The common prefix character is the greater than sign (>), although you can change that in the Options dialog box.

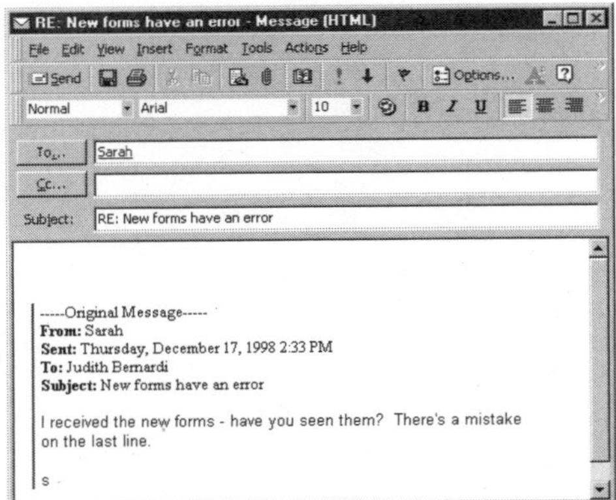

Figure 5-7. *The prefix character is replaced by a blue vertical line.*

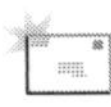

Note If you configure Outlook to use a prefix character on the original message, your spell-checker will check the original message in addition to your reply.

If the original message uses either the HTML or WordMail formats, when you click Reply, the original message has a vertical line instead of the prefix character (see Figure 5-7).

For HTML messages, there's nothing you can do. For WordMail messages, close the Reply form and close the original message. Then change your default mail format to either RTF or Plain Text. Open the message and then click Reply to open a message form in which the prefix character you selected is placed at the beginning of each line of the original message.

Mark My Comments Doesn't Work

Outlook's nifty Mark My Comments feature only works with HTML or RTF formats. In case you haven't used it, you can respond to the message within the message text, and each response is preceded with your name in brackets (see Figure 5-8). Both your name and your response appear in blue.

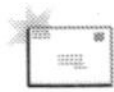

Note If you select the Mark My Comments feature, you cannot also configure Outlook to use a prefix character on the lines of the original message. The two features don't coexist.

Incidentally, Mark My Comments may work when you respond to a sender who uses other e-mail software. For example, the feature works in Eudora, except that the comments are not displayed in a different color.

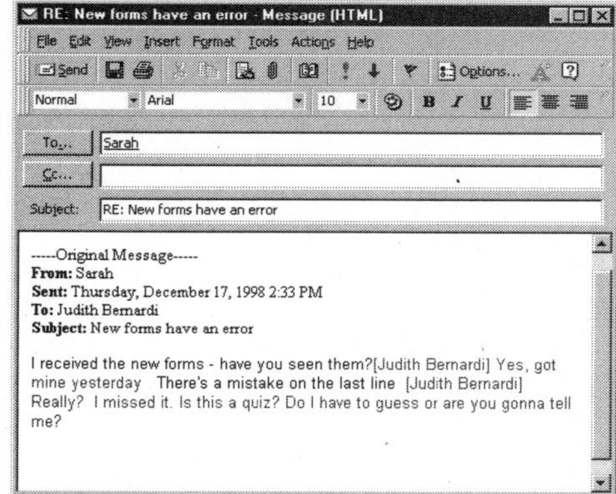

Figure 5-8. *It's easy to differentiate the response from the original text when you use the Mark My Comments feature.*

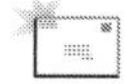

Note Even though the WordMail format doesn't support the Mark My Comments feature, it does support the Track Changes feature, which works the same way it does in Microsoft Word.

I found another problem with Mark My Comments that I've named "Mark My Comments Totally Weirds People Out," and we discovered it by accident in my office. Before I tell you the problem, I'll show you the result, which is a message one person on my Exchange system was sending to another person. Take a look at Figure 5-9, which is what the user named Judith saw when she entered a response to the user named Sarah. Judith is a touch typist, and after she positioned her insertion point where she wanted to begin her response, she didn't look at the screen until she'd completed the first sentence of her reply.

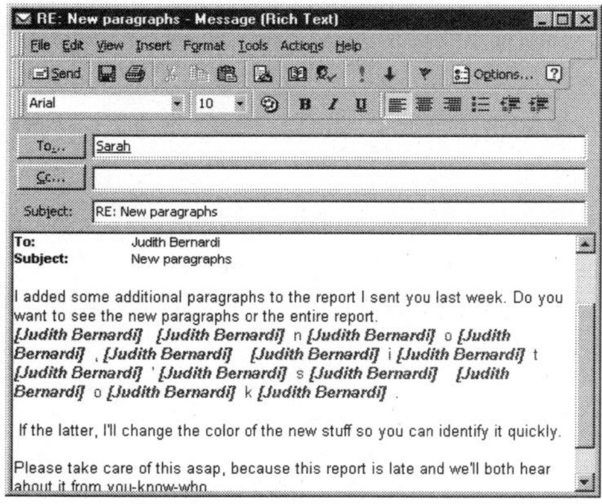

Figure 5-9. *If you look carefully you'll see that the response text is "No, it's OK."*

Judith had accidentally pressed the Insert key. If you do that when you're responding to an RTF message, the Mark My Comments feature kicks in between each letter you type. Incidentally, she calmly hit the Send key (she has a strange sense of humor).

Problems with Signatures in Replies

Many users create signatures that are automatically placed in every message. Outlook provides an option to turn off signatures for replies or forwarded mail, but most users are proud of their signatures and don't invoke that feature. (In fact, some users get a bit carried away, and I see far too many messages where the signature is longer than the actual message.)

Signature Formatting Is Lost

Sometimes signatures that are formatted with multiple fonts, or with attributes such as boldface or italic, appear as plain old text in a reply. The cause of this problem is that the format type of the original message is Plain Text. Therefore, the reply appears in Plain Text.

URL in Signature Is Changed

If your signature was created in HTML and your default mail format is also HTML, the signature that's inserted when you reply to a Plain Text message is changed (as described in the previous problem). If, however, you use a URL in your signature, the change is more than the absence of formatting—the format of the URL changes. Actually, it sort of duplicates itself.

For example, if the URL in your signature is *http://www.company.com/mypage*, it appears as *http://www.company.com/mypage* <*http://www.company.com/mypage*>, which can confuse the recipient.

One solution is to delete the second incarnation of the URL every time you reply to a Plain Text message. A more permanent solution, however, involves changing the default format for messages to Plain Text and editing your signature with the Outlook Advanced Editor while that default format is in effect. Here are the details:

1. From the Tools menu, choose Options, and go to the Mail Format tab.
2. In the Message Format section of the dialog box, select Plain Text.
3. Click the Signature Picker button at the bottom of the dialog box.
4. Select your signature and click Edit.
5. In the Edit Signature dialog box, click Advanced Edit. Outlook displays a message telling you that it's going to launch an editor that is not part of Outlook. Click Yes to continue.
6. Microsoft Notepad opens with your signature loaded.
7. Edit your signature so that it looks OK in Plain Text.

8. Save the document, and quit Notepad to return to the Mail Format page of the Options dialog box.
9. In the Message Format section, change the default format to HTML.
10. Click Apply, and then click OK.

Hereafter, your signature will work properly when you're replying to a Plain Text message. More important, the changes you made in the Plain Text version of your signature didn't change the format of your signature for HTML or RTF replies.

Meeting Requests Disappear After Replying

After responding to a meeting request, the original message disappears from the Inbox. The user who lost the message calls you, reporting that Outlook is "broken." Of course it's not, because that's the default behavior configuration.

If a user doesn't like the fact that the meeting request isn't retained, completing the following steps will change the default behavior:

1. From the Tools menu, choose Options.
2. On the Preferences tab, click E-Mail Options.
3. In the E-Mail Options dialog box, click Advanced E-Mail Options.
4. Click the option to delete meeting requests after responding to clear it (it's at the bottom of the dialog box).

Troubleshooting Attachments

For some reason, some users are intimidated by attachments. They're not sure what to do with them. Of course, real problems related to attachments do occasionally arise. This section covers some of the common calls that administrators receive when users need help with handling attachments.

Problems with Extensions of Attached Files

An attached file that has the wrong extension, no extension, or an unregistered extension causes problems for the recipient. Here are some things you can do to avoid, or solve, the problems.

Attaching a File Without an Extension

If you're working on a computer that is configured to hide the extensions of known file types (which is the default for Microsoft Windows 95, Microsoft Windows 98, and Windows NT 4.0), the same configuration applies to attachments. When you attach a file to a message, it's attached without an extension.

You can solve this within Windows Explorer or My Computer. From the View menu, choose Options, and go to the View tab. There, you may clear the option to hide file extensions. The client software will follow suit by using the extension when an attachment is added to a message.

Receiving a File Without an Extension

For the recipient of an attachment without a filename extension, the solution is to save the file and then change its name to include an extension. Here's how to accomplish this:

1. Call the sender and find out which software created the file so you know what extension it needs.
2. Open the message and right-click the icon for the attachment.
3. From the shortcut menu, choose Save As.
4. In the Save As dialog box, change the name to include the extension.

Handling Unregistered Extensions

If you receive a file with an extension that isn't registered on your system, you can register it. This assumes, of course, that you know which software to use with it (sometimes that requires a phone call or message to the sender).

When you attempt to open the file, Outlook 98 flashes a warning message (see Figure 5-10). Because the file extension isn't registered, Outlook suspects a virus.

Click Save It To Disk. (If you click Open It, you'll see a message that the file extension is not registered, along with the instruction that you should create an association. That's the hard way, because creating associations from scratch is real work.)

When the Save As dialog box opens, make a note of the folder in which the file is saved, or change the folder to one you'll remember. Then open Explorer and go to the file. Double-click the file (it won't open, but the Open With dialog box appears). Select the appropriate software in the Open With dialog box. Be sure the option Always Use This Program To Open This File is selected, because that creates the association in your system.

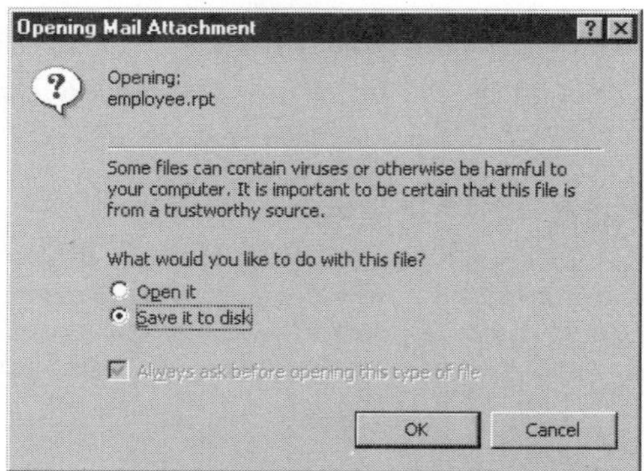

Figure 5-10. *Unregistered file types produce a warning, along with choices for action.*

Note Outlook 97 presents neither the virus warning message nor choices about saving to disk or opening the file. Right-click the attachment icon in the message and click Save As. Then follow the instructions in the previous section to associate the file extension to a software application.

Attachment Not Received by Internet Recipient

If you send a message with an attached file to an Internet recipient, you may receive a phone call or message asking, "Where's the attachment you mentioned in the message?" Your Sent Items folder shows the attachment, but the recipient insists there was no attachment. Don't get into an argument—instead check the format type you used for the message.

If the message was in RTF format and you use MIME encoding, and the recipient uses a POP3 e-mail program, the message probably didn't make it. Resend the attachment in a message that is not formatted for RTF.

Can't Rename an Attachment in a Message

There isn't a way to rename an attachment while you're working with it in the message. You have to open the attachment and change its name in the software with the Save As command. Alternatively, right-click the attachment and click Save As, then rename it.

Out of Memory Error When Attaching a File

If you see an Out Of Memory error, or an error indicating that you don't have sufficient resources to attach a file, you can probably ignore the message. The real problem is a path that's too complicated for Outlook to handle. If the path to the file exceeds 128 characters, or there are some very long folder names in the path, this specious error message may appear. After all, sometimes the document you want to attach is in a subfolder that's under another subfolder in your My Documents folder, which is under your profile folder, which is under the Windows folder, and so on. It can get long and complicated.

This is a known problem. If you encounter it, contact Microsoft to find out if a fix is available. In the meantime, open Windows Explorer and copy the file to a folder that's closer to the top of your folder hierarchy.

Troubleshooting Connectivity Problems

Unfortunately, it's not uncommon for LAN-connected clients to have problems connecting to the Exchange server. Sometimes a connection is so slow that it times out, and the user must work offline; sometimes users see a spurious error that the server is down and unavailable; and sometimes things just crawl.

Dial-in users have a longer list of complaints, because there's more that can go wrong when the connection is over telephone lines. This section provides helpful information for trying to solve communications problems for both remote and local users.

Understanding RPC Connections

The Exchange client uses remote procedure calls (RPCs) to communicate with Exchange Server (RPC is a core component of Windows NT Server). RPC is the application layer protocol, and it runs on top of a transport protocol. The RPC communication can be enabled over a variety of connection types.

Understanding Communication Protocols

As long as the network protocols are properly configured for a client machine, there shouldn't be any problem establishing RPC communication. You can tweak the protocol configuration (covered in the next section, "Tweaking the Binding Order"). RPC works with the following protocols (covered in the default binding order):

- **Local RPC (LRPC)** This is used when the computer with the client software is on the same network system as the server. The registry entry for LRPC is ncalrpc.
- **TCP/IP** This is used over Windows sockets. The client finds the server by using DNS, local host files, or an IP address. The registry entry for TCP/IP is ncacn_ip_tcp.
- **SPX** Client software RPCs use Novell's SPX and the NetWare bindery to find the server. (Windows sockets are used to implement this communication method.) The registry entry for SPX is ncacn_spx.
- **Named Pipes** RPC client calls locate the server using the server's NetBIOS computer name, LMHosts, or WINS. The registry entry for named pipes is ncacn_sp.
- **NetBIOS** RPC uses the default NetBIOS, which can be any protocol that supports NetBIOS. (NetBIOS works over NetBEUI, TCP/IP, and IPX.) The registry entry for NetBIOS is netbios.
- **Banyan Vines** This is supported for Microsoft Windows 3.x and Windows NT. The registry entry for Banyan Vines is ncacn_vns_spp.

Tweaking the Binding Order

The RPC tries each communication method, one at a time, to make a connection between the client software and the Exchange server. The order in which each communication type is tried is called the *binding order*. If the correct communication type is the last one in the binding order, it can take a long time for the Exchange client to access the Exchange server. In fact, it can take many minutes.

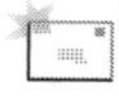

Note The binding order is not the order you see in the Network utility in the Control Panel when you're establishing network settings. Exchange Server keeps its own set of binding information.

There's a default binding order, given in the previous section, that's written to the local system when the client software is installed. You can tweak the speed of the connection by changing the binding order so that the right communication method (matching the network protocol configuration of the client computer) is first in the binding order.

Windows 95 and later clients have the worst history for slow connections between the Exchange client and the Exchange server. I've found that I can sometimes cure a client machine that takes more than five minutes to connect to the server with a change in the binding order. To change the binding order in Windows 9X machines, open Regedit and go to HKEY_LOCAL_MACHINE\SOFTWARE\Microsoft\Exchange\Exchange Provider (see Figure 5-11).

Double-click the data entry object in the right pane and edit it to match the protocol this computer relies on. Make sure there's a comma between each listing (you can eliminate protocols you haven't installed).

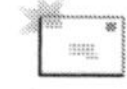

Note Microsoft Windows 9X registries have the Banyan Vines protocol listed, even though the operating system doesn't support this protocol. Feel free to delete it.

For Microsoft Windows 3.x clients, the binding order is found in the Exchange.ini file. The entry is named RPC_BINDING_ORDER=. The default binding order is Named Pipes, SPX, TCP/IP, NetBIOS.

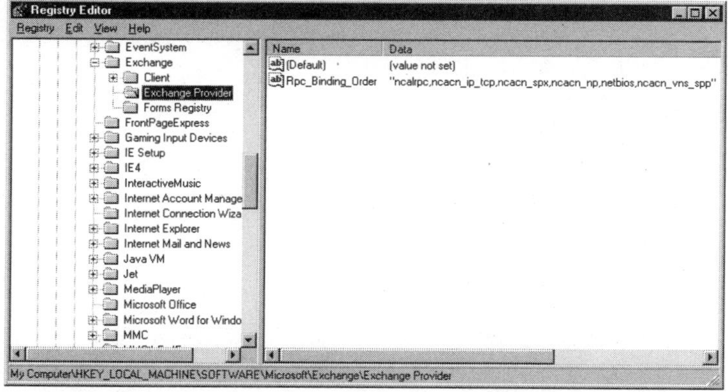

Figure 5-11. *Match the binding order to the protocol the computer is using.*

For DOS clients, the binding order is set in Autoexec.bat. The command line entry is set RPC_BINDING_ORDER=, and the default order is LRPC, Named Pipes, SPX, TCP/IP, NetBIOS.

Other Options for Slow LAN Connections

Sometimes changing the binding order doesn't work. I've seen identical binding orders on two Windows 95 or Windows 98 machines result in drastically different connection times—one machine connects immediately, and the other takes so much time that the user has learned to open Outlook and leave for a coffee break. I've checked other network settings, and they're also identical, so I am now out of explanations.

Sometimes (OK, frequently) a slow connection results in a time-out (see Figure 5-12).

If you know the server is up and running, click Retry (you may have to do this more than once). Then, if you can't find any settings that improve the connection speed, you can change the time-out specification. You can do this without making a connection to the server. Either choose to work offline (just to get the client software window up) or use the Mail utility in Control Panel.

- In the client software window, from the Tools menu, choose Services, and select Microsoft Exchange Server.
- In the Mail utility in Control Panel, go to the Services tab and select Microsoft Exchange Server.

Note If there are multiple mail profiles in the Control Panel Mail utility, select the appropriate profile before configuring the Microsoft Exchange Server service.

Click Properties and change the specification for the option Seconds Until Server Connection Timeout (see Figure 5-13). The default is 30; you may want to change that to several thousand.

Changing the time-out doesn't solve the real problem, but it means that the user doesn't have to click the Retry button (or at least doesn't have to click it as often).

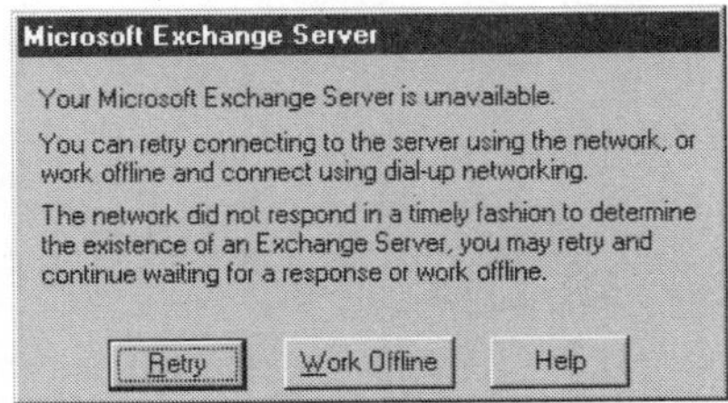

Figure 5-12. *The server is definitely available; it's just taking a long time.*

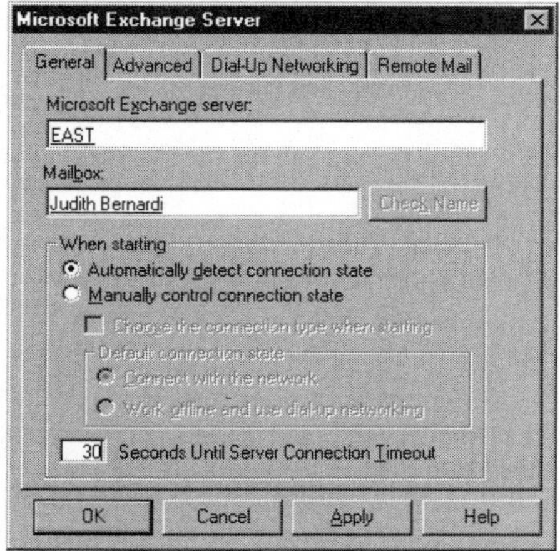

Figure 5-13. *You can use the Mail utility to configure the number of seconds that the client software spends trying to connect to the Exchange Server before issuing an error message.*

Troubleshooting POP3 Connections

If you have Outlook Express clients, you need to pay attention to POP3 (Post Office Protocol 3) communication. POP3 is a read-only protocol that allows an e-mail client to connect to a mail server and download messages. Popular POP3 clients include Outlook Express, Eudora, and Netscape Messenger.

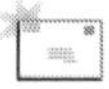

Note POP3 contains no provisions for sending mail. The SMTP protocol sends outgoing mail, so client software must point outgoing mail to an Exchange server that's running the Internet Mail Service.

It's important to realize that protocols such as POP3 must be enabled on the site in order to be enabled on a server. You can enable the protocols on every server in the site, or you can selectively disable any protocol on a specific server. When you decide to make changes to configuration options, you can apply those changes to the site or to a server (or multiple servers). Of course, if all the users who are reporting problems connect to the same server, it makes sense to change only the server's protocol options.

Check POP3 Connectivity

If your POP3 users are having connection problems, the first step in troubleshooting POP3 connectivity issues is to ensure that the POP3 protocol is enabled on the server. You can do this by establishing a Telnet connection to the appropriate port. Open a command prompt and enter **telnet <*server_name*> 110** or **telnet <*ip_address*> 110**.

If the connection fails, verify that POP3 is enabled—check the Protocols containers for both the site and the server.

Here is a sample successful login:

```
+OK Microsoft Exchange POP3 server version 5.5.2232.11 ready
USER domain\nt_id\mailbox_alias
+OK
PASS nt_password
+OK User successfully logged on
```

If you receive the error message "-ERR Logon failure: unknown user name or bad password," you probably entered one of the elements incorrectly.

Tip Don't forget that the mailbox has to be on the server you're using for this exercise.

Check Message Conversion Options

If users report difficulty in reading some messages or in receiving attachments, check the POP3 configuration on your Exchange server. POP3 clients cannot understand the native Exchange message format, so messages that are sent through your Exchange system are translated on the server before being downloaded by the POP3 client. You may have to experiment with a different message format type.

The options for the message format are in the Message Format tab in the POP3 Properties dialog box (see Figure 5-14).

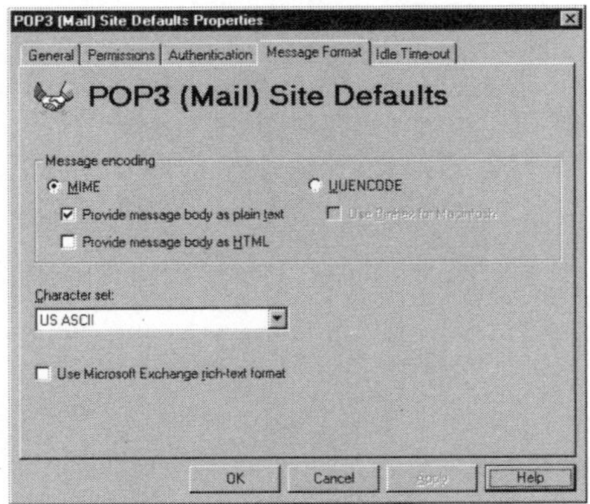

Figure 5-14. *Message conversion options are set on the Properties dialog box for the POP3 protocol.*

The settings in the Message Format property page allow you to specify the format that Microsoft Exchange Server messages are converted to when they're fetched by a POP3 client. These settings must be supported by the POP3 client.

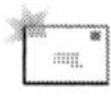

Note You can also set the message content format and the character set option on individual mailboxes, servers, and sites.

Tip Messages that are sent by Internet users are not converted on the Exchange server. The POP3 clients retrieve those messages in the format in which the message was composed.

For message encoding, MIME and UUENCODE are available.

Multipurpose Internet Mail Extensions (MIME) is the standard for sending multimedia messages over the Internet. If a non-MIME-aware client receives a MIME message, the text and attachments are generally scrambled and not readable. MIME is the default for Exchange Server because most of the client software you'll work with is capable of handling that standard. By default, the option Provide Message Body As Plain Text is selected. You can also select the option Provide Message Body As HTML. If both options are selected, Exchange Server provides both HTML and Plain Text in a MIME multipart alternative message.

UUENCODE is used by the UNIX operating system to encode 8-bit data sent across the Internet. If you select the UUENCODE option, Exchange Server renders the body of the message as text and encodes any attachments using UUENCODE. Select Use BinHex For Macintosh Attachments to render the body of the message as text, and encode any attachments with the BinHex method (used by the Macintosh operating system to encode 8-bit data that's sent across the Internet).

Check Character Set Options

You can select the character set that Exchange uses to generate MIME and non-MIME messages that originate from an Exchange Server system. The default character set, of course, is matched to the language installed on your server.

Select the option Use Microsoft Exchange Rich-Text Format to enable RTF formatting in messages. This means that messages sent with character formatting (bold, italic, font colors, and so on) are received with the formatting intact. When RTF is enabled, messages that are retrieved by a POP3 client that cannot handle RTF see plain text. The information about formatting is contained in an attachment (which is useless).

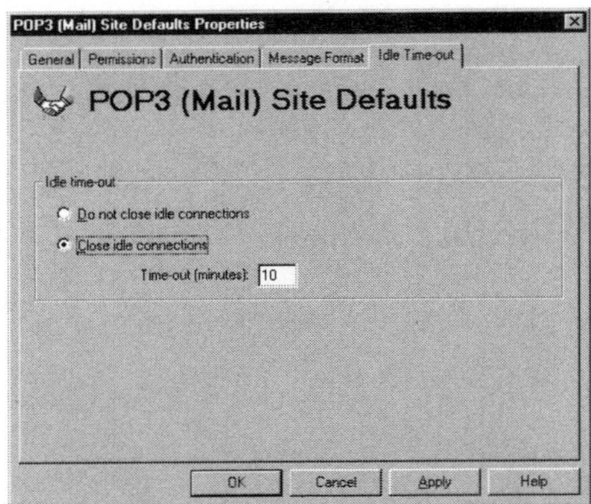

Figure 5-15. *Specify the time out duration that keeps your system responsive.*

Set Connection Limits

A lot of POP3 connection activity can strain a server, resulting in a slowdown. You may want to consider tightening the limits for the amount of time that a POP3 client can stay connected without activity. Go to the Idle Time-out tab of the POP3 Properties dialog box (see Figure 5-15).

Log POP3 Activity

If you're having a problem identifying or solving POP3 problems, consider logging the protocol activity. This gives you a chance to see what's going on over an extended period of time—a perspective that often provides some clues.

Tip Troubleshooting by logging is a server-based, not a site-based, solution.

To enable POP3 protocol logging, you'll need to change the registry as follows:

1. On the Exchange server computer, run either Regedit or Regedit32 and go to HKEY_LOCAL_MACHINE\SYSTEM\CurrentControlSet\Services\MSExchangeIS\ParametersSystem (see Figure 5-16).
2. Change the value of the POP3 Protocol Logging Level to a value between 1 and 4. The values are 0 = no logging, the default value; 1 = minimum logging; or 4 = maximum logging.
3. If you have a good reason for it, you can change the value of POP3 Protocol Log Path (where the log file is saved).

Caution You must stop and start the Information Store in order to have protocol logging take effect.

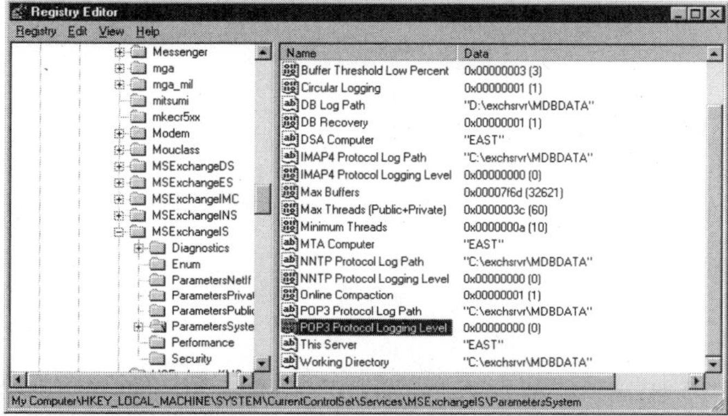

Figure 5-16. *Values for POP3 logging and the path of the logging file are both in the same registry key.*

After you've finished troubleshooting, return the POP3 Protocol Logging Level to its original value.

Troubleshooting IMAP4

IMAP4 (Internet Message Access Protocol 4), like POP3, is a protocol for retrieving messages from a server. The features in IMAP4, however, are more robust and advanced than those in POP3. For example, you can perform the following tasks with IMAP4:

- View the header and sender of a message prior to downloading
- Create multiple folders on the server
- Move messages between mailboxes and folders on the server

IMAP4 tends to be a much more useful protocol than POP3 when connecting to an Exchange server, but because most people are more familiar with POP3, it isn't implemented as commonly.

Check the IMAP4 Connection

The first step in troubleshooting IMAP4 connectivity is verifying that the protocol is enabled on the server in question. This can be done via telnet, using the following syntax: **telnet server_name 143** or **telnet ip_address 143.**

A successful connection and login attempt might look something like this:

```
telnet mail.server.com 143

* OK Microsoft Exchange IMAP4rev1 server version 5.5.2232.11
(mail.server.com) ready

AA0 login domain/nt_id/mailbox_alias password
```

```
AA0 OK LOGIN
AA1 select inbox
* 242 EXISTS
* 0 RECENT
* FLAGS (\Seen \Answered \Flagged \Deleted \Draft)
* OK [PERMANENTFLAGS (\Seen \Answered \Flagged \Deleted \Draft)]
* OK [UNSEEN 1] Is the first unseen message
* OK [UIDVALIDITY 9795] UIDVALIDITY value
AA1 OK [READ-WRITE] SELECT completed
```

Note that each command issued to the IMAP4 server is prefixed with a command identifier (AA0 and AA1). Also, remember that IMAP4 requires forward slashes rather than backslashes when you're entering the username.

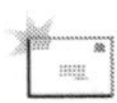

Note For Windows NT Challenge/Response to work with the Outlook Express Client, the mailbox alias and Windows NT username must be the same.

Log IMAP4 Activity

When obvious solutions elude you, you can enable protocol logging on the Exchange server. IMAP4 protocol logging, like POP3 protocol logging, should be turned on only to troubleshoot a specific issue and should be turned off during normal operations.

To enable IMAP4 protocol logging, you'll need to edit the registry as follows:

1. On the Exchange server, run Regedit or Regedit32 and go to HKEY_LOCAL_-MACHINE\SYSTEM\CurrentControlSet\Services\MSExchangeIS\ParametersSystem.
2. Change the value of IMAP4_Protocol_Logging_Level to a value between 1 and 4 (1 = minimum; 4 = Maximum).
3. If there's a reason to change it, you can alter the value of the IMAP4 Protocol Log Path (where the log file is written).

Caution Stop and start the Information Store to have protocol logging take effect.

After you've finished troubleshooting, return the IMAP4 Protocol Logging Level to its original value.

Tip Remember that you must enable protocols on the site before you can enable them on any server in that site. You can disable POP3 on any server in the site by clearing the Enable Protocol option on the General tab of the server's POP3 Properties dialog box.

Troubleshooting LDAP

LDAP (Lightweight Directory Access Protocol) allows users to perform lookups against a server. This is especially useful for users who are working remotely or use a platform on which a Microsoft Outlook client is not available (for example, UNIX). See Chapter 4 for information on Outlook Web Access for clients who connect using a browser.

Check the Connection

The first step in troubleshooting LDAP connectivity is verifying that the protocol is enabled on the server in question. This can be done via telnet, using the following syntax: **telnet server_name 389** or **telnet ip_address 389**. Unlike the connection checks for POP3 or IMAP4, there is no welcome message when you connect successfully to port 389. Unless you get a "Connect failed" message, you can assume that your server is listening on port 389.

Check User Authentication

If you're not using anonymous access for users, they will need to authenticate their connections. Here is the format for the username and password when connecting to an LDAP server:

```
Username: cn=domain, cn=nt_id
Password: nt_password
```

If you have restricted search rights on the Global Address List, users might receive the following error message even though they are connecting using appropriate credentials: "The specified Directory Service has denied access. Check the Properties for this Directory Service and verify that your Authentication Type settings and parameters are correct."

This is a normal result of restricted search rights for this client type. You have to weigh the alternatives and make decisions according to your security mandates.

Note Additional LDAP referral servers can be specified in Exchange Server. This can be a handy tool for extending the ability of your users to look up users in other companies or organizations without cluttering your Global Address List with additional entries. Up to 350 additional LDAP referral servers can be specified.

Troubleshooting Client Machine Recovery

Restoring a client machine isn't too complicated most of the time. Whether it's a new hard drive, a reformatted hard drive, or a new computer, you install the operating system, then install the software, and then restore backed-up data files.

Client computers that run Windows, Microsoft Office, Microsoft Internet Explorer, and Outlook 98, however, can drive you crazy for months if you don't put everything back in the proper order. To organize, do the following:

1. Install the operating system (Windows 95, Windows 98, or Windows NT). If the operating system is Windows NT, install the appropriate Windows NT Service Pack.
2. Make sure that you have a clean, trouble-free boot process.
3. Configure the peripherals.
4. Install Office using the guidelines that follow.
5. Install any Service Release Patches for individual Office applications (this usually means Microsoft Excel, but by the time you read this there may be others).
6. Install Internet Explorer 4.0 (or later).

Here are the guidelines for installing the various flavors of Office:

- If you're installing Microsoft Office 2000, just install it. Microsoft Outlook 2000 is part of the installation process, as is Internet Explorer 5.0.
- If you're installing Office 97 and you're using Outlook 97, just install it. Install any Service Release Patches for Office 97.
- If you're installing Office 97 but also want to install Outlook 98, install Office but select Custom Install and clear the Outlook 97 check box. Install any Service Release Patches for Office 97. Then install Outlook 98.

Part III

Site Components

Microsoft Exchange Server administrators have to keep an eye on sites, servers, folders, and all the other containers in the left pane of the Exchange Server Administrator window.

Most of the time, Exchange Server runs smoothly and efficiently. With a little tweaking here and a few changes there, administrators manage to keep all the services running smoothly. It's important, however, to know what needs tweaking or changing, and when to perform those tasks. It's also important to be able to move swiftly and efficiently when things go awry.

The chapters in this section are designed to help you understand, maintain, and troubleshoot the Exchange components in the site for which you have responsibility.

Chapter 6

Maintaining Servers and Sites

Maintaining and troubleshooting servers and sites is an ongoing responsibility, and the best approach to this obligation is to make sure you schedule preventive maintenance tasks. Don't worry; many of these tasks are nothing more than checking into the system statistics and behavior. If everything's cool, there's no additional work. If something's amiss, fixing it early prevents major headaches.

In this chapter I discuss the maintenance routines you should be performing (or delegating to other members of your department). I also cover some of the troubleshooting tasks you might face. It's impossible to address every potential problem that could arise on your Exchange servers or at your site, so I'll focus on the problems that administrators tell me are most likely to occur.

Maintaining Servers

In the Microsoft Exchange Server hierarchy (see Figure 6-1), a server is the parent container for a number of server-based core components: Directory Service; System Attendant; Public Information Store (Public IS); Private Information Store (Private IS); and the Message Transfer Agent (MTA). In addition, each Exchange server has a Server Recipients container, which holds all recipients that call the server home.

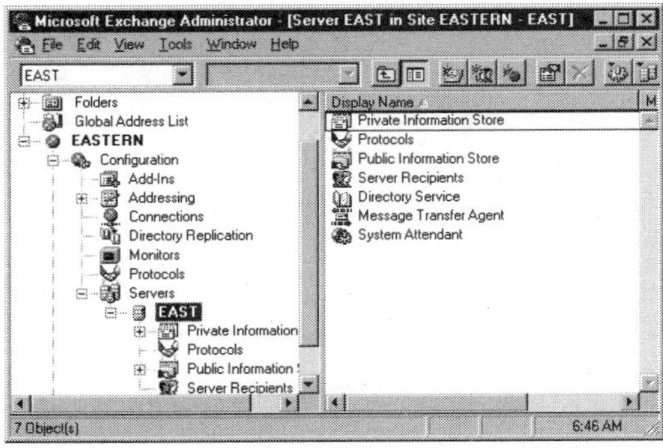

Figure 6-1. *Each Exchange server contains core components.*

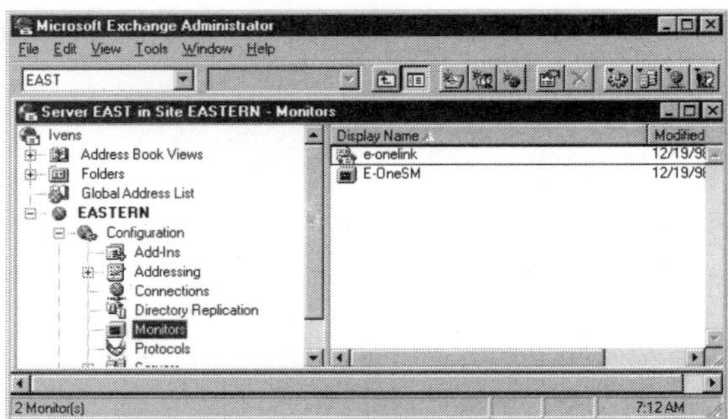

Figure 6-2. *A Server Monitor is installed in this site.*

Using Server Monitors

If a server monitor wasn't created and configured immediately after Exchange Server was installed, it's time to correct that oversight. The server monitor keeps an eye on the behavior and health of Microsoft Windows NT services on Exchange servers in a site. You can determine whether a Server Monitor is already installed through the Exchange Administrator window. Select a site and open its Configuration container object. Then select the Monitors container. The right pane of the window displays the monitors that have been created for the site (see Figure 6-2).

The Monitors container holds both Server Monitors and Link Monitors. You can tell which is which by the icon for the monitor object. A Server Monitor icon looks like a computer monitor. A Link Monitor icon has several little artistic objects, but you can usually spot the magnifying glass or the red curved arrow (or, if you can't make out the details, it's the icon that is *not* a computer monitor).

Creating a Server Monitor

If you check the Monitors container and find that there's no Server Monitor, you can create one quite easily. From the File menu, choose New Other, and then choose Server Monitor. The Properties dialog box for a Server Monitor appears (see Figure 6-3), and you can begin the configuration process.

Server Monitor General Properties

The General tab is where you take care of the basic configuration for the monitor. Here are some guidelines:

- **Directory Name** This can have up to 64 characters and must be unique. The name can't be changed, because it's the name used internally by your Exchange and Windows NT systems.
- **Display Name** This is the name you see in the Exchange Administrator window. You can use up to 256 characters for this name.

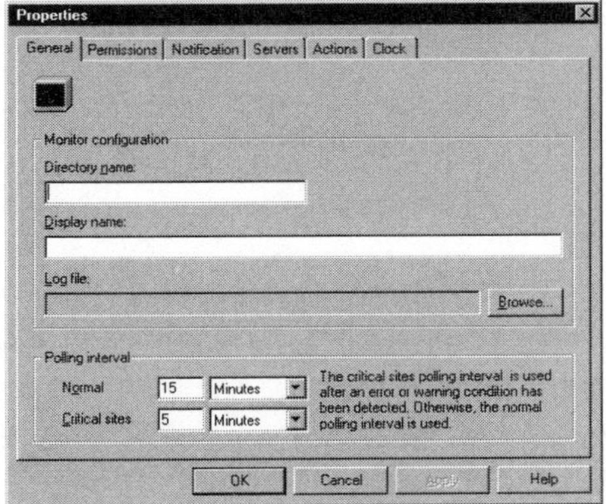

Figure 6-3. *Start the configuration by naming the monitor and setting the polling interval.*

- **Log File Entry** This is the path and name of the monitor's log file. If you omit this field, there's no log file (the log is not required).
- **Polling Intervals** These specify how often the monitor checks services. There's an interval for normal checking, and a shorter interval that becomes effective if the server is in a warning or an alert state.

Configuring Server Monitor Notification Actions

The Notification tab of the Server Monitor Properties dialog box (see Figure 6-4) is the place to design a plan for notifying you (and/or the people you designate) when a monitor finds something wrong.

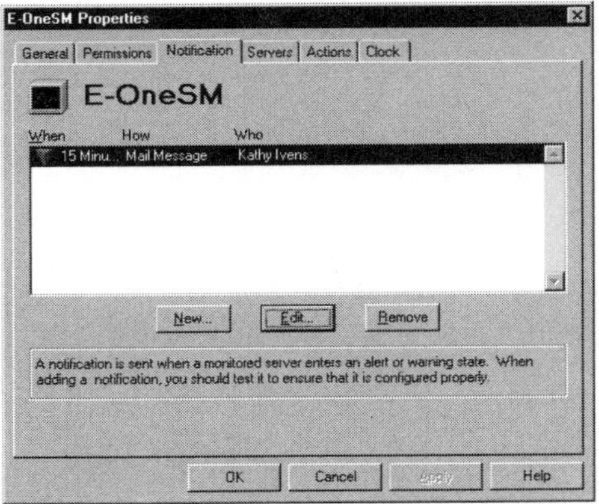

Figure 6-4. *It doesn't make sense to monitor your server without having a way to find out there's a problem.*

Click New to create a notification event. There are three types of notification events:

- **Launch A Process** This kicks off an application that's external to Exchange Server. A common use for this is launching software that activates a message to a beeper. If you have software that shoots off cannons to get your attention or releases balloons emblazoned with the message "server in trouble," you can use this event type.

  The dialog box for this event type (seen in Figure 6-5) isn't difficult to configure. Remember that Exchange Server doesn't do anything except launch the application.
- **Mail Message** This sends e-mail automatically to a recipient whom you specify. This notification type permits only one recipient, so if you have several people who should be told when there's a problem, create additional mail message notifications.
- **Windows NT Alert** This uses the Messenger service that's built into Windows NT to notify users. Of course, that service sends on-screen messages to computers, so this alert type doesn't work unless the target computer is running and the user has logged on.

You can have multiple alerts and alert types. You should test each alert as you create it (there's a Test button for this purpose on each alert type dialog box).

Choosing the Servers for This Monitor

Use the Servers tab of the monitor's Properties dialog box to select the servers connected to this Server Monitor. All the servers in the site are listed, and you can select one or more to be attached to this monitor.

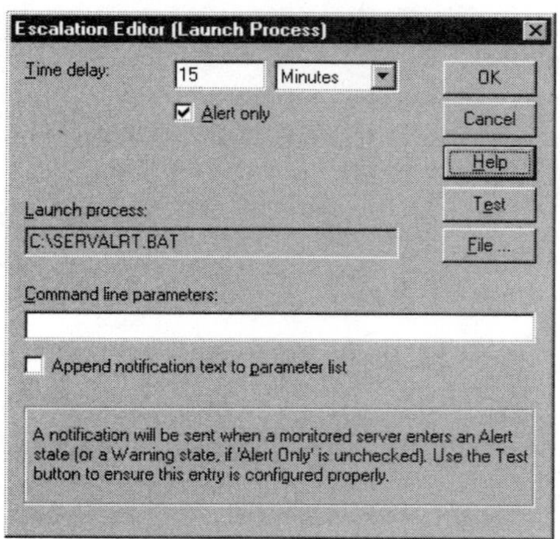

Figure 6-5. *Kick off a program to take care of notifying the appropriate people when there's a problem.*

Caution You cannot put clustered and nonclustered servers on the same monitor.

If the configurations you're applying to the Server Monitor should differ for different servers (perhaps there are administrators in charge of specific servers who should be notified only when their own servers have a problem), create separate Server Monitors.

Configuring Server Monitor Actions

By default, when a monitored service fails, the Server Monitor takes no further action (except for the notifications you establish in the Notification tab). In the Actions tab (see Figure 6-6) you can design actions that will be applied when there's a problem.

Tip The actions you configure are unrelated to the notifications you've created. They occur independently.

There are three choices for actions, and you can apply any choice to any of the three attempts displayed in the dialog box:

- **Take No Action** The Server Monitor does nothing about the problem (except send any notifications you've configured).
- **Restart The Service** Send a command to restart a service that has stopped.
- **Restart The Computer** Send a command to restart the server. If you use this option, specify the amount of time that must elapse before applying this remedy in the Restart delay text box. Also enter a message that displays on the server before the restart action takes places (this gives a user working on the computer time to close any applications or save data).

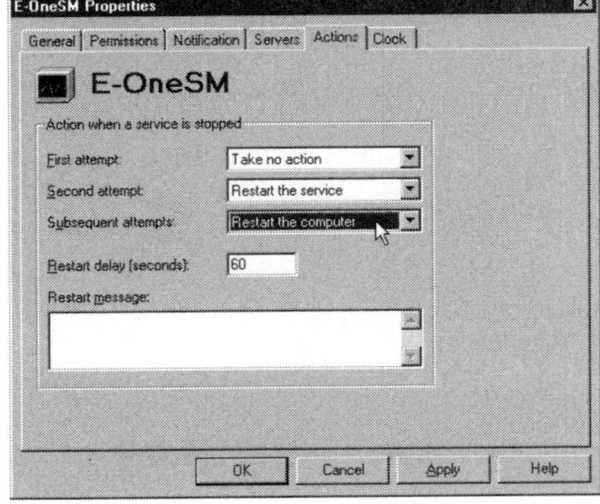

Figure 6-6. *You have three chances to apply an action to correct a problem with a service.*

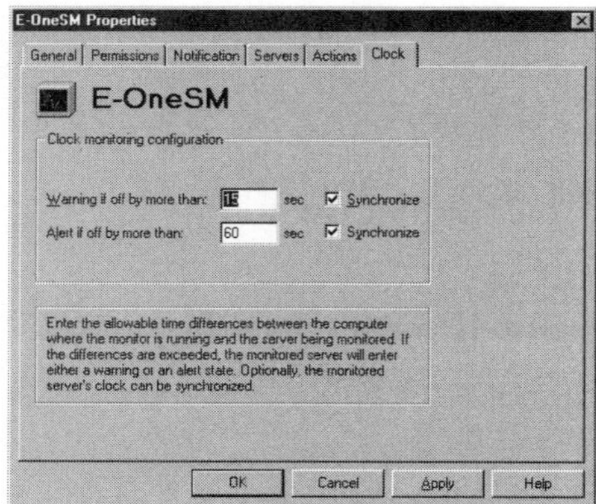

Figure 6-7. *You can either issue an alert or synchronize the clocks.*

You can set any of these actions for each attempt. The first attempt action is launched the first time a monitored server is polled and a problem is found. The second attempt action is launched the second time that a problem is found. Actions tied to Subsequent Attempts are taken after the first two attempts (meaning that neither of the actions in the first two attempts provided a solution).

Caution The action you specify for the Subsequent Attempts category will repeat continuously at an interval specified in the General tab (the Critical Sites interval setting). Be sure you allow enough time in the Critical Sites interval for the action to occur. If restarts take 4 minutes, don't set a 2-minute interval on the General tab.

Setting Clock Time Corrections

Use the Clock tab (see Figure 6-7) to monitor the difference in time between the computer that's running the monitor and the server(s) being monitored. Exchange Server has many time-related functions, and all sorts of events kick off every so-many minutes. If a server is out of synch with time, the effects on your system can be deleterious.

Tip If you're monitoring servers in different time zones, Windows NT will use the time zone information in the target server so that the time difference doesn't set off a specious alert.

Determining the Services to Monitor

By default, a Server Monitor tracks the following Windows NT services:

- Microsoft Exchange Directory
- Microsoft Exchange Information Store
- Microsoft Exchange Message Transfer Agent

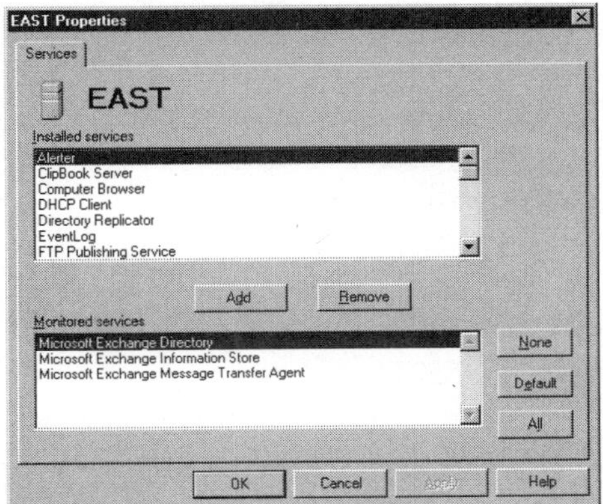

Figure 6-8. *The list of services installed on this server are displayed, and any of them can be added to the list of monitored services.*

You can change the list of monitored services in the Services dialog box, which is available on the Servers tab. Select each server you've added to this monitor and click the Services button to determine which services you want to monitor on this server (see Figure 6-8).

Running a Server Monitor

After the monitor is created and configured, you have to start it. Select the monitor and, from the Tools menu, choose Start Monitor (you can perform this task from a remote server). A dialog box appears in which you enter the name of the server you want to connect to, then the monitor window appears (see Figure 6-9, on the following page).

You can also start a monitor from the command line, with the syntax ExchangeServerFolder\Bin\Admin.exe /M<*site*>\Monitor\Server. The monitor name in this syntax is the directory name you gave the monitor, not the display name.

The monitor in Figure 6-9 was started with the command C:\Exchsrvr\Bin\Admin.exe/Meastern\E-one\East. In fact, that command, followed by the command exit, is a batch file I put into the Startup folder of my Exchange server's Programs menu. Exchange Server and the monitor both start when the computer starts. However, Exchange Server starts without being connected to a server (the Administrator window is empty). Choosing the File menu and clicking Connect To Server displays my usual Exchange Server Administrator window.

The most important thing to remember is that if you close the monitor window, you stop the monitor. Minimize it to keep it running.

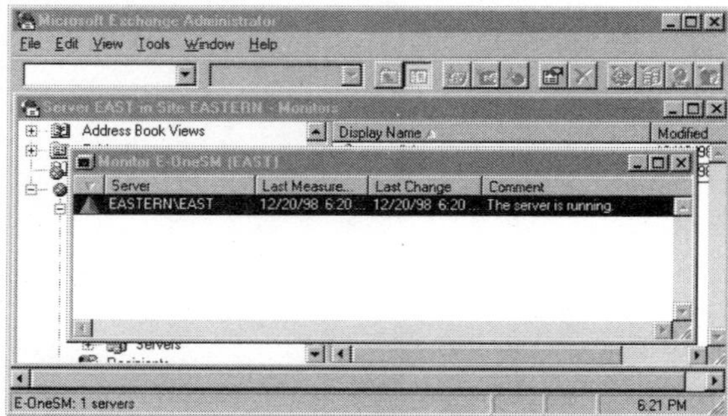

Figure 6-9. *Use the monitor window to keep an eye on things.*

Using the Server Monitor Window

The monitor window displays each server being monitored on its own line, using four columns.

The icon column contains one of four icons to indicate the status of the target server:

- A green triangle pointing up means that the server is up (working).
- A red triangle pointing down means that the server is down (if any monitored component is down, the server is deemed to be down).
- An exclamation point indicates that the server is in a warning state.
- A question mark indicates that the server is not being monitored.

The Server column lists the name of the target server.

The Last Measure column displays the time at which the latest RPC was sent to test the status of the Windows NT services being monitored.

The Last Change column displays the time at which the condition of a monitored service changed.

Double-click anywhere on a server's line to see the Properties dialog box for the monitored server (see Figure 6-10).

You can stop or start services on the Actions tab, check the results of clock synchronization on the Clock tab, see if any notifications were dispatched on the Notification tab, and determine whether the server was taken down for maintenance on the Maintenance Status tab.

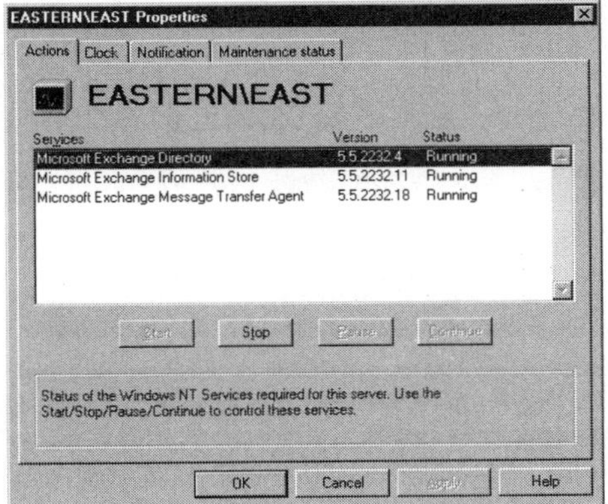

Figure 6-10. *Get a status report, or stop and start services, in the monitor window.*

Notifying the Monitor About Server Maintenance

What do you do when you want to take an Exchange server down for maintenance, and the monitor that's watching that server is also watching other servers?

You could shut down the monitor and hope nothing happens to the other servers while you perform maintenance tasks on one server, but you don't have to take that risk. Exchange Server provides an alternative: notify the monitor that a server is about to undergo maintenance. Essentially, this tells the monitor that it can ignore any problems it senses until the server is back up. Notifications aren't sent, and no actions to restart services occur.

To notify the monitor that you're putting a server into maintenance mode, enter the command **admin /t nr** on the server you're taking down. (The admin executable is in \ExchangeServerDirectory\Bin, so either enter the command in that directory or include the path in the command.) Otherwise, as soon as you stop a service in order to maintain the server, the monitor will restart the service.

The monitor receives this notification at the next scheduled polling, so don't take the server down or stop Exchange Server services until that occurs. Also, make sure that the monitor has received the message by opening the server's listing in the monitor window and checking the Maintenance Status tab (the Notifications And Repairs should be marked as suspended). To take the server out of maintenance mode, enter **admin** at the command line and connect to the appropriate server.

Now that you know how to perform this maintenance task, here's my personal advice: shut down server monitors whenever you're doing maintenance on an Exchange server. The processes I just described don't always work. Once I was making a change or adding something to my Exchange system (I can't remember what), and I had to shut down some Exchange services. I notified the Server Monitor with the right keystrokes (incidentally, the *nr* parameter I used in the command line means "suspend *n*otifications, suspend *r*epairs"). I performed the work I needed to do, but it took a while (there were a couple of phone calls I had to take), which is important to mention because the delay meant I ran into the next polling time for the Server Monitor. I even noticed that and glanced at my workstation (next to the Exchange server) to make sure that no notifications were received in my Inbox. I was admiring the efficiency of this feature when I got an error message telling me that the work I was doing couldn't proceed because the System Attendant service had to be stopped. I'd just stopped the System Attendant service! The Server Monitor Maintenance Status tab indicated that notifications and repairs were suspended. Regardless, the monitor was repairing the server, restarting the Exchange System Attendant. Arrghh! I learned that this is a known problem (if you encounter it, contact Microsoft to find out if a fix is available). In the meantime, if you want to do any maintenance work on a server that's covered by a Server Monitor, close the Server Monitor to shut it down, or you may end up in a tug-of-war (I turn off a service, the monitor turns it on) the way I did.

Maintaining the Information Stores

The Information Stores on a server hold all the mailboxes and data for those who use that server as the home server (in the Private IS); they also hold the public folders residing on that server (in the Public IS).

Tweaking the IS Maintenance Settings

Periodic maintenance routines occur automatically for the Information Stores on a server. During the periodic maintenance, the IS files are defragmented and compacted. You need to make sure that the schedule doesn't interfere with other important routines (such as automated backups).

To check (and possibly change) the schedule, select the server you want to use in the left pane of the Exchange Administrator window. From the File menu, choose Properties, and go to the IS Maintenance tab (see Figure 6-11).

A problem that administrators frequently encounter is an overlap between automated backups and IS maintenance. If your backup starts at midnight and takes more than two hours, don't start IS maintenance before 3 or 4 A.M. Online defragmentation, an important part of the IS maintenance, will not run if a backup is running.

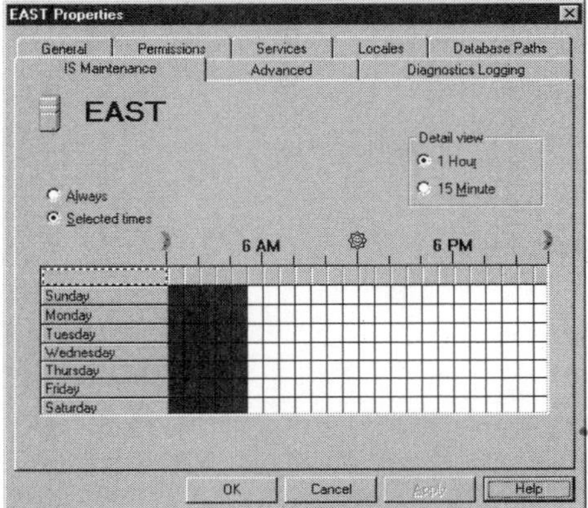

Figure 6-11. *Check the maintenance schedule to make sure it doesn't interfere with other important tasks.*

On the other hand, if the IS maintenance takes a long time, you need to make sure it's finished before users show up and start accessing mailboxes and public folders.

The larger your IS, the longer maintenance takes (and the longer backup takes). You might want to think about sharing the load by putting another Exchange server on the site and relocating some mailboxes to the new server.

Offline Defragmentation

You should run an offline defrag every so often, because it's far more effective and efficient than the scheduled online defrag. For one thing, the online defrag is stopped and started by the IS maintenance schedule, and it is allotted a specific amount of time. If the entire IS isn't defragged within the time limit, a marker is left behind, and at the next scheduled maintenance defragging picks up where it left off. As your IS gets larger and larger with use, less and less defragging takes place online. This means that you don't get the speed and efficiency that defragging is supposed to deliver. An offline defrag, on the other hand, is a total defrag, and you should see increased efficiency each time you perform this task. See the section "Automatic IS Maintenance" in Chapter 2 for detailed instructions on performing an offline defrag.

Diagnostics Logging for the Information Stores

If your system seems slow, or if users are reporting untoward events, it may be useful to log specific events for the IS. You can specify the logging levels you want to achieve in the Diagnostics Logging tab of the server's Properties dialog box (see Figure 6-12, on the following page).

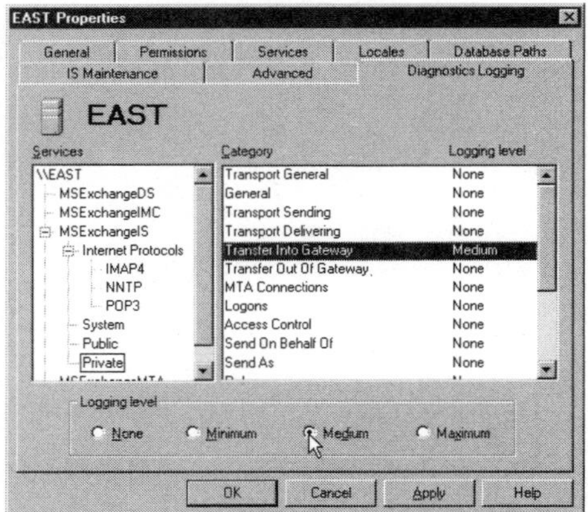

Figure 6-12. *Turn on diagnostic logging for the Information Store to locate bottlenecks or problems.*

Maintaining the Message Transfer Agent

Each Exchange server has an MTA that delivers the messages in its queue to all the other servers. To perform that task, the MTA uses the routing table, which calculates the path for delivering each message. If there are changes in your Exchange system that affect the routing, such as a change in the address space of a connector, the MTA learns about the changes during the automatic daily rebuild of the routing table.

Recalculating the Routing Table

If you've made a lot of changes or added connections, you should rebuild the routing table manually:

1. Select the appropriate server in the left pane of the Exchange Administrator window.
2. Double-click the MTA object in the right pane to display its Properties dialog box.
3. On the General tab, click Recalculate Routing.
4. A dialog box with a message telling you it will take several minutes to replicate the new routing information across the site appears. Click OK.
5. The routing table is recalculated. (No message appears to tell you when the task is finished.)

Diagnostics Logging for the MTA

If there are Event Viewer messages for the MTA, you may want to turn up the level of diagnostics logging to find and solve the problem (see Figure 6-13). Use the Diagnostics Logging tab to select the service and level of logging.

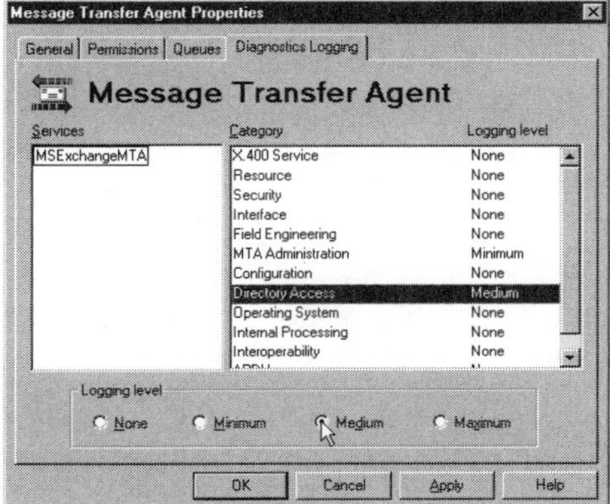

Figure 6-13. *Push the logging level of services reporting problems, even if they're minor problems.*

Checking MTA Queues

The Queues tab of the MTA Properties dialog box lists the messages that are awaiting delivery by the MTA (see Figure 6-14). The Queue Name drop-down box lets you choose the Public IS, the Private IS, and any additional mail services or gateways. An empty message list box means that everything is sailing through the MTA and no item is waiting for delivery (a rare occurrence in a busy Exchange system). Click the Refresh button to see the latest list.

Manipulating the Messages in the MTA Queue

You can make changes to the delivery of the messages in the MTA queue. Double-click the message you want to manipulate, then change the priority level or

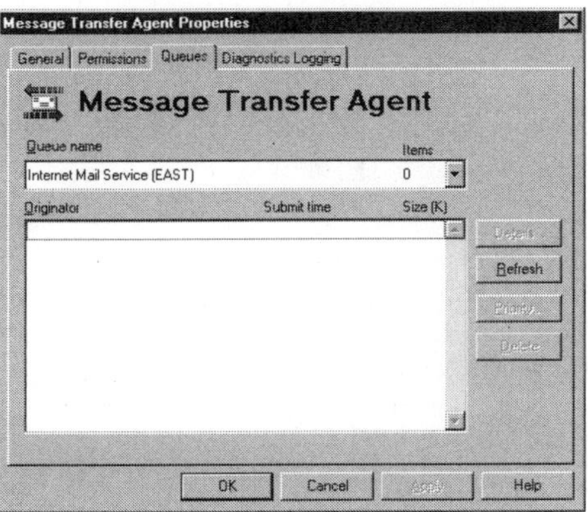

Figure 6-14. *The Internet Mail Service has a Message Transfer Agent queue, and there's nothing awaiting delivery at this moment.*

delete the message. This is useful if a message seems to be hanging around too long, and may be causing a bottleneck for the messages behind it. Lowering the priority level lets the messages behind it pass through, and deleting it eliminates all problems (except the one you'll have when you tell the originator).

Preventive Maintenance for Servers

You should take some steps to make sure you can get your Exchange system up and running again after a server disaster. The most important preventive measure, of course, is doing a full backup every day (or night). Microsoft Backup, which comes with Windows NT, handles all the special functions required for backing up Exchange information.

Beyond the backup, however, consider these additional safeguards for your server(s).

- Use an uninterruptible power supply.
- After installation, and periodically thereafter, make a copy of the server directory, Dir.edb, and take it offsite. This file is computer-specific and can't be regenerated if it's destroyed. It's in the \Dsadata subdirectory.
- Keep a document offsite that contains all the important information about the server, such as:
    - Directory name structure for the Organization, Site, and Server
    - All the service packs and hot fixes you've installed
    - Exchange service account and password
    - Paths to all the Exchange databases (update the information after you run the optimizer, if it results in moved files)
    - Settings for all connectors

Maintaining Sites

Even if you have only one Exchange server on your site, some objects in the Exchange hierarchy are site-specific. Of course, if your site connects with other Exchange sites, you have plenty of maintenance tasks.

Using Link Monitors

Link Monitors are used to monitor connections between two points in your Exchange system in order to test the messaging system (you can also configure a Link Monitor to test a foreign messaging point). Essentially, a Link Monitor pings the target computer with a test message (a ping message). Responding to an alert from a Link Monitor is easier and more pleasant than responding to a user who is receiving NDRs.

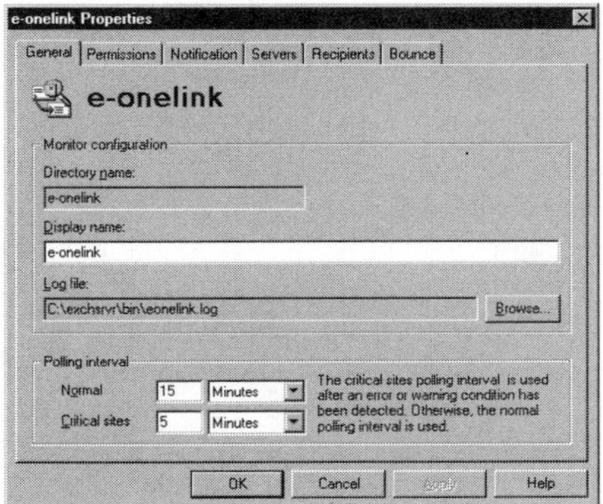

Figure 6-15. *Set up a Link Monitor to keep an eye on messaging.*

Link Monitors are in the site hierarchy, and you can create the monitor from an external site (with the proper permission levels, of course):

1. Expand the Configuration container for the site.
2. Select the Monitors container.
3. From the File menu, choose New Other, and then choose Link Monitor.

The Monitor Properties dialog box displays the General tab (see Figure 6-15), where you name the monitor and set the polling interval. You can also select a location for a log file (this is optional, but a good idea).

The Notification and Servers tabs are configured in the same manner as Server Monitors (explained earlier in this chapter).

The Recipients tab is used to establish a link monitor procedure with foreign systems. Remember that the important part of a link test is the connection to the system. The only way to accomplish this is to send the test message to a non-existent recipient (at a good address) so that you get an NDR. This means that the test message reached the system (which returned the message "That person isn't here"). If you send a message to a real recipient, you have to pick up the telephone and call that recipient to ask if he or she got the message.

The Bounce tab is where you specify the durations for warnings and alerts. The duration is the amount of time you believe to be sufficient for a round-trip message (your message ping and a response). Essentially, a warning occurs if the round trip takes longer than the specified duration (the default duration is 30 minutes). An alert occurs if the trip is much longer than specified (the default is 60 minutes). The times you specify should vary depending on the type of connection. A foreign system, for example, should be given more time than another site in your own organization.

After your Link Monitor is created, you need to start it. Use the instructions earlier in this chapter for starting Server Monitors.

Managing X.400 Connectors

Most Exchange systems that require X.400 connectors install them during the initial deployment of Exchange Server, so I won't cover the installation procedure here. I've asked a lot of Exchange administrators, however, to tell me about X.400 problems or tricks they've discovered. Several items showed up in multiple lists, so it's safe to assume that these experiences are common enough to pass along to you.

Connector Never Used

Picture this: a site has two servers, and each server has an X.400 connector. Users send messages to custom X.400 recipients. The server that takes the mail routes the mail to the other server instead of using its own X.400 connector. The second server's X.400 connector sends the mail. OK, that's strange, but the mail gets through, so there's no compulsion to figure out the problem if you're a busy administrator (I'm quoting their excuses; do not assume this is my advice).

If the second server goes down, the original server does not use its own X.400 connector. Instead, the mail waits in the MTA queue until the second server is available. Now there's a reason to figure out what's going on. What's the problem?

Believe it or not, the original X.400 connector isn't "broken"; it has one teeny configuration error. The routing cost is so high that Exchange won't use it. If you have multiple X.400 connectors in a site, be sure you set the routing cost to 1 for both of them.

Here's the interesting part: every administrator swore that he or she didn't set the high routing cost. Apparently, if you're setting up a second X.400 connector in a site, a routing cost that's way too high (90) might be applied automatically. Go to the Routing Cost text box on each connector's Properties dialog box and equalize the specifications (1 is a good choice).

Client Software Can't Handle Message Replies or Forwards

Messages sent from one Exchange server X.400 connector to another Exchange server X.400 connector caused problems for the clients if the messages contained attachments. Because an Exchange server to Exchange server message should be the easiest, most trouble-free type of transaction, this was puzzling.

It turns out that in each case, the General tab of the X.400 Connector Properties dialog box had the setting named Remote Clients Support MAPI disabled. Don't assume that the setting isn't needed because you're passing messages between Exchange servers. The only time you can disable this setting is when your X.400 connector is communicating with third-party transfer agents.

Bad Address Space Configuration Can Cause NDRs

If outbound mail using an X.400 is bouncing with a "no route to recipient" message, check the address space configuration for the connector. The MTA uses this information to decide which connector should handle a given message. Here are some guidelines for the address space entry:

- You don't need an address space entry if the connector is used only to connect to another site's Exchange MTA. However, you must configure the Connected Sites tab.
- The pecking order for matching a recipient address to the information in the address space is: exact match; wildcard match; substring match (which can be partial). No match causes an NDR.

Dealing with That Annoying Winmail.dat Attachment

Exchange users get telephone calls and messages from recipients who demand to know why messages arrive with an attachment named Winmail.dat. The attachment is tiny (usually 1 or 2 bytes). If you open it, you can see that this is not a normal attachment (see Figure 6-16).

This attachment only shows up with messages that are sent using RTF. Winmail.dat is used to tell the receiving system how to handle the RTF formatting in the message. If the receiving system doesn't know how to take Winmail.dat apart and use it, the result is this incomprehensible attachment. If the recipient uses e-mail software that treats attachments as discrete objects (for example, Eudora) and sends them to a specified attachment directory, that directory can contain a great many Winmail.dat files. Windows, of course, adds a number to each file as it is placed in the directory, so the recipient may find files named

Figure 6-16. *I have a whole collection of files named* Winmail.dat, *and they all have contents similar to this.*

Winmail.dat, Winmail1.dat, Winmail2.dat, and so on. Eventually, tired of cleaning out the directory, the recipient tells your Exchange user to cease and desist.

If the complaints are bothersome, you have two choices:

- Instruct your users to avoid RTF messages to users not on Exchange Server.
- From the X.400 Connector Properties dialog box, click the General tab and clear Remote Clients Support MAPI.

If the complaints don't bother your users, you don't have to do anything.

Note It's actually the MTA that sends the Winmail.dat attachment, but the solution is in the X.400 Connector.

Site Connectors

Some Exchange administrators prefer to connect sites via Site Connectors instead of using X.400 Connectors.

Site Connectors vs. X.400 Connectors

Here are some guidelines you might want to consider:

- If you have the standard version of Exchange Server (instead of the Enterprise version), X.400 Connectors aren't included on your CD-ROM, and you must purchase an X.400 Connector CD.
- Site Connectors are direct links between Exchange sites in your organization. Servers in each site communicate directly via RPCs (through the MTA), and messages are sent without any need for conversions to a different format. The downside of this is that RPCs run on top of the base protocol (usually TCP/IP) and therefore require more bandwidth to avoid massive slowdowns during periods of heavy traffic.
- Site Connectors are easier to set up, maintain, and troubleshoot than X.400 connectors, especially if the links are between sites in the same domain or trusting domains.
- You cannot set message size limits when you use a Site Connector. Instead, you must set limits on the MTA, which is a global setting, affecting all other connectors. This may cause problems. X.400 Connectors can be configured for message size limits.
- Delivery configuration (such as delayed sending) is supported by X.400 Connectors and is not supported by Site Connectors.

Creating Site Connectors

Setting up a Site Connector is a two-step process, because you must set up the connector in your own site and then establish its partner in the remote site. It's much easier to do this by getting the necessary permissions to perform both steps yourself. If that isn't possible, arrange to have an administrator at the remote site working on creating a Site Connector at the same time you're creating one on your site. (During the procedure, Exchange prompts for the creation of the target Site Connector.)

1. In the Exchange Administrator window, expand the local site and select the Connections object in the left pane.
2. From the File menu, choose New Other, and then choose Site Connector.
3. In the New Site Connector dialog box, enter the name of a server in the target site and click OK.

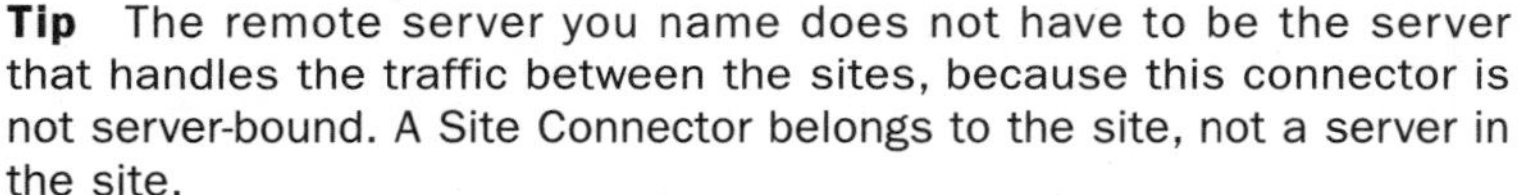

Tip The remote server you name does not have to be the server that handles the traffic between the sites, because this connector is not server-bound. A Site Connector belongs to the site, not a server in the site.

Now your Exchange system locates and accesses the server you named. If it cannot make a connection, the process terminates. Here are some of the problems you might encounter:

- If the target site is in another domain, you must establish the appropriate level of rights before beginning this process. This means that you must have administrative rights in the target domain and also have administrative rights for the Exchange server you're trying to connect with.
- A name resolution mechanism must be in place so that you can resolve the name of the target server (WINS, DNS, or LMHOSTS file).
- If a Site Connector already exists between the sites, you won't be able to continue.

Configuring Site Connectors

If you have a successful connection, you can move to the next step. A Properties dialog box for the connector appears so you can begin the configuration process.

General Tab of the Site Connector In the General tab, you can rename the connector (there is a directory name and a display name), but the default name of Site Connector <*site name*> should work just fine. The following information is also entered in the General tab:

- **Cost** Enter a routing cost (the default is 1). Exchange makes decisions about using connections based on cost (the lowest and best is 0; the highest and worst is 100).
- **Bridgehead** Optionally, specify a bridgehead server to manage communications with the target site. By default, any server in the site can take on this task, so use a bridgehead specification only if there's a reason to name a specific server.

Target Servers Tab of the Site Connector The Target Servers tab is the place to specify which servers at the target site will receive messages. The left pane of the window lists all the servers on the site, and the right pane displays the servers you elect to use for the Site Connector (click Add to move a server to the right pane).

For each selected server, enter the routing cost and click Set Value.

Address Space Tab of the Site Connector You have to configure the connector for the address types it's going to handle. Select an address type (X.400, Internet, MS Mail, and so on) to add it to the connector.

Override Tab of the Site Connector Use the Override tab for Site Connectors that have target sites in a different domain or an untrusted domain. You need to provide logon information for the connector, including the account name and password.

Configuring the Remote Site

When you've completed the configuration of your local Site Connector, click OK. Exchange asks if you want to create a Site Connector in the remote site. Click Yes to continue. Click No if you want to perform this step later, but remember that you don't have a working Site Connector until you perform this step.

When you opt to create the remote Site Connector, a Properties dialog box appears for the remote site. Use the guidelines and rules for configuring your local site connector to configure the remote site. If an administrator at the remote site has already configured the Site Connector, there's not a lot of work for you to do.

Remote sites that are linked to your site via a Site Connector appear in the left pane of your Exchange Administrator window—they're a part of your site hierarchy. You can view information about the objects in the remote site, but you cannot change anything until you log on to a server in that site.

Tip Don't forget to set up a directory replication connector to the remote site so that you can share address lists.

Troubleshooting Directory Replication Between Sites

When I was preparing for this book I polled Exchange administrators about the tasks they performed regularly. I was surprised at how few of them talked about nursing, babysitting, or otherwise spending time on directory replication between Exchange sites. Apparently replication works smoothly most of the time (if you set it up properly).

Problems do occur, however, and this section describes the steps you can take to try to figure out what's causing a problem and what will solve it.

- **Look for connection (not connector) problems** Bandwidth is important (I consider it a replication error if it takes many hours to complete replication). If you're using a Site Connector, insufficient bandwidth can result in an aborted replication. The best test for a connection is a message, so send a test message before starting replication if you've had problems previously.

Check modems, ports, lines, or whatever elements are involved in your connection.

- **Check for security problems** If the sites are not in the same domain, make sure there are properly configured trusts in both directions. If these trusts don't exist, you must use identical Exchange service accounts and passwords (if you're using a Site Connector, you can configure the Override tab of the Properties dialog box to configure the accounts more specifically).
- **Check the event logs** Scrutinize the event logs to see if you can find an error related to your replication problems.
- **Turn up diagnostics logging** Use the Diagnostics Logging tab on the MTA and Directory Properties dialog boxes to turn up logging levels. (Select the server, and then open the MTA and Directory objects.)
  - In the MTA, set the logging level to Maximum for these categories: X.400 Service, Interface, Configuration, Directory Access, and Internal Processing.
  - In the Directory, set the logging level to Maximum for these categories: ExDS Interface, Replication, and Directory Access.

Then keep an eye on the Event Viewer.

Exchange Server and Windows NT

Exchange Server is inextricably linked to Windows NT, and beyond its dependency, it uses many Windows NT features and functions. In this section I discuss two important maintenance tasks: backing up (which is a daily chore) and disaster recovery (which you may never have to do, but you should know how just in case).

Backing Up

The purpose of backing up is to restore as quickly as possible. That means that you don't create a backup scheme that's convenient, easy, and fast—you create a backup scheme that makes restoring convenient, easy, and fast.

When you install Exchange Server on a Windows NT server, the Windows NT backup software (Ntbackup.exe) is changed too. It's enhanced so that it can handle the complicated functions necessary for backing up Exchange Server data.

Exchange Server Files

Backing up Exchange Server is a complicated procedure because of the variety and type of files that must be backed up. There are three sets of files:

- The Information Store files that contain the public folders and private folders (mailboxes)
- The Directory Store file that contains information about recipients, connectors, and servers
- The Transaction Logs that contain the transaction data

The Information Store has two database files: Priv.edb and Pub.edb. They're located in the \Mdbdata directory.

The Directory Store has its information in the file Dir.edb, which is located in the \Dsadata directory.

The Transaction Logs include Edb.log for the current IS transactions, Ebd.log for the Directory Service (DS) transactions, backup copies of those files (made automatically), reservation log files (which reserve space on the disk), and Edb.chk, which is a database checkpoint file. The transaction log files are in the \Mdbdta directory.

Transactions are written to the databases in a manner designed to prevent interruption and slowdown. Transactions that are in the log files but haven't yet been committed to the database are called outstanding transactions.

Every time the Exchange Server databases are started, the transaction log is checked and the process of writing transactions to the databases starts.

If there's a computer problem, whether an inadvertent shutdown (Exchange servers, like all mail services, should run 24x7) or a major hardware failure, the restored transaction logs and databases can resume their communication so that transactions are written as intended.

Using Ntbackup.exe

When you launch the Windows backup software, Ntbackup.exe, you see a window for Microsoft Exchange Server in addition to the icons for your server's drives (see Figure 6-17). Use the normal Windows NT procedures to begin the backup.

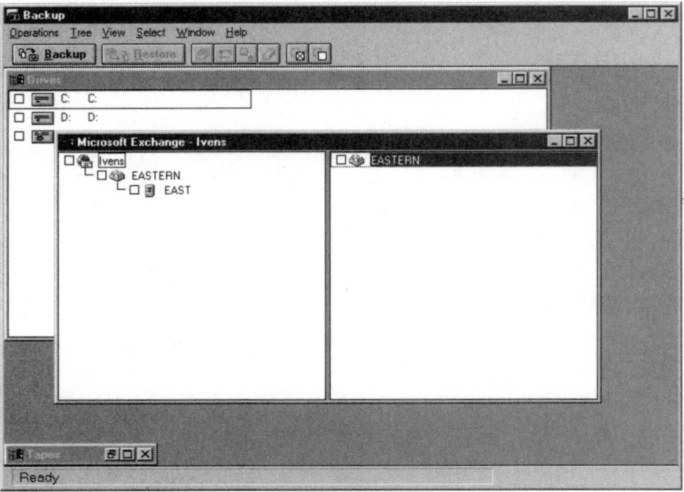

Figure 6-17. *Exchange Server adds services to the Windows backup software.*

Exchange Server's structure permits online backups while users are connected to the server and accessing the databases. To allow the activity to continue, Exchange uses special files to track the transactions. The files are called *patch files*, and there's one for each store:

- Pub.pat for the Public IS
- Priv.pat for the Private IS
- Dir.pat for the DS

When the backup software starts working, the patch files are created. The transaction log is locked (disabled), and both the database and log files are written to the backup media. Transactions that occur during this time are written to the patch file.

When the store backup is complete, the lock on the transaction log is removed and the contents of the patch file are written to the backup file. When that is completed, the patch file is deleted.

Tip After the backup is completed, check the \Mdbdata directory to make sure there's no patch file. If there is, you probably didn't have a successful backup, and you should repeat the procedure.

Recovering an Exchange Server

The worst-case restore process is a server or hard drive replacement, so it seems appropriate to discuss that eventuality. If your problem is something less tragic such as the accidental deletion of files, you won't have to go through all the operating system restoration steps. Because the backup is a backup of databases, not mailboxes, however, you have to do a complete restore if you want to restore only a mailbox. There's a workaround for this, and I'll discuss it after I explain the restore procedure.

1. Install Windows NT and give the server the same role and name as the server you're replacing. (For example, if the server that failed was a Backup Domain Controller [BDC], you should make this server a BDC).
2. Install any required service packs.
3. Install Exchange Server. Use the same organization and site names as the previous server. Use the same Exchange service account.

Caution If the server is not the only server in the site, use Setup /r when you install Exchange Server. This prevents automatic replication of this server's data to the rest of the system.

4. Install Exchange service packs.
5. Install Exchange client software. This will let you test your system after you restore the Exchange data.

6. Run Ntbackup.exe and restore the IS and DS.
7. Use the client software to check the system by sending yourself a message.
8. Open the Exchange Administrator window and make sure that mailboxes and Windows NT accounts are linked properly.
9. Run the Exchange Performance Optimizer.

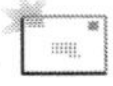

Note If the Exchange server is also a BDC (not a great idea, but I know that it happens), use the Windows NT features for rebuilding the Security Accounts Manager (SAM). You'll have to use Server Manager to demote the BDC and then promote it back. I'm assuming nobody would ever use a Primary Domain Controller (PDC) as an Exchange server.

If you need to restore only a mailbox, you don't have to perform all the tasks in the previous list, but you still won't have an easy time of it. Here are the steps for restoring the Information Store:

1. Shut down all the services on the Exchange server.
2. Back up the IS.
3. Find the previous backup (before the mailbox was deleted) and restore the IS.
4. Start the Exchange IS service, but don't allow users to log on (disconnect the cable to the NIC).
5. Log into the restored mailbox and move the messages to a .pst file.
6. Shut down Exchange services.
7. Restore the backup you just made.
8. Start all the Exchange services and reconnect the network cable (listen for the cheering and clapping coming from users).
9. Give the owner of the deleted mailbox the .pst file so that he or she can access the messages.

There are less disruptive methods that are available to you if you've purchased additional software or hardware for the express purpose of disaster-planning.

The preferred method, which causes the least or no interruption to your messaging services, is to use the single mailbox recovery feature of a third-party backup software program such as BackupExec or ArcServe with the Microsoft Exchange Agent modules installed. These backup software programs provide you with the capability to recover a single mailbox without forcing you to restore the entire Directory Store and Information Store.

Chapter 7

Maintaining Public Folders

The toughest part of administering public folders is the amount of control you don't have. Users create the folders and can give other users permissions. Of course, when things go awry, it's up to you to resolve the problems. However, you can do some things to protect your system from user-powered anarchy and this chapter discusses them, along with other maintenance and troubleshooting pointers.

Public Folder Hierarchy and Locations

Public folders exist in a tree structure, which is organization-wide (see Figure 7-1). The hierarchy consists of the organization's Public Folders container, folders, and subfolders.

A public folder can contain messages (both headers and bodies), attachments, forms associated with the folder, and subfolders.

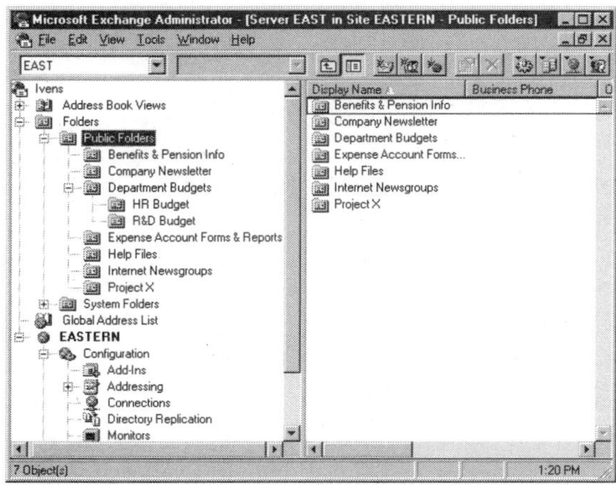

Figure 7-1. *Public folders are organization-wide.*

Public Folder Servers

The user's view of the public folder structure is supplied by the server that provides that user with public folders. This may or may not be the same server that contains the user's mailbox (depending on the configuration choices you made when you installed Microsoft Exchange Server).

To view (or change) the server that is assigned to hold public folders, open the Private Information Store object on the server. The General tab has an entry that indicates the server for public folders. Every server that is designated to hold public folders contains the complete hierarchy for the organization.

The contents of a public folder reside on the server that is configured to hold that folder's contents. The contents can be replicated to other servers, but that isn't automatic; it's a configuration choice. This means that sometimes users can see a public folder but can't access its contents.

When a user creates a folder, it's created on that user's public folder server. The creator can create subfolders and give other users the right to create subfolders.

If the top-level folder is not replicated, those subfolders are created on the server that holds the top-level folder (regardless of the server assigned to the user who created the subfolder).

If the top-level folder is replicated, the subfolder is created on the server assigned to the user who created it, but of course it travels back to the server of the original creator, contents and all, because subfolders inherit the replication configuration of the parent folder.

Hierarchy Replication

When a user creates a new folder, the new hierarchy and the contents of the folder are stored on the public folder server for that user (the data is written to Pub.edb, the Public Information Store database). That server is the originating server for the public folder.

The new hierarchy is automatically sent to all the servers throughout the organization, until it's written to every local Pub.edb. Remember, I'm talking about the hierarchy, not the folders' contents. The replication of the public folder hierarchy is sometimes called *dissemination*.

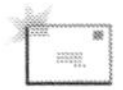

Note The hierarchy is propagated via a Public IS IPM (basically, a mail message), and the MTA delivers it across any connector transports.

User Rights for Public Folders

Public folders can be created only by users, through client software (such as Microsoft Outlook or Microsoft Exchange Client). By default, Exchange Server permits any user to create a public folder. Table 7-1 describes the available roles for public folders.

Owner Rights

The user that creates a folder is the Owner; he or she has the permission levels assigned to the Owner role (see Figure 7-2, on the following page).

Two other users are automatically added to the Permissions tab of the public folder dialog box: Default and Anonymous.

- The Default user is a stand-in for all users who access the public folder (the assumption is that every user in the organization can access the folder).
- The Anonymous user is a stand-in for any person who accesses this public folder via the Internet. If the public folder isn't exposed to the Internet, the user is meaningless.

The Owner can add any users in the GAL to the list of users, assigning any role or combination of permissions. Another powerful feature is the ability to assign client permissions for a public folder through a Distribution List (DL). In the same way that Microsoft Windows NT allows you to assign permissions to Global and Local groups, you can use DLs in Exchange Server. This makes the administration of permissions much easier, since you can put a certain group of users into a large DL and then assign that DL one set of permissions instead of having to add 200 people manually to the client permissions list.

Table 7-1 Public Folder Roles and Their Associated Permissions

Role	Permitted Behavior
Owner	Performs any task. Creates subfolders, gives permissions to others, deletes anything, and generally runs amok.
Publishing Editor	Same permissions as the owner; used by the owner to give full permissions to another user.
Editor	Creates and deletes items but cannot create subfolders.
Publishing Author	Creates items; edits and deletes only those items. Creates subfolders.
Author	Creates and reads items; edits and deletes only the items he or she creates.
Non Editing Author	Same as Author, but cannot edit his or her own items.
Reviewer	Reads items.
Contributor	Creates items (used for automated processes that place information into public folders).
None	Self-explanatory; you're a potted plant and can't do anything on this folder.
Custom	Permissions assigned by the owner that do not match a preconfigured role.

The three users who exist in a public folder when it's created, along with their related roles, can have their permissions changed, but the accounts cannot be deleted from the folder through client software. If a user removes any of these accounts from the client software and clicks OK, all three accounts will be back

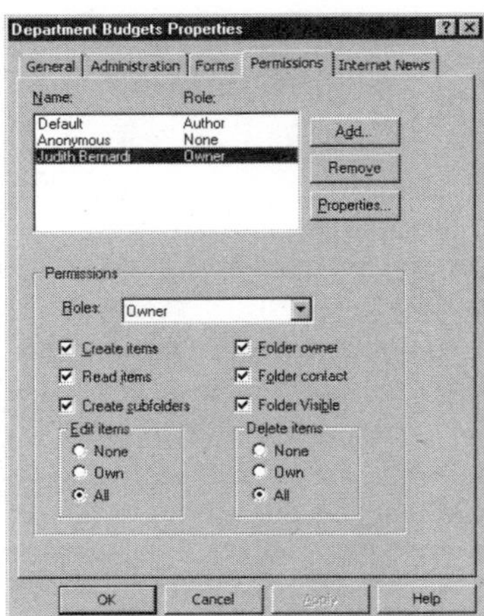

Figure 7-2. *The Owner of a public folder has unlimited permissions to manipulate the folder.*

when he or she opens the folder Properties dialog box again. The roles have been modified, however, as seen in Figure 7-3.

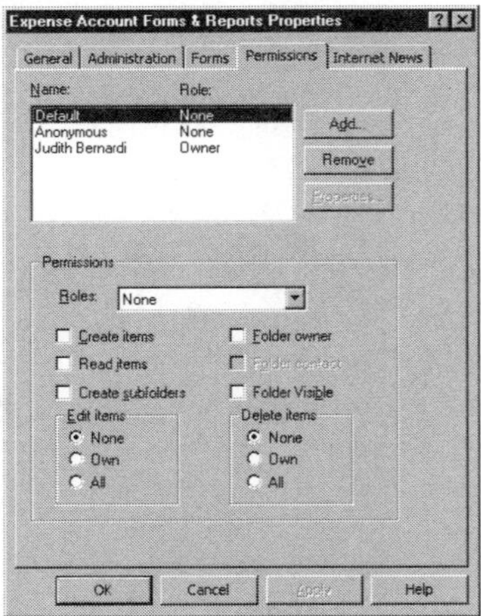

Figure 7-3. *After you delete the default accounts from the client software window, they return with reduced permissions.*

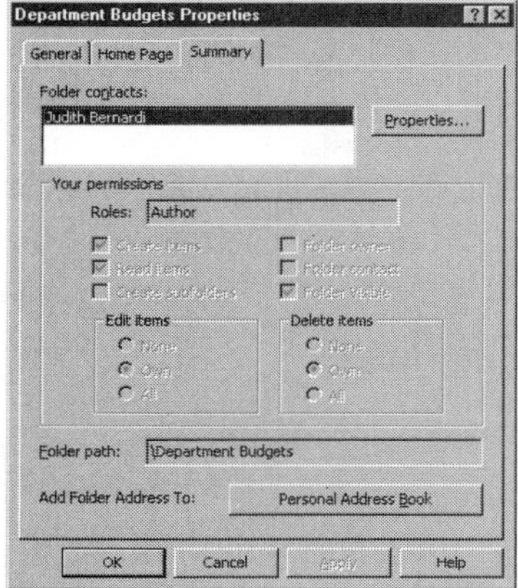

Figure 7-4. *Users cannot change their own permissions in a public folder.*

Note This works differently in the Exchange Server Administrator window (see the section "Administrator Rights for Public Folders," below).

Nonowner Rights

Other users who access the Properties dialog box of a public folder do not see a Permissions tab. The Summary tab, as seen in Figure 7-4, displays the name of the owner, along with the user's own permissions (which are not accessible and cannot be altered).

Administrator Rights for Public Folders

In Microsoft Exchange 5.5, administrators can manipulate permissions for the folder, and for the way the folder is used (permissions for manipulating contents).

Folder Permissions

As with all previous versions of Exchange Server, you can set permissions for a public folder in the Permissions tab of the folder's Properties dialog box (see Figure 7-5, on the next page). These permissions are for administrative tasks, affecting the folder itself, not the permissions that affect the folder contents.

The Windows NT accounts with permissions are the *only* Windows NT accounts that can perform any administrative functions for this folder. Add yourself to the list of Windows NT accounts with inherited permissions. Otherwise, if you try to perform a task (for example, replication), you'll generate an error indicating that you have insufficient privileges to perform that task.

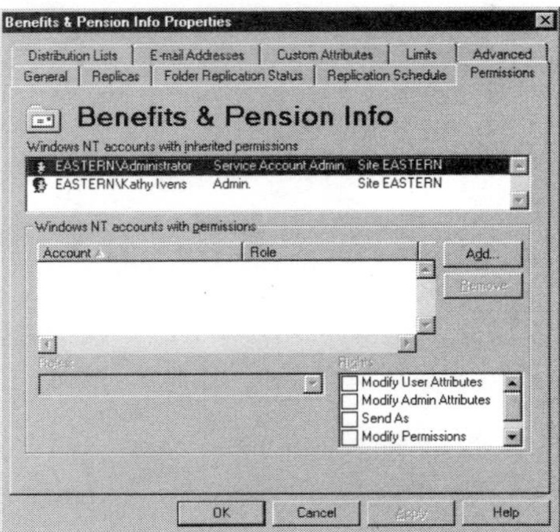

Figure 7-5. *Administrator permissions are not for folder contents.*

User Permissions

New to Exchange Server 5.5 is the ability to view and manipulate the client permissions (the user permissions set by the owner) at the Administrator window. Open the folder's Properties dialog box and click the Client Permissions button on the General tab to open the Client Permissions dialog box seen in Figure 7-6.

One quirk in the way that permissions are set on public folders is the difference between using the Administrator window and the client software window. For example, the Administrator can remove all the default accounts. This means the folder is ownerless. However, if you check the Client Permissions dialog box

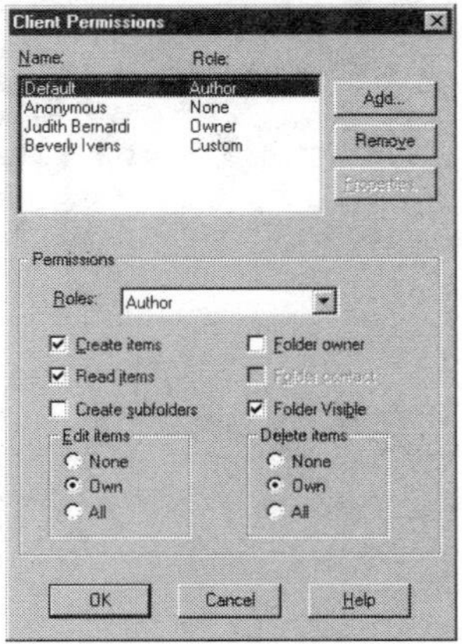

Figure 7-6. *View the folder's client permissions from the Administrator window.*

again (after you remove the three default accounts and click OK), the Default and Anonymous accounts are back with their access set to None. This makes it impossible to lose control of a folder, stranding it in never–never land. Just add an owner (make it yourself).

It's a good idea to remove the owners of folders you think are not well maintained, are over-maintained (too many high-level permissions are granted), or seem unnecessary. Make yourself, or an assistant, the owner.

Administering User Rights for Public Folders

By default, Exchange Server invites every user on the system to create public folders. This can create chaos, and by the time your Exchange system has been up and running for a while, you probably have encountered one or more of these problems:

- There are more public folders than could possibly be necessary (look for lots of similar folders, as different users had the same "great idea for a public folder").
- Many users are indiscriminate in the granting of permissions, so items are created and deleted rapidly, making the folder less useful.
- Public folder replication takes forever.

Now is the time to take back the control of your public folders!

Limiting the Right to Create a Public Folder

Start by limiting the right to create a public folder. This task is performed at the site level (and needs to be performed on each site in the organization). In the Administrator window, take these steps:

1. In the left pane, select the Configuration object under the Site container.
2. In the right pane, select the Information Store Site Configuration object.
3. From the File menu, choose Properties to open the IS Site Configuration dialog box (see Figure 7-7, on the following page).
4. Select List in one of the windows, then click the Modify button to display the GAL so you can add names to the window:
    - Use the Allowed To Create Top Level Folders window if you want to enter a small list or give permissions to the members of a DL.
    - Use the Not Allowed To Create Top Level Folders window if you want to exclude a small list of users.

Tip You can use both windows if necessary. For example, you may have an existing DL you want to add to the list of users allowed to create top-level folders. Then use the other window to exclude certain members of that list.

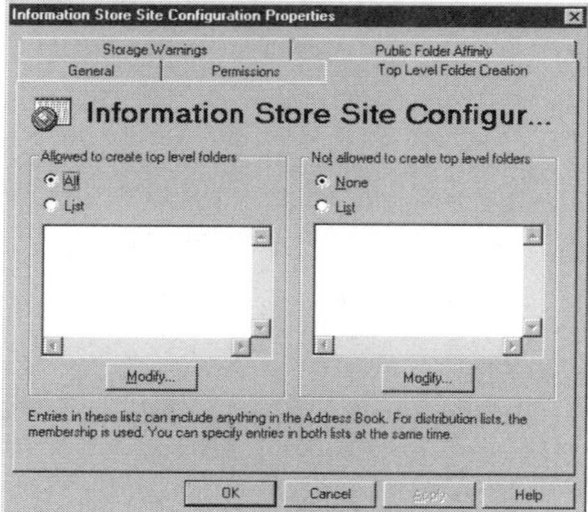

Figure 7-7. *The default setting is that everybody in your world can create a public folder whenever the whim strikes.*

Consider limiting the users who can create top-level folders to yourself and perhaps one or two assistant administrators. Then you can give additional users the right to add subfolders in those folders you create (see the next section).

Controlling the Top-Level Folders

The creator of a top-level folder can restrict user access to the folder and its subfolders and also restrict the users who can create subfolders. For real control, create the top-level folders yourself. Make these folders rather generic, because they'll hold subfolders for more specific collections of items. Perhaps you need a top-level folder for customers, company forms, or other broad topics.

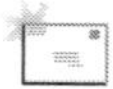

Note While permissions are inherited by lower-level folders, the inherited permissions are merely established as the default. The permissions aren't etched in cement, and anyone with the appropriate rights can change those permissions for the lower-level folders.

Replicating Public Folders

Public folder replication is an administrative task; it's unrelated to any configuration options that the folder's creating user chooses in client software. Replicas of public folders can be placed on any public folder server in your organization, which could be another server in the same site or a server in a different site.

Public Folders Require Two Replication Processes

There are actually two replication processes for public folders: replication of the hierarchy and replication of the content. The hierarchy travels throughout the organization based on the schedule for directory service replication. The content replicates on the schedule for folders. The timing of both replication services depends on the connector schedule. Sometimes the two replications arrive at targets separately. If the hierarchy arrives before the content, users can see the folders, but they get access errors when they try to open them.

Some public folders serve the user community perfectly well with only a single instance of the folder. For example, a public folder that a department or division uses to disseminate documents of interest to its employees can serve that group (assuming there's an easy way for everyone to connect to the folder's server).

On the other hand, public folders that are accessed frequently by the entire user community should be replicated, even if there's not a geographic separation between offices and departments. This balances the load, avoiding bottlenecks. More important, the redundancy means that if something happens to the originating server, users can still get to the forms and messages they need.

Of course, if your organization has offices that are geographically separated, replication of public folders that are used by everyone in the organization is a necessity.

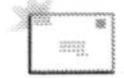

Note Overreplicating can be as disadvantageous as underreplicating, because it uses time, computer resources, and disk space.

Maintaining the Replication Schedule

You can set an individual replication schedule for each public folder, which is a terrifically efficient feature. Select the folder and then, from the File menu, choose Properties. In the Properties dialog box, go to the Replication Schedule tab (see Figure 7-8).

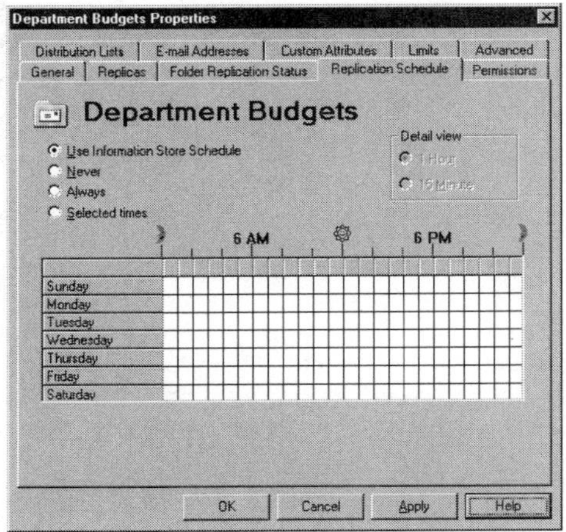

Figure 7-8. *By default, public folders take on the replication schedule for the server's Information Store.*

Use the choices on the Replication Schedule tab as follows:

- Select **Never** to stop replicating this folder. Use this option for a public folder that doesn't need to have its contents shared with users outside of this site.
- Select **Always** to replicate the folder every fifteen minutes. This option is useful for folders that have constantly changing items that users connected to other servers need to see. This is not a great choice if you replicate over a slow connection.
- Select **Selected Times** to specify a schedule in the Schedule Grid.

Caution If replication is implemented across wide area networks (WANs) with slow connections, it may take more than fifteen minutes to complete the task. In that case, don't use the Always option—instead set a schedule on the grid that takes all factors into consideration.

Note You can modify the default value of Always, which is fifteen minutes, by typing a different value in the Replicate Always Interval (Minutes). You'll find this option on the Advanced tab of the Properties dialog box for the Public Information Store.

Replication scheduling for a public folder overrides the schedule for the IS. If you have a lot of public folders, however, you may want to change the replication schedule on the server's IS instead of changing each public folder:

1. In the Exchange Administrator window, select the Server object.
2. In the right pane, select the Public Information Store.
3. From the File menu, choose Properties.
4. Go to the Replication Schedule tab and make the desired changes.

Tip Unlike the replication process in Windows NT, you cannot manually force replication of public folders. There is no command line utility or dialog box that performs a "replicate now" process.

Choosing Replication Targets

Not all public folders need to be replicated to all servers in your organization. You can balance the load of a public folder that contains items of interest to users in your site by replicating the folder to another server in that site. Or you can replicate a public folder to a server in any other site. From the folder's Properties dialog box, move to the Replicas tab and select the target servers you want to include in the replication schedule.

You can check the current status of replication for any public folder on the Folder Replication Status tab of the Properties dialog box. The target server name, last received time, and average transmission time appear, and you can add more columns to the display if you want to see additional (or different) information.

Pulling In Replicas from Other Sites

It's common for administrators to set up replication of the public folders on the sites they administer. If your organization has multiple sites, an administrator at each site takes care of deciding which public folders are replicated and where they're sent. You can also set up replication of a public folder at another site in order to bring it to your site. Here's how:

1. In the left pane of the Administrator window, select the server you want to use as the recipient of the replica(s).
2. In the right pane, select the Public Information Store.
3. From the File menu, choose Properties.
4. When the Properties dialog box appears, move to the Instances tab, where the initial view is of your own public folder server. The public folders listed in the right pane are your local folders.
5. From the drop-down list at the bottom of the left pane, select a site to see all the public folders in the public folder server for that site (see Figure 7-9).
6. Select each public folder you want to replicate and click Add. The folder name moves to the right pane.

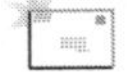

Note There's a Remove button you can use to remove a replica from your home site, but it doesn't work on public folders that belong to this site. You can remove only a replica you've brought in from another site.

After replication occurs, open your client software and access the public folder you replicated into your site. You should have no trouble opening it and using

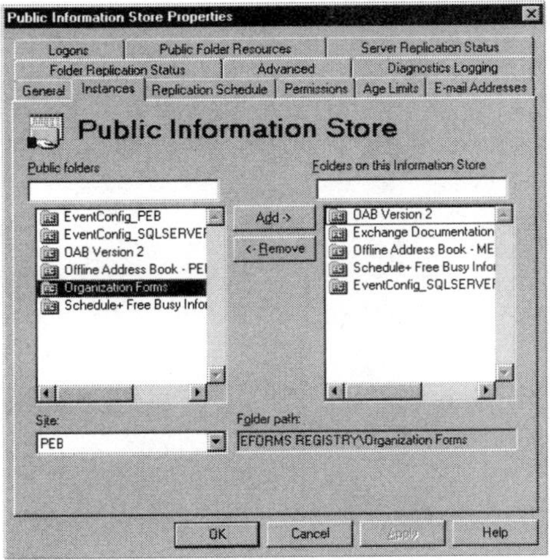

Figure 7-9. *Use the Instances tab to locate and replicate public folders on other sites.*

the contents. If you get an error message indicating that the folder is not accessible, make sure replication has occurred. If it has, retrace your steps and repeat the process (you may have done something wrong).

Working with Public Folder Affinity

You may have a public folder that you don't replicate, or is replicated to one site but not to others. Usually you make that decision because users at other sites don't have any need to access the contents of this public folder. If the folder is large (has a great many items) and is not needed throughout the organization, eliminating or limiting replication makes sense.

If a site doesn't receive a replication of the public folder, but a user needs to access the folder, you can enable the connection through a feature called *affinity*. Affinity gives users in one site the ability to access all the public servers in another site. The user must be able to reach the site through a connection within Exchange Server (affinity connections use RPCs). In some ways, it's a replacement for replication.

Setting Public Folder Affinity

Affinity is a site feature, not a server feature. The affinity you configure is from one site to another site, and it's a one-way process. If users at Site A have affinity to public folders at Site B, users at Site B do not have a complementary affinity back to Site A. You must set affinity from Site B to Site A.

To set affinity, follow these steps:

1. In the left pane of the Exchange Administrator window, select the site.
2. In the right pane, select the Information Store Site Configuration object.
3. From the File menu, choose Properties.
4. Move to the Public Folder Affinity tab of the dialog box and select a site to add to the affinity for this site.
5. Set a value for the connected site cost, or accept the default value.

Tip The cost is used only if there is more than one site with the public folder that the user wants to access. This occurs if you replicate public folders to limited sites, but not to the site of the user trying to access the folder.

After you set the affinity, open your client software and test it by selecting a folder. Be sure you can access the contents.

Troubleshooting Public Folder Affinity

The most common problem that users encounter when trying to access a public folder through an affinity setting is that they cannot get into the site. If the site is not part of the user's domain, you must have a trust relationship from the target site's domain to the user's domain in order to give the user the right to open a folder on the site.

Tip The short explanation of the authentication task is this: the public folder domain is the trusting domain; the client's domain is the trusted domain.

Administrators get confused about the need to establish a trust across domains for affinity because IS replication and other Exchange services don't need the explicit trust. Many of the functions you initiate as an administrator are performed by the Exchange service account, which has the equivalent of a master domain account.

Test the authentication by opening the client software and using the net view command to try to access the shares on each server that has a public folder you're trying to reach. The syntax is net view *computername* | domain: *domain_name*. If you get an "access is denied" message, you're going to have to create a trust to authenticate the users in your domain.

The second most common problem is that trying to establish a connection to the target site produces an error message ("not accessible"). You cannot use connections across the Internet or any other connection except an Exchange Server connector.

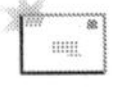

Note A user accessing Exchange Server with the Outlook Web Access version of client software cannot access a public folder by affinity. Only folders on the local server (including replicas) are available.

Moving Public Folders

If you need to balance the load for busy public folders, you might want to move some of them to another server. You can move a public folder to another server on the same site, or to another site, although the latter is far more complicated and is rarely necessary. If you don't have another server running Exchange Server on your site, you should think about adding one if the public folders on the site are busy.

Moving Public Folders to Another Server

If the site does not already have a server running Exchange Server, you must create an Exchange server on the site. Then, moving a public folder between servers in the same site requires just a few steps:

1. In the left pane of the Administrator window, expand both the Folders container and the Public Folders container.
2. Select the public folder you want to move, then from the File menu, choose Properties.

3. Move to the Replicas tab.
4. In the Servers box, select the target server and click Add.
5. In the Replicate Folders To box, select the original server and click Remove.

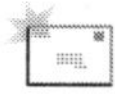

Note The folder remains on the original server until replication has occurred.

Selecting Remove on the Replicas tab does not delete the folder; it just removes the folder from one server after it has been replicated on another server. In fact, you cannot delete a public folder from the Administrator window. A public folder can be deleted from client software only by a user with Owner permissions.

Moving a Public Folder to Another Site

It's not common to move a public folder to another site, but if you have to perform this task, it's more complicated. You cannot use the same steps as moving a public folder between servers in the same site, because after you set up the replication to another site, the system will not let you remove the server from the current site.

The only way to move a public folder to another site is to export its contents, delete it from the first site, and then re-create it on the second site. This is all done with client software (which is the only way to delete and create public folders).

Exporting the Contents of a Public Folder

The first step in moving a public folder to another site is to export it to a file you can use as an import source on the second site. To do this, open client software and log on to Exchange Server (the server that has the public folder you want to move to another site). Then take these steps:

1. From the File menu, choose Import And Export.
2. Select the option Export To A File, and click Next.
3. In the Create A File Of Type box, select Personal Folder File (.pst), and click Next.
4. Select the public folder you want to move to another site (see Figure 7-10), and click Next.
5. Enter the path and filename for the .pst file you want to use. (The options for handling duplicates are irrelevant.)
6. Click Finish.

The contents of the public folder are transferred to the .pst file. Put the .pst file in a location you can access from the other site (some people e-mail it to themselves or to a recipient at the new site). Do not delete the public folder from the current site at this time.

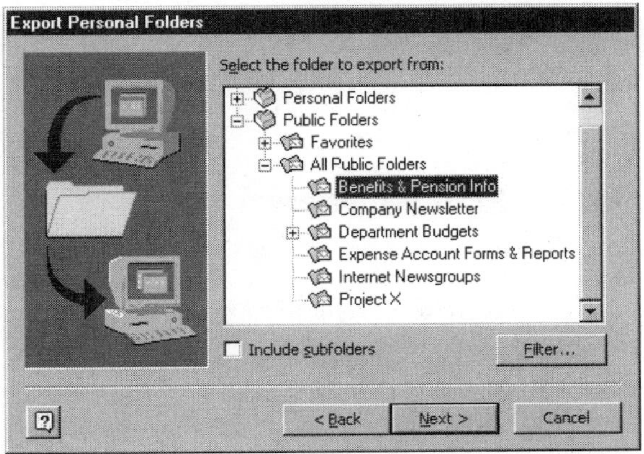

Figure 7-10. *Scroll through the folder hierarchy to the public folder you want to move.*

Importing Public Folder Contents at a New Site

To put the public folder onto the new site, open client software at that site and log on to the Exchange server that will hold the public folder. Create both a personal folder and a public folder using the same name as the public folder you want to move from the first site. (Imported files are brought into personal folders, not public folders, hence the need for a personal folder.) Then use these steps:

1. From the File menu, choose Import And Export.
2. Select Import From Another Program Or File.

Note Earlier versions of Outlook or Exchange may have an Import From The .pst option.

3. Select Personal Folder File (.pst).
4. Select the .pst export file you created as the file to import.
5. Select the new personal folder as the target and select the option Import Items Into The Same Folder In Public Folders.

Set up the replication and have users test the new public folder. When everything is working properly, delete the original public folder using client software (the folder owner must be the logged-on user of the client software, because only the Owner can delete the folder).

Maintaining Limits for Public Folders

If a public folder is popular and users constantly add items, the size of the folder can get out of hand. Imposing a size limit or an aging limit (or both) can help keep the folder manageable.

Additionally, as the Exchange administrator you're going to get calls from users who start their conversations with "Oops." Because users are aware that they can recover deleted messages in their mailboxes, they expect the same ability with public folders. The ability to recover a deleted item from a public folder, however, isn't automatic, the way it is with mailboxes.

Setting Aging Limits for Public Folders

An age limit is a specification of the amount of time a message can be stored in a public folder. When a message's time runs out, the message expires and dies. Aging is a tool you use to keep public folders from being cluttered with items that are no longer needed. Keeping your public folders lean makes replication easier, and also makes it easier for users to find items.

Configuring Age Limits for the Public IS

Because the Public IS is the container for all the public folders on a server, it's a logical place to set aging limits. Setting individual aging limits on specific folders, however, overrides the Public IS setting. Here's how to establish aging limits for the Public IS:

1. In the left pane of the Administrator window, select a server.
2. In the right pane, select the Public Information Store.
3. From the File menu, choose Properties.
4. In the Properties dialog box, go to the Age Limits tab (see Figure 7-11).
5. Select the Age Limit For All Folders On This Information Store check box, and then specify a number of days.

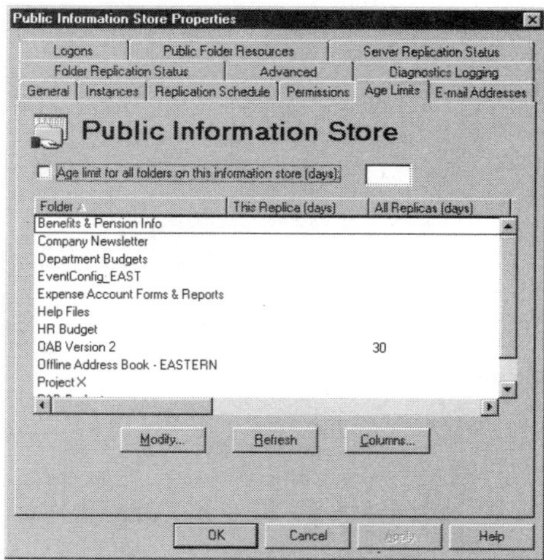

Figure 7-11. *The Public Information Store has no default settings for public folder age limits.*

Tip Use the horizontal scroll bar on the dialog box to view additional information about the contents of the public folders.

Items that are deleted as a result of the age limit you set are gone forever.

Configuring Age Limits for Individual Public Folders

You can set age limits for individual public folders instead of, or in addition to, setting a global limit on the Public IS. There are two places to set the limits: in the Public IS dialog box, or in the folder's Properties dialog box.

If you're working in the Public IS dialog box, double-click a public folder in the list that displays on the Age Limits tab. The Modify Age Limits dialog box for that folder appears (see Figure 7-12).

This dialog box lets you set age limits for the replica of a public folder on this Public IS, and for all replicas of the public folder throughout the organization. If you opt to set limits for all replicas, administrators on other sites can override those limits for their own Public IS.

Note The Effective Age Limit for the folder is displayed at the bottom of the dialog box. It represents the value you entered in the Public IS Age Limits dialog box and cannot be changed here.

You can also set an age limit in the Properties dialog box for a specific folder: in the Administrator window, expand the Public Folders container and select the public folder of interest. Then follow these steps:

1. From the File menu, choose Properties to open the folder's Properties dialog box (see Figure 7-13, on the following page).
2. Move to the Limits tab and select Age Limits, then specify a number of days.

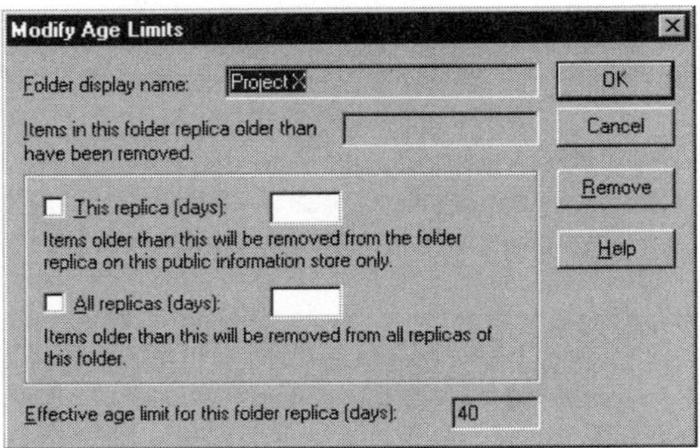

Figure 7-12. *You can configure age limits for specific folders from the Public Information Store dialog box.*

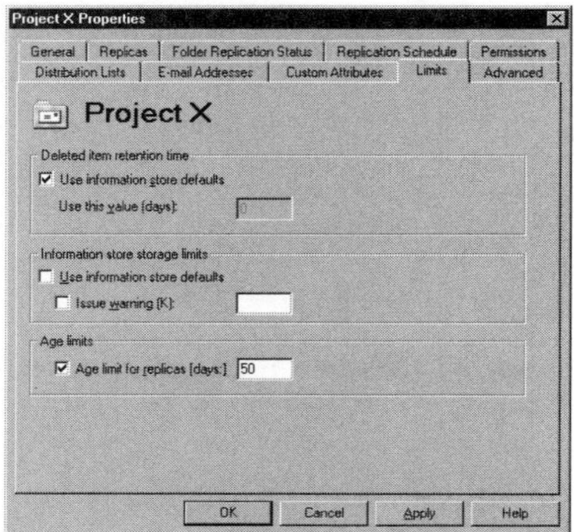

Figure 7-13. *Set an age limit for this folder in the Properties dialog box.*

Configuring Deleted Item Recovery

By default, the ability to recover deleted items from a public folder is disabled, so if you delete an item, it's gone. If you don't specify a deleted item's recovery option, the only way to recover a deleted item is to restore the entire server and logs from the last backup (which would cause complications you don't even want to *think* about) or use a "brick" backup and recovery technique software application that allows you to recover the contents of one mailbox or public folder.

Item Recovery is the Recycle Bin for the Information Store. With the appropriate settings on the Public or Private Information Stores, you can ensure that items are not permanently deleted until the age limits for a folder kick in.

You can establish item recovery settings for individual folders on the Limits tab of their Properties dialog boxes (see Figure 7-14), or for the entire Public IS on the General tab of the Properties dialog box.

By default, individual public folders use the item recovery setting for the Public IS. Deselect that option to enter a value for a specific public folder (remember, the default option for the Public IS is that there is no item recovery available).

Tip If you use the Public IS to establish the item recovery setting, you are also offered an option to hold on to deleted items until the store is backed up. Because you should be backing up daily, this shouldn't be an important selection.

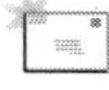

The IS service must be stopped and started again for the changes to take effect.

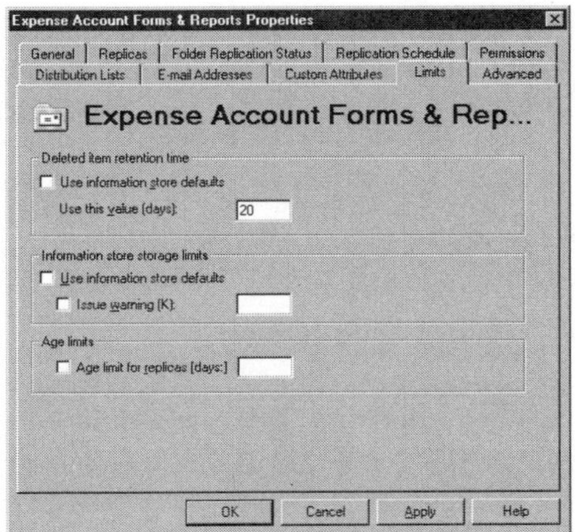

Figure 7-14. *Set specific item recovery values for individual public folders.*

Age Limits vs. Deleted Item Retention Limits

If you configure the Public IS and public folders for age limits and deleted item retention limits, it's important to know the pecking order. Age limits have precedence. This means that if you set a longer limit for deleted items than for age limits, any deleted item that reaches the age limit is permanently deleted, even if it should have a couple more days of life according to the deleted item retention setting.

Recovering Deleted Items

You cannot recover an item that was deleted from a public folder in the Administrator window; this is a task for client software. After you configure the Public IS or any individual folder(s) for deleted item recovery, the client software on your system gains a new command on the Tools menu—Recover Deleted Items.

Tip To recover a deleted item you must have read/write/delete permissions on the public folder (Editor Role).

In the client software, select the public folder for which you need to recover an item and choose Recover Deleted Items from the Tools menu. A window opens, displaying any items that were deleted from this folder and still exist because they're within the limits you established on the server (see Figure 7-15, on the following page).

- Select the items you want to recover (or click the Select All button on the toolbar).

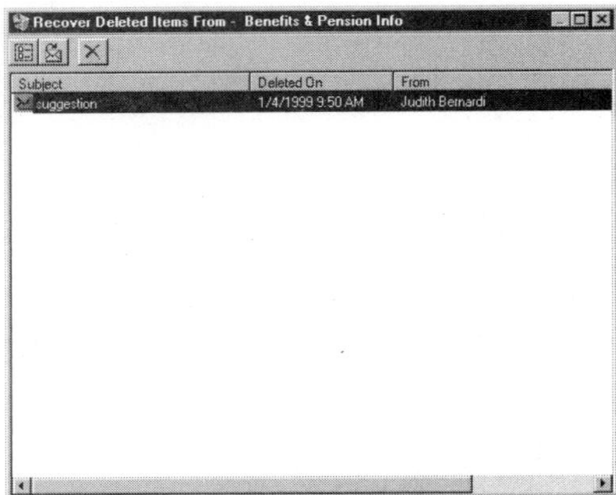

Figure 7-15. *You can recover any items that haven't been permanently deleted.*

- Click Recover Selected Items to put the items back into the public folder.
- Click Purge Selected Items to permanently delete the items.

> **Deleted Public Folder Items Are Not Handled Like Deleted Mail** When an item is deleted from a public folder, it remains in the folder, but it's hidden. This is not the same as the way Exchange Server handles deleted mail messages, which are removed from the folder in which they were placed (the Inbox or another folder chosen by the user). Then a new, discrete item is created in the Deleted Items folder of the user mailbox.

Setting Storage Size Limits

Even though aging limits can help keep the size of a public folder to a manageable proportion, you might want to consider imposing storage limits on busy and popular public folders.

Like the other limitations available to you, you can establish size limits for the entire Public IS, for individual public folders, or for a combination of both. Use the General tab of the Public IS Properties dialog box or the Limits tab of the public folder's Properties dialog box to set the storage limits.

When the items in a public folder exceed the size limit you configure, posting to the folder continues, and no items are refused or removed. However, the designated contact for the folder is sent a warning message. The contact is usually the folder's owner—check the Summary tab of a folder for which you are not the owner to see the name of the folder contact.

Using Public Folders for Newsgroups

Most of the work involved in setting up and configuring public folders that are used for newsgroup feeds was accomplished during the setup and configuration of your Exchange Server system. Because these public folders tend to grow quite large and have more security concerns than the public folders that aren't exposed to the Internet there are some guidelines you should be aware of.

- Newsgroup public folders do not hold on to deleted items.
- The top-level folder should not be exposed to the Internet but should exist only for the purpose of creating subfolders.
- Permissions to create subfolders should be limited to yourself and an assistant (or a couple of assistants).

Administrators who manage newsgroup public folders spend a lot of time interacting with their ISPs. The amount and type of work you have to do to fetch information depends on your arrangement with your ISP. Some administrators maintain Windows NT accounts for the ISP in order to receive a feed (a push feed).

An important task is the maintenance of the active file. This file is really the basis of the newsgroup hierarchies, and it's needed to receive a news feed. The active file is simply a text file that starts with a valid newsgroup name on the first line, ends with a period on the last line, and in between contains a listing of every newsgroup that your server knows about. You can configure Exchange so it pulls this file from your ISP. For load balancing reasons, however, your ISP may turn this feature off, and you will have to provide the file manually.

The best way to get an active file if Exchange is not performing this task is to use Telnet. This bypasses the normal server handshaking and instead uses client authentication to talk to the host server. You log on with the username your ISP provided for you, and then manually extract the newsgroup list from their server. Here are the steps:

1. Start Telnet.
2. Click Terminal, then choose Preferences and turn on local echo (this is essential).
3. Choose connect, and then choose Remote System and enter either the IP address or the Site Name for the news server in the Host Name Box. Enter **119** in the Port box (unless your ISP has given you a different port value).
4. Click OK.

The Telnet window should return a string indicating the server is ready. Assuming there are security standards in place, you should next begin establishing authorization. To do this, you must enter information in the Telnet window:

1. Enter **Authinfo user *<username>*** where *<username>* is the user ID your ISP provided for you.
2. The server returns 381 PASS required.
3. Enter **Authinfo pass *<password>*** where *<password>* is the password attached to the user ID.
4. The server returns 281 OK.
5. Choose Terminal, and then choose Start Logging. When you're prompted for a name, enter **Active** and click OK.

6. In the window, enter the word **list** and press Enter. A list comprising every newsgroup that your news server knows about scrolls through the window. (It can take quite some time, depending on your connection speed.)
7. When the list is complete, choose Terminal, then choose Stop Logging.

Now open the list in a text editor (it's too big for Microsoft Notepad) and run through the following checklist:

- Eliminate any garbage characters.
- Be sure the first line is a valid newsgroup name.
- Be sure the last line is a period followed by a carriage return.

Tip The easiest way to make sure that the end of the file is correct is to position your cursor to the right of the last character on the last line; then hit Delete until there's nothing past the cursor, and then hit Enter twice.

Save the file as Active.txt.

Now you can start the newsfeed. The Newsfeed Wizard walks you through windows in which you answer questions and specify options. There's no way to guess which combination of options you're using, so I'm not going to walk through the Wizard. However, there are some important issues to think about and plan around and this section gives you food for thought.

The Wizard wants to know what Site Name you want to use on the Internet. You should carefully reflect on how your organization is set up with respect to firewalls and Domain Name System (DNS) Servers. To receive a feed inbound, your newsfeed server must have an address record in your DNS server so that your ISP's news server can find you. Many firewalls are established to be very restrictive (as they should be), so you should make sure your firewall is configured to allow access to port 119 inbound if the newsfeed server is inside your company.

You have two choices for the type of feed, Push feed or Pull feed. A Push feed occurs when the ISP sends, or pushes, data from its news server to you. A Pull feed occurs when you connect to the ISP and draw data at whatever interval you specify. These choices present some possible obstacles, and they have to be worked out carefully with your ISP. Exchange Server is strictly Request for Comments (RFC)-compliant in its implementation of Network News Transport Protocol (NNTP), the protocol used over TCP to get and send news. Problems arise because many news servers are UNIX based, and their implementation of NNTP is based on the Berber draft, another news server guideline. Strict compliance with RFC standards requires servers to search their newsgroups and create a horrendous amount of overhead for servers when they attempt to send or receive updates from the host server (these are the Ihave and NewNews commands). Because many ISPs are feeding extremely large amounts of data both to and from themselves and anyone who is pulling a feed from them, your ISP is most likely going to be unwilling to allow a Pull feed from them and will likely want to set up a Push feed to you.

There are some issues with the Ihave and NewNews commands used by NNTP that result in serious performance problems when doing a Pull feed. The most notable is that these commands force servers to search their entire news hierarchy for updated or new information for the requesting server. With a small newsgroup tree to look through, this is no big deal. But when a full 45gb feed has to be examined, the magnitude of the problem grows. This is why many servers are not strictly RFC-compliant, but rather follow the Berber draft, which offers different techniques for managing feeds.

Understanding Forms and Scripts

Part of the great power and flexibility of Exchange Server is its extensibility. It's beyond the scope of this book to present a detailed discussion of using forms and scripts (that's a whole book in itself). But because both forms and scripts are so useful with public folders, it's a good idea to spend some time on an overview of these features.

Electronic forms provide a great way to automate routine chores like submitting time cards, screening data to be posted, and serving clients by allowing them to submit support requests, and they also make for fun and games (literally). You can create forms that ask users for information that you used to get in writing, or via telephone calls. Now you can have a form post that information to a public folder so the information can be tracked. With electronic forms, you can make the form do most of the work for you, so you can focus on more important things, like playing Freecell. The Electronic Forms Designer is available from any flavor of Microsoft Outlook from the Tools menu.

Instead of (or in addition to) forms, you can use the Server Scripting Agent. This feature allows you to automate many processes without having to do much programming. Any Microsoft Outlook 8.03 or later client can be used to administer these scripts.

The Server Scripting Agent is not designed to handle large streams or great volumes of mail (such as parsing every message that arrives). Because the Scripting agent uses Microsoft Jscript, Microsoft Visual Basic, Microsoft VBScript, or some other extensible language, there is overhead associated with processing the language first, then processing the messages.

The Server Scripting Agent is perfect for routing or workflow type applications, since it allows you to use Collaborative Data Objects (CDO) to look up user information in the Directory, to check on the current location and state of a message, or to provide an automated solution when a stepped approval process is necessary.

Tip There's an advantage to using Microsoft Visual Interdev (VI) instead of Notepad for scripts. With VI you can interactively debug your files while you are creating them.

Part IV

Appendices

Most computer books have at least one appendix. It's a reference zone, detailing information that doesn't work well as prose.

This book has multiple appendices, because there's an abundant amount of useful information for Exchange administrators who sometimes need some extra assistance.

In this section you'll find knowledge above and beyond instructions for manipulating Exchange components. There's a copious amount of resource data as well as information about some utilities you may find are helpful to you as you perform your administrative tasks.

Appendix A

Handling Basic User Issues

The preceding chapters covered the tasks and problems that Microsoft Exchange administrators face frequently. There are, of course, other issues that arise, albeit less commonly, and in this appendix I go over some of them. These are client issues, notably Microsoft Outlook issues, that you're likely to be asked about as users call you for assistance.

Archiving

The Microsoft Outlook AutoArchive feature automatically creates an archive, and periodically copies Outlook items into the archive. All original Outlook folders, with the exception of Contacts, can be AutoArchived. (Because contacts are more or less permanent entries, they are not considered candidates for AutoArchiving.) AutoArchiving rules are based on the last modification dates of items. Manual archiving is available also, and it works either instead of or in addition to automatic archiving.

Configuring AutoArchiving

Setting AutoArchive options requires two separate operations:

- Set the global options.
- Set the individual folder options.

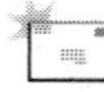

Note Folder-specific AutoArchive configuration options take precedence over the global AutoArchive options.

To set global options complete the following steps:

1. From the Tools menu, choose Options to open the Options dialog box.
2. In Microsoft Outlook 98 or Microsoft Outlook 2000, move to the Other tab, and click the AutoArchive button.
3. In Microsoft Outlook 97, go to the AutoArchive tab.

The first option is to enable or disable AutoArchiving. If you disable AutoArchiving, no other options are available. If you enable it, the remaining options are the frequency of AutoArchiving, whether to display a prompt before AutoArchiving, an option to delete expired e-mail, and naming the archive file (there's a default file that is an appropriate choice). After AutoArchiving is turned on, go into the individual Outlook folders and set the archive options.

Archiving Manually

To archive manually, from the File menu, choose Archive. Then either archive all folders or a specific folder. Archiving proceeds using the options established for each folder. There's also a check box to archive folders that are set to Do Not AutoArchive.

Retrieving Archived Items

If a user needs to view or use an archived item, use the Import feature (from the File menu, choose Import And Export). The archive file is a .pst file. Use the filter feature in the Import Wizard to retrieve specific items instead of the entire file. If you need access to the entire archive, Archive.pst can be added to the user's profile, just like another personal folder.

Calendar

Very few issues in Outlook's Calendar feature are complicated enough to require assistance, but you might want to publish some tips. Additionally, in a mixed environment (several versions of Outlook and Exchange Client are installed on user workstations), there are some issues you should be aware of, specifically regarding Schedule+.

Calendar Tips

- Calendar uses English commands, so users can enter **next Friday** or **two weeks from tomorrow** when they're creating an appointment. This is often faster and more instinctive than looking up the date and selecting it on the Calendar icon.
- When editing a recurring appointment, it's important to indicate whether the configuration of the recurring appointment is being altered, or only one instance is being changed.
- A quick way to change the time of an appointment is to drag its icon from one time slot to another in the Daily Calendar view.
- You can copy or move an appointment in the Week or Month view by right-dragging it to the new date. When you release the mouse, a pop-up menu asks if you are copying or moving the appointment.
- If you create a calendar of company holidays in a public folder, users can drag the dates from the public folder to their calendars.

Using vCalendar Files

New to Outlook 98 is support for vCalendar, a handy Personal Data Interchange (PDI) feature. vCalendar files are used to exchange appointment and schedule data with users who are not in your organization.

- To create a vCalendar file, select an appointment and then, from the File menu, choose Save As. Then select vCalendar (.vcs) as the file type.
- To distribute a vCalendar file, attach it to an e-mail message.
- To use a vCalendar file you receive as a mail attachment, double-click it and then choose Save And Close. The appointment is added to your Calendar.
- If you receive a vCalendar file as a file (perhaps on a disk), use the Outlook Import feature to import it to your Outlook calendar.

Mixing Schedule+ and Calendar

If you and your users rely on the shared calendar features and need the ability to see everyone's calendar, you must take some special steps if you have a mixed environment that includes both Outlook and Schedule+.

Users of Schedule+ may not be able to view some of the calendar information for Outlook users unless the Outlook users have selected the option Use Schedule+ As My Primary Calendar.

While this means that your Outlook users lose some of the advanced features available in Outlook Calendar, at least you'll have seamless schedule sharing across the network. Most of the time, it's necessary to use these options only during a transition period, until all your users have been updated to Outlook.

To make this more complicated (sorry), the Outlook option to use Schedule+ for calendar features only exists if Schedule+ was running on the computer before Outlook was installed. Outlook itself does not provide installation of all the Schedule+ functions.

Contacts

This is another Outlook feature that doesn't cause numerous problems, but a lot of users don't employ the Contacts feature (or don't use it fully) because they find it laborious. Tell your users about these tips to make the Contacts database more effective and attractive.

Contacts Shortcuts

Here are some easy-to-use and easy-to-teach shortcuts for Contacts.

- If you have multiple contacts in the same company, you don't have to reinvent the wheel. Open the Contact form for a person who works at that company and, from the menu bar, choose Contact, and then choose New Contact From Same Company. Outlook opens a new Contact form with the company information filled in—just add the name and other name-related details.

- Use the Import feature to import a Personal Address Book to the Contacts database. This results in some duplication, however, if the PAB has distribution lists, because the individual names are imported (the lists are not imported), and, of course, they also exist in the PAB as discrete entries. Just sort the Contacts list alphabetically, select every duplicate name, and delete the duplicates.
- Add the name of a person who sent you e-mail to your Contacts database by right-clicking the From entry in the message and selecting Add To Contacts.
- To print a list of specific contacts, select each contact by holding down the Ctrl key as you click. Then, from the File menu, choose Print, and then choose Only Selected Items.
- Drag a contact to the Inbox icon on the Outlook bar to open an e-mail message already addressed.
- Drag a contact to the Calendar icon to create an appointment with the contact.

Using vCards

Outlook 98 supports vCards, a PDI device used to exchange contact information.

- When a vCard arrives as an e-mail attachment, double-click the vCard, and then choose Save And Close to add it to your Contacts folder.
- To create your own vCard, enter yourself in the Contacts database. Then select the entry and, from the File menu, choose Save As to save it as a vCard file type (.vcf).

Tasks

You can use the Outlook Tasks feature to track large projects. Most large projects involve a series of tasks, and in most organizations I notice that the tasks are discrete, independent items in a user's Tasks folder. Project tracking is frequently accomplished via outside software (such as a project management application or a spreadsheet). For some projects, this is overkill.

You can create a project out of all the individual tasks involved in that project by taking advantage of the Outlook Categories feature. Create a category for each project, then associate each task with that project by assigning it to the category. Because you can view and print any item in Outlook sorted by category, this automatically helps you keep the project on track.

Appendix B

Using BackOffice Resource Kit Utilities

There is no Microsoft Exchange Resource Kit, so you need the Microsoft BackOffice Resource Kit (BORK) if you want to use any of the nifty utilities available for Microsoft Exchange Server. This appendix is an overview of some of the Exchange utilities in BORK. It's not my purpose (or goal) to provide complete installation, configuration, and usage information about all the tools available. Rather, I discuss basic information about some of the tools that administrators use frequently.

The splash screen for the BackOffice Resource Kit CD-ROM (see Figure B-1) offers several choices. You can install the BORK, browse the CD-ROM, or install additional Exchange tools ("additional" means above and beyond the Exchange tools that are part of the basic BORK).

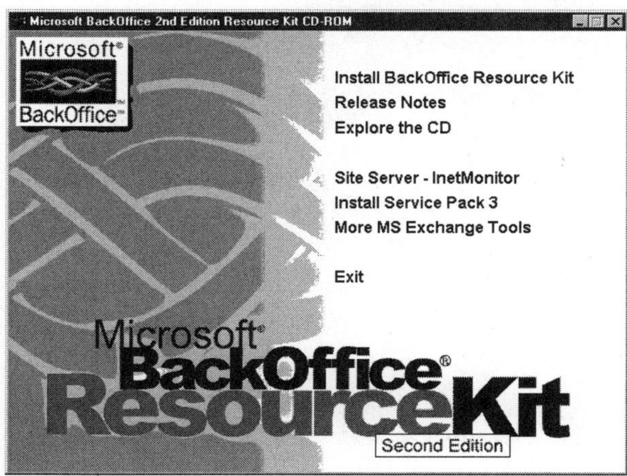

Figure B-1. *If you have a different edition of the BackOffice Resource Kit, your splash screen may have different choices.*

Installing BORK

If you opt to install the BackOffice Resource Kit, you need Administrator privileges. There are two installation choices: Typical Setup and Complete/Custom Setup. The Typical installation (using about 50mb of disk space) installs the following files:

- Help, documentation, and Tools Management Console files
- For SMS, SQL, SNA, and INETMON, all tools and utilities that do not require a special installation
- For Exchange, the tools from the Administration And Public Folder category that do not require a special installation

Tip If you aren't running Microsoft Internet Explorer 4.0 or later, the Setup program will install it before installing BORK.

The Complete/Custom installation option installs the files you select. If Exchange Server is the only BackOffice application for which you want to install utilities, choose this option. When the dialog box that offers the installation choices appears (see Figure B-2), clear everything except Exchange Server.

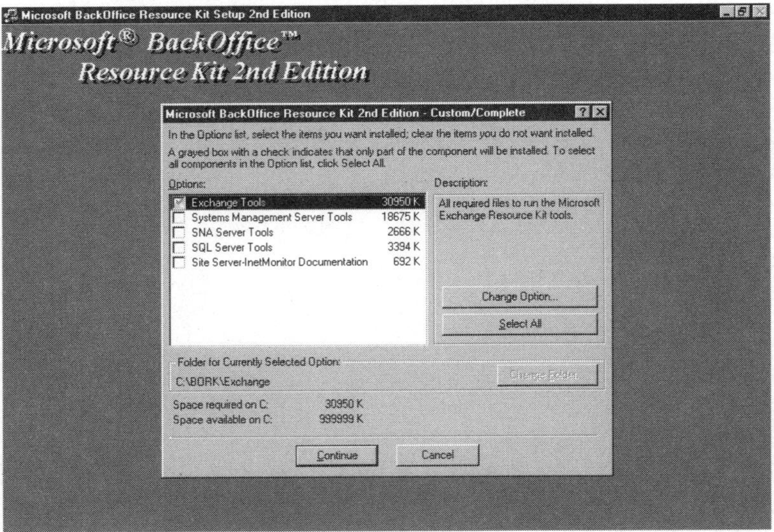

Figure B-2. *You can install only the Exchange Server BackOffice utilities.*

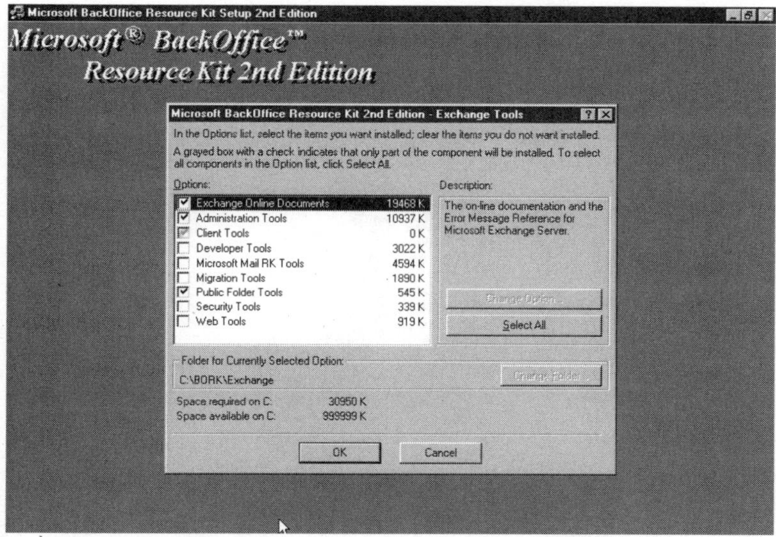

Figure B-3. *Select the specific utilities you need.*

Notice that the check box in the Exchange Server listing has gray shading. This means there are multiple tools available, and not all of them are selected for installation. Click Change Option to see a list of the utilities you can install (see Figure B-3).

Select or deselect tools as you require—click each listing to see a description of that tool. After you've made your selections, return to the first dialog box and click Continue. The appropriate files are transferred to your hard drive.

Installing More Exchange Server Tools

There's an entry named More MS Exchange Tools on the BORK splash screen. When you select it, the list you see depends on the version of BORK you have, although the majority of tools are on all versions (see figure B-4, on the following page).

These programs (and others) are also available for download from Microsoft's BackOffice site (I'd give you the specific URL, but it seems to change often). All of these tools and other downloadable tools are installed discretely. Always perform these installations after you've installed the basic BORK files, because that installation puts the file Exchtool.chm on your drive (which has installation information and help for the additional tools).

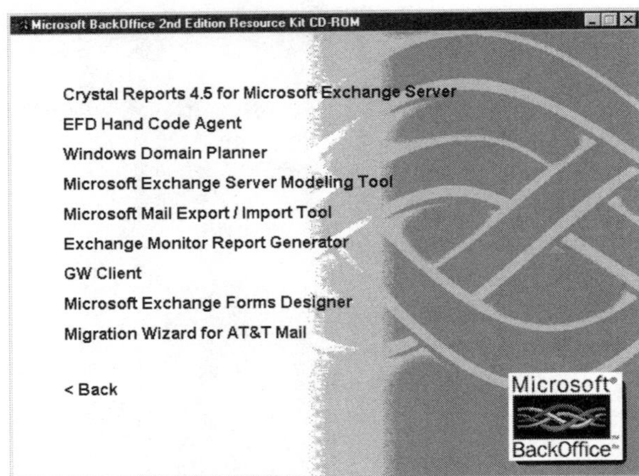

Figure B-4. *Click a listing to install the program.*

Crystal Reports

Crystal Reports for Exchange Server is a very popular program. Administrators can create reports about almost every aspect of Exchange, and most administrators take advantage of all this available power. I've seen administrators build some very detailed reports that are filled with more information about an event than I would have thought possible. The administrators who design these reports claim that they use them to fine-tune Exchange.

You can use Crystal Reports to build reports from all kinds of Exchange data, including data on the server and on client computers. For example, you can use the following data sources (this is not a complete list by any means):

- Address Books, including the GAL (and subsets), user PABs, and Distribution Lists. The data can include any information available in those containers, such as names, addresses, phone numbers, company names, and so on.
- Message tracking logs, including any data in the logs (sender names, dates, message size, and so on).
- E-mail messages.
- Form data.

Note Crystal Reports treats each data source as a table, so if you're reasonably comfortable with database structures, you can easily combine data from different sources within a single report. For instance, you can use an e-mail address to integrate a PAB with a message tracking log.

The following features are installed with Crystal Reports for Exchange Server:

- A set of predefined reports called Microsoft Exchange Reports. You can use these reports as is or as templates to build your own reports. (The reports are installed in a samples directory as well as in a sample .pst file.)
- Crystal Extension for the Microsoft Exchange Client is included so that access to the Crystal Reports components is available to users from within client software.
- Crystal Reports Designer provides a quick method for designing reports, using properties to select the data type you want to include. You can also use the Reports Designer to modify existing reports.
- Crystal Reports Viewer is an application that's launched from within the Exchange client; it provides display, printing, and export functions for reports.

Import Header Tool

A friend who is an Exchange Server consultant to large companies tells me that all his clients use the Import Header tool. This utility provides an easy way to update directory objects.

The Import Header tool is an import/export utility that you can use on a wide variety of directory objects in Exchange. It runs on the Exchange server (the directory service must be running).

Installing the Import Header Tool

No complicated program is needed to install this tool, just copy Header.exe from the BORK CD-ROM. It's located in the \Exchange\\<*Os*>\\<*Platform*>\Migrate\Header folder. (For example, I copied the program from\Exchange\Winnt\I386\Migrate\Header to \BORK\Exchange on my Exchange Server.)

Using the Import Header Tool

When you launch Header.exe, it spends a few seconds loading information (the *schema*), then presents the software window (see Figure B-5, on the following page).

The software window is designed to be an easy do-it-yourself import/export utility. You just click your way through the appropriate options, making the selections you need:

1. In the Directory Mode section of the window, select either Import or Export.
2. In the Object Class text box, click the arrow to select the object class you're earmarking for import or export.
3. In the Available Attributes list, select the attributes you want to include in the header file and click Add to move them to the Selected Attributes list. Attributes displayed in bold type are required.

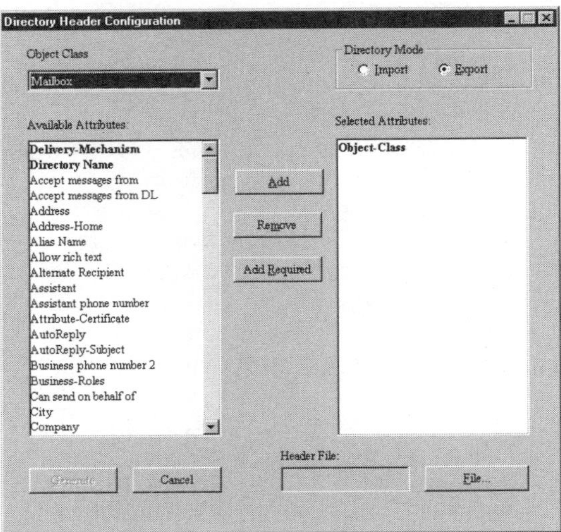

Figure B-5. *The Import Header utility loads the header configuration for a variety of objects.*

Tip Click the Add Required button to move all the required attributes to the Selected Attributes list automatically.

Note If you're importing, there are fewer attributes available (the ones you can't use are shaded).

Tip To remove an attribute from the Selected Attributes list, select it and click Remove.

4. Click File and enter a filename to hold the information—the file is a text file.
5. Click Generate to create the file, which you can use to import or export header information.

Tip You can click the File button and load a file you saved previously (which is easier than re-inventing the wheel each time you want to import or export header information).

Public Folder Administration Tool

The Public Folder Admin tool (Pfadmin.exe) is a command line program you can use to monitor and modify various aspects of public folders. An Exchange administrator I know told me he uses this tool "to fix those things that break in the night." Many administrators use Pfadmin.exe to set permissions (or reset permissions that have gone awry for reasons you'll never figure out), to report on folder contents, and to monitor message contents by type.

To install the program, copy the following files from the \Exchange\<*Os*>\<*Platform*>\ Pftools\Pfadmin directory on the BORK CD-ROM to the Exchange server:

- Pfadmin.exe
- Dapi.dll
- Mapi32.dll
- Mfc42.dll
- Msvcirt.dll
- Msvrct.dll

To get help, enter **pfadmin ?** at the command prompt. For help on a specific task, enter one of the following commands:

- **pfadmin ? setacl**
- **pfadmin ? rehome**
- **pfadmin ? setreplicas**
- **pfadmin ? listacl**
- **pfadmin ? listreplicas**
- **pfadmin ? messageclass**

Profile Generation Tool

The profile generation tool, Profgen.exe, is a handy utility for creating user profiles automatically. This means that you, as the administrator, can control and define the services configured for client users in the user profiles (mail profiles, not logon profiles).

Tip Profgen.exe is especially useful for administrators who have to manage roaming users.

To install this utility, copy the following files from the \Exchange\<*Os*>\<*Platform*>\Admin\Profgen directory on the BORK CD-ROM to your computer:

- Profgen.exe
- Profgen.ini
- Profgen.txt
- Profgen.doc

The program modifies profile descriptor files (.prf) to include the appropriate settings for Microsoft Exchange Server as a service, the name of the Exchange server, and the name of the new mailbox. Then it runs Newprog.exe to create a profile based on the .prf file.

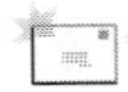

Note Newproof.exe is installed on computers when Windows messaging is installed.

Mailbox Cleanup

This is the ultimate tool for enforcing the rules you set to control the size of mailboxes. It's the heavy-handed, take-charge utility for administrators who don't countenance rebellion or disobedience in the ranks. You can use the mailbox cleanup tool to delete and move outdated messages from user mailboxes.

Caution Messages deleted by the mailbox cleanup tool are gone forever, there's no going back, no undelete, no recovery. This is a tool for administrators who are serious about controlling disk space (or making sure old messages don't cause problems by appearing in the courtroom during a lawsuit).

Installing the Mailbox Cleanup Agent

To install this tool, shut down the Exchange administrator window. Then copy the \Exchange\<*Operatingsystem*>\<*Platform*>\Admin\Mbclean subdirectory from the BORK CD-ROM to the Exchange server on which you want to use this tool (copy the directory, not just the files). Then run Setup.exe from the directory. This installs the Mailbox Cleanup Agent, a service that will run on this server.

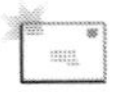

Note You cannot install the agent remotely; you must perform all the installation tasks from the server on which you'll be running the agent.

You'll be asked to specify the name of the Exchange server, following which the installation program finds and displays the site information. Select the site and click Continue. A list of site containers is displayed (see Figure B-6). Choose a recipient container to hold the agent.

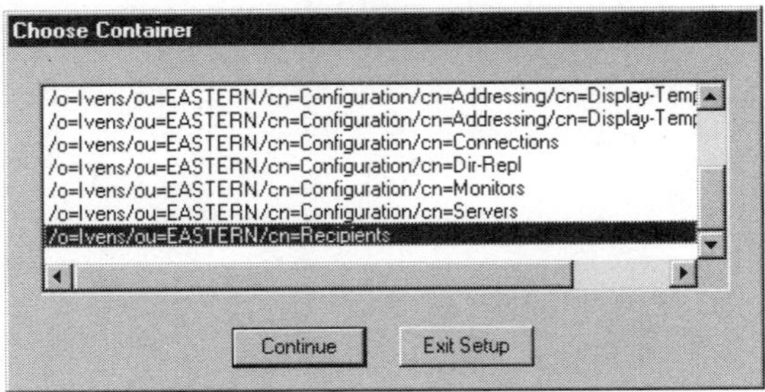

Figure B-6. *Select a recipient container for the mailbox agent.*

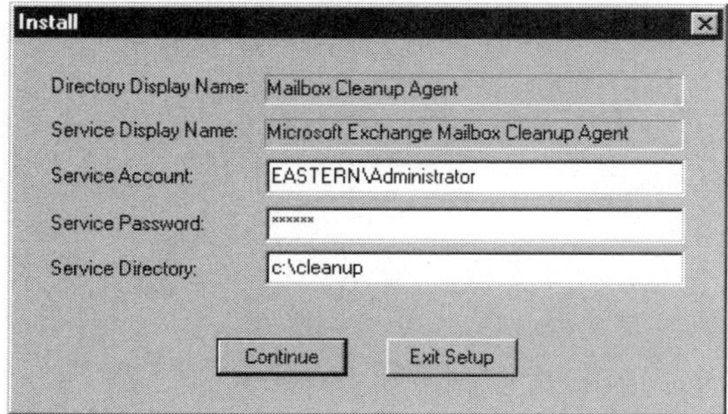

Figure B-7. *Provide the necessary information for the Mailbox Cleanup Agent.*

The next dialog box presents the information for the Mailbox Cleanup Agent. As you can see in Figure B-7, directory and display names are needed, along with the name of the service account for the agent.

The service directory text box in the dialog box is the path to the directory where the agent is installed. This entry must include a drive letter.

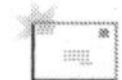

Note The service account (which must contain both the domain name and a Microsoft Windows NT user name) provides the security context for the agent. The service account must be a user with administrative rights. It's a good idea to use the same service account you use for the Microsoft Exchange Server services.

Installing the Agent for Use on RISC-Based Boxes

If you're planning to use the Mailbox Cleanup Agent in a site that consists of RISC-based computers, you must install the Mailbox Cleanup Agent on an Intel server that is connected to the site.

Follow the installation procedures described here, and in the dialog box that asks for the server name, specify the server that will be the target of the agent's work. That server can be any RISC or Intel computer in the site.

Configuring the Mailbox Cleanup Agent Properties

Now you must configure the agent; then you can run it. To configure the agent, open the Exchange Administrator window and select the Recipients container into which you placed the agent. Double-click its entry in the right pane to bring up its Properties dialog box (see Figure B-8, on the following page). Then click the container against which you'll run the agent.

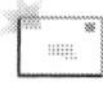

Note If you start the service before you complete the configuration process, the service shuts down and logs an event (which includes the information that the service was stopped because it isn't configured).

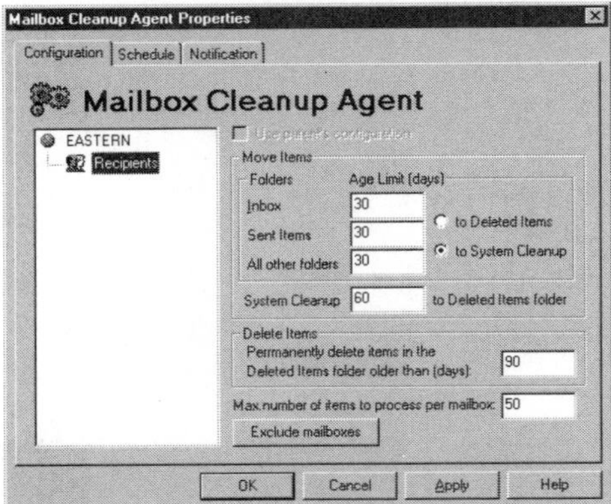

Figure B-8. *Start by configuring the specifications for cleanup.*

The items in the dialog box are straightforward, and you need only specify the limits you want to apply. System Cleanup is a private folder that's created by the Mailbox Cleanup Agent (there's one for every mailbox). It's a holding area for messages that the agent removes from mailboxes. Specify the number of days that messages can remain in this folder for user action (such as moving the message to a personal folder) before the messages are moved into the Deleted Items folder.

The dialog box option for permanent deletion determines how old messages in the Deleted Items folder can be before they are permanently deleted by the Mailbox Cleanup Agent. If you don't specify an age limit, the configuration defaults to the user's configuration options.

You can exclude mailboxes from the agent's processes. Click Exclude Mailboxes to produce a list of all the mailboxes in the recipient container. Use the buttons in the Exclude Mailbox dialog box (see Figure B-9) to remove any mailboxes from the automatic cleaning.

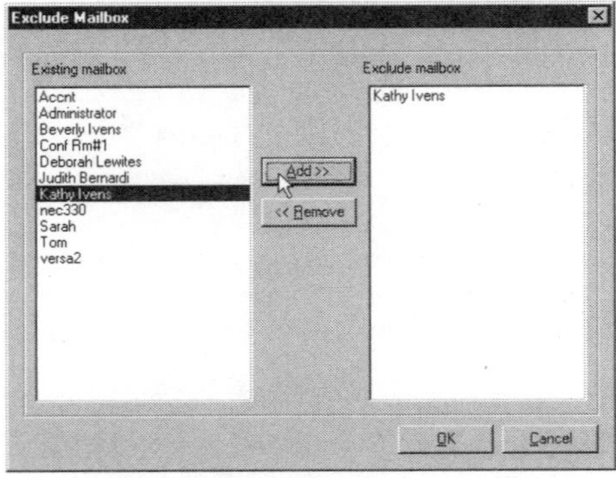

Figure B-9. *There may be some mailboxes you don't want to clean automatically.*

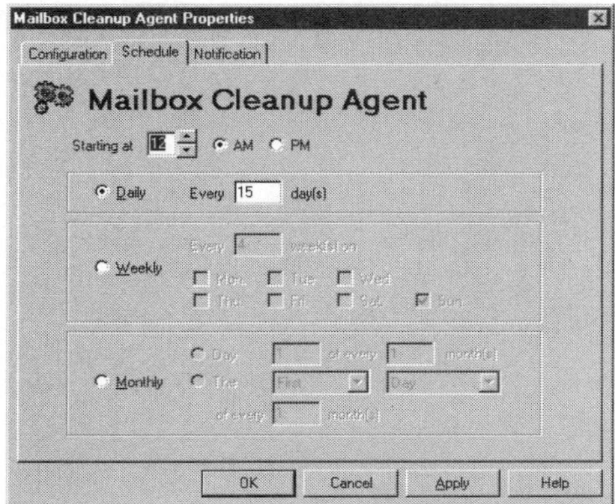

Figure B-10. *Choose a basic interval, then narrow the schedule options.*

Configuring the Mailbox Cleanup Agent Schedule

Move to the Schedule tab to set the cleanup schedule. As you can see in Figure B-10, you have quite a bit of flexibility for scheduling.

Configuring User Notifications

The Cleanup Mailbox Agent is by nature a polite and thoughtful character. By default, the agent sends a notification message after sweeping through a user's mailbox. As seen in Figure B-11, you can deselect the notification check box or replace the default notification message with one of your own.

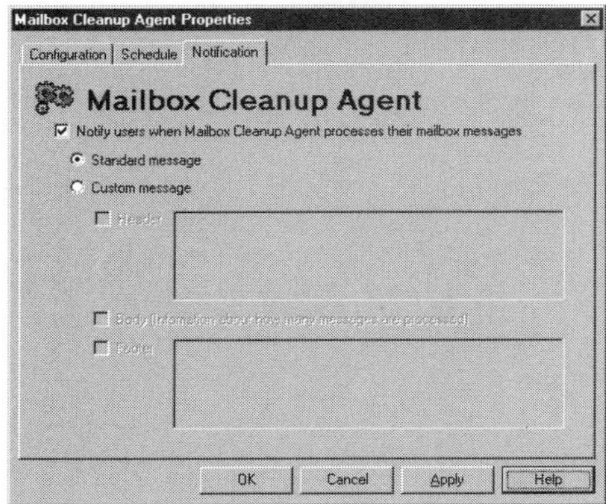

Figure B-11. *You can create your own message to users after cleaning out their mailboxes.*

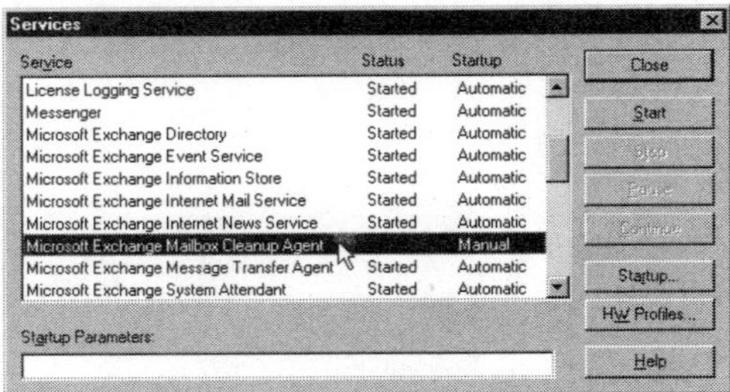

Figure B-12. *The Cleanup Agent is a service and must be started like any other service running in Windows NT.*

Starting the Mailbox Cleanup Service

After you've configured the service (don't forget to click OK to close the dialog box), you must start the service. From the Control Panel, open the Services utility. Look for the service named Microsoft Exchange Mailbox Cleanup Agent (see Figure B-12). Set the service for Automatic startup.

Caution Microsoft Exchange services must be running before you start the Cleanup Agent service.

Event Log Tools

The Windows NT Event Viewer service is a terrific aid when you have a problem, but it has quite a few shortcomings. You have to scan a lot of events to find the one you think might be responsible for your current dilemma, and if there are several meaningful events logged, they're rarely contiguous in the list. If you want to filter events, you have to open the Event Viewer and manually apply your filters—there's no way to ask the Event Viewer service to do this automatically in the background.

In addition, the Event Log service monitors only the current server, and except for a notice that a service failed during boot-up, you're not notified about problems—you have to take the initiative and check the logs yourself to keep an eye on everything. If you find a problem, you have to start a recalcitrant service yourself (or stop one that's causing a problem).

The solution to these shortcomings is the Event Log Tools utility in the BORK. This nifty addition to your Exchange toolkit provides the following services that are on every administrator's wish list:

- Automatic event filtering for service, type, and event ID
- Multiple server monitoring
- Automatic stopping or restarting of services
- Notification when important events occur

Installing the Event Log Tools

To put the Event Log tools on a server, copy the \Exchange\<*Os*>\<*Platform*>\Admin\EventLog directory to the hard drive (the instructions in the BORK help files have the wrong path; trust me, this is the right path).

Creating the Event Log Configuration File

The Event Log tools perform the actions you specify in a configuration file. You need to create that configuration file, which has a line for each event you want to monitor (much like a batch file). The format of each line is:

```
EventID;Source;Action;AlertList;MailList;Command line;Comment
string;
```

Insert contiguous semicolons to skip an entry. Table B-1 describes the entries for the line.

Table B-1. Elements in Each Line of the Event Log Tools Configuration File

Entry	Description
Event ID	The numerical ID for the event ID.
Source	The source name for the service that's being monitored.
Action	The action to take (either Restart or Stop).
AlertList	A list of computers to which a pop-up message is sent when this event occurs (separate multiple computers with commas).
MailList	A list of mailboxes (e-mail aliases) to which a message is sent when the event occurs (separate multiple e-mail aliases with commas).
Command line	A command to launch a program (usually a notification utility or a batch file). The command line can include parameters and can contain up to 256 characters.
Comment string	Text for the alert pop-up message and/or e-mail message.

Note To use e-mail notification, this utility must be running on a MAPI-enabled computer (if the computer is running Exchange Server or an Exchange client, it is running MAPI).

As an example, here's the beginning of my own configuration file, which is named ExcEvnts.cfg:

```
;ExcEvnts configuration file
;Ivens Consulting, Inc-running on Server East in Domain Eastern
;configuration file for logging Exchange Server events.
;EventID;Source;Action;AlertList;MailList;Command;CommentString
9278;MSExchangeMTA;stop;AdminWKS;jbernardi,kivens;tellall.bat;Event
9278 MTA in trouble
```

Running the Event Log Tool

Run Evtscan.exe from the command line, with the following syntax:

```
Evtscan -f config_file -u profile_name [-p password] [-t delay_
in_seconds] server_list
```

where:

- **config_file** is the name of the configuration file.
- **profile name** is the name of the Exchange profile to be used.
- **password** is the password for that profile.
- **delay_in_seconds** is the time to wait between scans (in seconds).
- **server_list** is a list of servers to monitor for events (separate servers with commas).

As an example, here's the command I use:

```
Evtscan -f excevnts.cfg -u events -p scanning -t 30 East,West
```

Minimize the command window and let the program run.

Tip This tool works for any event, not just events involving Exchange services. It's a handy Windows NT utility.

Using the Initialize Event Log Tool

When you attempt to view the Event Log of a remote computer, the files and registry keys you need aren't present. Use the Initialize Event Log tool on the BORK to remedy this problem. Copy \Exchange\<*Os*>\<*Platform*>\Admin\Initlog\Initlog.exe to your computer.

Launch the program and enter the name of the server that has the registry keys you need. Then select the keys that are connected to the programs you want to view. If you have administrative rights on the remote computer, the keys and associated files are copied automatically. If you don't have administrative rights on the remote computer, a list of files is written to a text file (EventLogFilesToBeCopied.txt), and you can copy the files you need manually.

Appendix C

Using Microsoft Windows NT Resource Kit Utilities

Microsoft Exchange Server and Windows NT are joined at the hip, and sometimes it's hard to tell when one leaves off and the other begins. Mailboxes, functions, features, and a lot of other important maintenance items in Exchange owe their existence to the functionality of Windows NT Server. A solid, robust, well-functioning Windows NT system is the backbone of a good Exchange Server system.

A Windows NT system with extra functions and features that are useful to Exchange and Exchange administrators makes everything even better. For that reason, this Appendix covers some of the nifty software available in the Windows NT Resource Kit.

Associate

Many companies create file extensions for certain file types, using them to keep track of reports, database forms, certain types of documents, and so on. For example, your homegrown customer database may be programmed to report out customer financial information with text files that have the extension .cfi. Perhaps your word processing department has rules about document extensions so that budget reports use the extension .brp, and documents relating to personnel matters use the extension .per.

It's far easier to work with these documents if users can open them automatically from Explorer or My Computer. However, the extensions have no association, so that doesn't work. You can either go through all the steps of associating an extension with a program, or use the handy utility in the Windows NT Resource Kit, which is faster and easier than any of the native Windows procedures.

In fact, you can change associations quickly with this utility because it has a switch for removing existing associations.

Associate.exe runs from the command line with the following syntax: **Associate *.ext filename* [/q] [/d] [/f] [/?]** where:

- ***.ext*** is the extension for which you're setting up an association.
- ***filename*** is the program with which you're associating the extension.

- **/q** suppresses interactive prompts (it stands for quiet).
- **/d** deletes the association.
- **/f** forces an overwrite of the existing association.
- **/?** displays help for Associate.exe.

Tip Enter **Associate *.ext*** to learn the name of the associated executable for that extension.

For example, if your Human Resources department, using Microsoft Word, uses the extension .per for all documents relating to personnel policies, use the following command to force .per files to open in Word: **associate .per winword.exe**.

If you want to change the association for bitmapped files to a graphics program named LoveToDraw, enter **associate .bmp lovetodraw.exe /f**. This overwrites the current associate for .bmp files (probably Microsoft Paint).

AddUsers

Addusers.exe is an administrative tool you can use to create, delete, and report on user accounts. It's often used for reporting, because it reports out lots of useful information about the user accounts on a computer. The utility works in conjunction with a comma-delimited file.

AddUsers is a command line utility that has the following syntax: **addusers [*computername*] [/c] [/d] [/e] *filename* [/s:*x*] [?]** where:

- ***computername*** is the computer that holds the user accounts you want to use. Omit this parameter to use the local computer.
- **/c** creates user accounts as specified by the file (***filename*** parameter).
- **/d** dumps user accounts to the file.
- **/e** deletes user accounts specified in the file.
- ***filename*** is the name of the file the program uses.
- **/s:*x*** changes the delimiter character—replace the *x* with the new character.
- **/?** displays a help screen.

The best way to use this software is to make your first use of it a dump. The resulting file has the following information:

- User accounts
- Local groups
- Global groups
- Headings (User, Global, Local)

You can import this file into a spreadsheet and use it to create the files you need for subsequent uses of AddUser.

For example, from my workstation I entered the following command: **addusers \\east /d c:\aureport.txt**. (The name of the PDC of my domain is east.)

Here are some selected sections of the resulting file, Aureport.txt. You can see which users are members of groups (in this case some groups have no members).

```
[User]
Accnt,Accnt,,,,,
admin,,,,,,
Administrator,,,Built-in account for administering the computer/
domain,,,,
Beverly Ivens,Beverly Ivens,,,,,
Conf Rm#1,Conf Rm#1,,,,,
Deborah Lewites,Deborah Lewites,,,,,
Guest,,,Built-in account for guest access to the computer/
domain,,,,
IUSR_EAST,Internet Guest Account,,Internet Server Anonymous
Access,,,,
Judith Bernardi,Judith Bernardi,,,,,
Kathy Ivens,Kathy Ivens,,,,,
Paul Goldstein,Paul Goldstein,,,,,
Richard Gold,,,,,,
Sarah,,,,,,
[Global]
Domain Admins,Designated administrators of the
domain,Administrator,Accnt,Kathy Ivens,
Domain Guests,All domain guests,Guest,Domain Users,All domain
users,Administrator,EAST$,IUSR_EAST,Accnt,Kathy Ivens,Judith
Bernardi,Deborah Lewites,Beverly
Ivens,admin,ADMIN$,New98,new98$,Sarah,Tom,versa2,nec330,Conf
Rm#1,Paul Goldstein,Richard Gold,
[Local]
Account Operators,Members can administer domain user and group
accounts,
Administrators,Members can fully administer the computer/
domain,EASTERN\Administrator,EASTERN\Domain
Admins,EASTERN\Accnt,EASTERN\Kathy Ivens,
Guests,Users granted guest access to the computer/
domain,EASTERN\Domain Guests,EASTERN\IUSR_EAST,
Print Operators,Members can administer domain printers,
Replicator,Supports file replication in a domain,
Server Operators,Members can administer domain servers,
Users,Ordinary users,EASTERN\Domain Users,
```

The file shows you the structure of the comma-delimited file you must use to make changes to your system. The headings must exist in the files you use with the AddUser program.

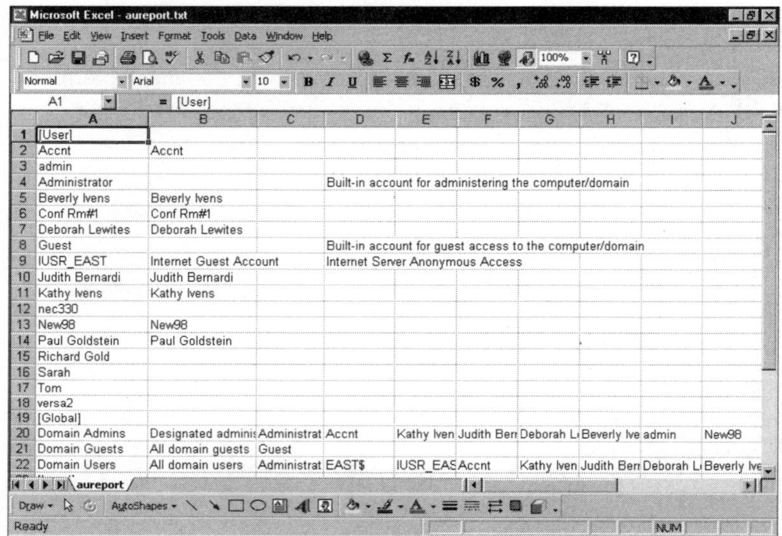

Figure C-1. *A spreadsheet format lets you see user and group information in a format that's neat and categorized.*

You can import the file into a spreadsheet program such as Microsoft Excel, which is a good way to view the groups and accounts on your system (see Figure C-1).

Usrtogrp

Usrtogrp.exe lets you add users to groups. This utility saves you the steps involved in adding users to groups in User Manager or User Manager for Domains. Here are the highlights of this utility's functional power:

- Adds users to local groups
- Adds users to global groups
- Adds users to groups you're inventing (the group is created automatically)
- Performs across trusted domains
- Works from Microsoft Windows NT Workstation or Microsoft Windows NT Server

Usrtogrp cannot create users; the users you specify must already exist. However, if you're working across trusted domains, you don't have to know which domain is home to any user because the program ascertains that information for you.

The syntax for Usrtogrp is **usertogrp *filename***. Like addusers.exe, Usrtogrp works with an associated text file. The file has the following format:

```
Domain: domainname
Localgroup group: groupname (or globalgroup: groupname)
Username1
Username2
```

If you're adding users to a global group, the users listed in the file must have an account in the domain you specified in the file. If you're adding users to a local group, the user accounts can be on your local computer, the domain you specified, or in any trusted domain.

Global

Global.exe is a command line utility that reports members of global groups. The software works for remote servers or domains. The syntax is **global *groupname* [*domainname* | *server*]** where:

- ***groupname*** is the group for which you want to know the names of the members.
- ***domainname*** is the name of a domain.
- ***server*** is the name of a network server.

Caution If the name of the group has a space (for instance, Print Operators), you must enclose the name in quotation marks ("print operators").

Autolog

Autolog.exe configures a workstation to log on a specific user when the computer boots. The user doesn't see the logon dialog box and doesn't have to press Ctrl+Alt+Del. The program works only with the currently logged-on user.

To use Autolog, log on as the user for whom you want to create an automatic logon. Then open Autolog.exe from Explorer or My Computer. The Windows NT Auto Logon Setter window opens, as seen in Figure C-2, on the following page.

After you enter your password and click OK, Autolog writes the automatic logon information to the registry. Hereafter, no logon dialog box appears. This, of course, means that nobody else can log on to this computer. If another user needs to log on, you'll have to turn off the autolog feature. Just open the software and select the Remove Auto Logon radio button, then click OK.

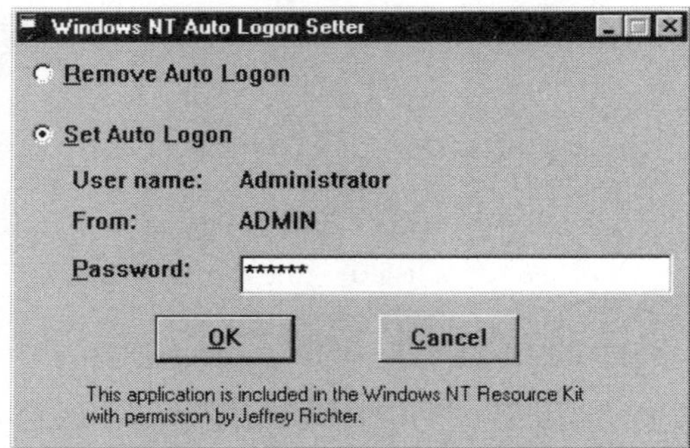

Figure C-2. *Enter your password to log on automatically from now on.*

Delprof

This utility deletes profiles. Users change offices, jobs, and assignments, and after they move their stuff, they must log on to the computer in the new location. After a while, computers can contain a lot of profiles for users who no longer log on. A profile can grow very large before the user moves to another computer, and the disk space it occupies can be reclaimed with this utility.

You can run Delprof.exe from the command line on any Windows NT computer and act on any other Windows NT computer on the network. This means you could work at your own desk and clean up all the workstations that have this "useless profile" problem.

The syntax for Delprof is **delprof [/q] [/i] [/p] [/c:*computername*] [/d:*days*] [/?]** where:

- **/q** suppresses confirmation requests (it stands for quiet mode).
- **/i** ignores errors and continue to delete.
- **/p** prompts for confirmation before deleting a profile.
- **/c:*computername*** specifies a remote computer as the target.
- **/d: *days* (in integer)** specifies the number of days since activity, beyond which profiles are deleted.
- **/?** displays help.

Diruse

Diruse.exe is a handy command line utility that reports how much disk space is being used on directories. It's the information you wish Windows Explorer would show you when you select a folder that has subfolders. The syntax is **diruse {/s | /v} {/m | /k | /b} [/c] [/,] [/q:# [/l] [/a] [/d] [/o]] [/*] dirs** where:

- **/s** includes any subfolders of the specified folders.

- **/v** displays progress reports when scanning subfolders (this doesn't work if **/s** is specified).
- **/m** displays usage in megabytes.
- **/k** displays usage in kilobytes.
- **/b** displays usage in bytes (this is the default).
- **/c** uses compressed file sizes.
- **/,** displays a thousands separator in the display of file sizes.
- **/q:#** marks folders that exceed the size you specify with the # by displaying an exclamation point.
- **/l** outputs overflows to a logfile named Diruse.log (located in the current folder).
- **/a** requests an alert if sizes specified by **/q:#** are exceeded. (The Alerter service must be running.)
- **/d** displays only folders that exceed the size you specified.
- **/o** skips subfolders when checking for a specified size.
- /* uses the top-level folders in the specified directories.
- **dirs** specifies the list of paths to check. This parameter is required.

Tip The order of parameters doesn't matter. You can use a dash instead of a forward slash in front of any parameter.

I use Diruse.exe across the network by mapping the hard drive of a remote computer. I also make sure I always have a file report by redirecting the command. For example, if I map drive C of a remote computer to drive F, I enter **diruse /s f:*directoryname* > *filename.txt*.**

For example, here's a report from my workstation about the directory use of Exchange Server on drive C (mapped as drive F) of the server (there are additional Exchange files on drive D):

```
   Size  (b) Files Directory  123904  1 F:\EXCHSRVR   0  0
F:\EXCHSRVR\ADD-INS  515  1 F:\EXCHSRVR\ADD-INS\INS   0  0
F:\EXCHSRVR\ADD-INS\MBClean

  108725    2 F:\EXCHSRVR\ADD-INS\MBClean\i386
       0    0 F:\EXCHSRVR\ADD-INS\SMTP
  440592    1 F:\EXCHSRVR\ADD-INS\SMTP\I386
       0    0 F:\EXCHSRVR\ADDRESS
       0    0 F:\EXCHSRVR\ADDRESS\CCMAIL
  108816    1 F:\EXCHSRVR\ADDRESS\CCMAIL\ALPHA
   54032    1 F:\EXCHSRVR\ADDRESS\CCMAIL\I386
   21776    1 F:\EXCHSRVR\ADDRESS\CCMAIL\MIPS
   21264    1 F:\EXCHSRVR\ADDRESS\CCMAIL\PPC
       0    0 F:\EXCHSRVR\ADDRESS\MS
  110352    1 F:\EXCHSRVR\ADDRESS\MS\ALPHA
   41744    1 F:\EXCHSRVR\ADDRESS\MS\I386
```

```
       0   0 F:\EXCHSRVR\ADDRESS\SMTP
  115984   1 F:\EXCHSRVR\ADDRESS\SMTP\ALPHA
   46352   1 F:\EXCHSRVR\ADDRESS\SMTP\I386
       0   0 F:\EXCHSRVR\ADDRESS\X400
  113424   1 F:\EXCHSRVR\ADDRESS\X400\ALPHA
   60688   1 F:\EXCHSRVR\ADDRESS\X400\I386
19645340 120 F:\EXCHSRVR\bin
 6027494  23 F:\EXCHSRVR\bin\movesrvr
 2105344   1 F:\EXCHSRVR\bin\movesrvr\dsadata
  419056 142 F:\EXCHSRVR\bin\movesrvr\htm
 1060562  32 F:\EXCHSRVR\bin\movesrvr\misc
       0   0 F:\EXCHSRVR\CONNECT
       0   0 F:\EXCHSRVR\CONNECT\MSEXCIMC
  526369   3 F:\EXCHSRVR\CONNECT\MSEXCIMC\BIN
    5003  11 F:\EXCHSRVR\CONNECT\TRN
 4218880   3 F:\EXCHSRVR\DSADATA
 2048000   1 F:\EXCHSRVR\imcdata
       0   0 F:\EXCHSRVR\imcdata\in
     718   1 F:\EXCHSRVR\imcdata\in\Archive
    1060   2 F:\EXCHSRVR\imcdata\log
       0   0 F:\EXCHSRVR\imcdata\out
     718   1 F:\EXCHSRVR\imcdata\out\Archive
       0   0 F:\EXCHSRVR\imcdata\Pickup
       0   0 F:\EXCHSRVR\imcdata\Pickup\Archive
       0   0 F:\EXCHSRVR\imcdata\work
    2560   1 F:\EXCHSRVR\insdata
       0   0 F:\EXCHSRVR\insdata\log
       0   0 F:\EXCHSRVR\KMSDATA
 3178496   4 F:\EXCHSRVR\mdbdata
 3304707 126 F:\EXCHSRVR\MTADATA
    2237   1 F:\EXCHSRVR\MTADATA\MTACHECK.OUT
 1955216   9 F:\EXCHSRVR\RES
     991   2 F:\EXCHSRVR\tracking.log
       0   0 F:\EXCHSRVR\WebTemp
45870919 498 SUB-TOTAL: F:\EXCHSRVR
45870919 498 TOTAL: F:\EXCHSRVR
```

Diskmap

Use Diskmap.exe at the command line to get a report on the configuration of a hard drive. The information that's returned includes partition data, logical drive data, and disk characteristics information from the registry.

The syntax is **diskmap /d <*drive#*> [/h]** where:

- **/d <*drive#*>** is the number of the target physical disk.
- **/h** requests hex output (the default is decimal output).

Caution Some fields are predetermined as decimal or hex and will use their assigned format regardless of your use of the /h switch.

This is another utility I always use with a redirector to a file. Print the file and tape it to the box in case of a calamity.

For example, examining disk0 on my workstation, I redirect to a file named Admin.txt (the workstation name is admin) with the following command: **diskmap /d0 > admin.txt**. Here is the output of the file:

```
Cylinders  HeadsPerCylinder  SectorsPerHead  BytesPerSector  MediaType
     2047                64              32             512         12

TrackSize = 16384, CylinderSize = 1048576, DiskSize = 2146435072 (2047MB)

Signature = 0xcd000636
StartingOffset   PartitionLength   StartingSector   PartitionNumber
*        32256        2146765824               63                 1

MBR:
        Starting                      Ending             System  Relative  Total
Cylinder  Head  Sector   Cylinder  Head  Sector       ID    Sector  Sectors
*      0     1       1        260   254      63     0x06       63  4192902
       0     0       0          0     0       0     0x00        0        0
       0     0       0          0     0       0     0x00        0        0
       0     0       0          0     0       0     0x00        0        0
```

Disksave

Disksave.exe is a command-line utility that saves the Master Boot Record (MBR) and the Partition Boot Sector (PBS) as binary image files. If either of these disk structures is damaged, you can use the image file to fix the disk. This is extremely helpful if you pick up an MBR virus. (Each image file is 512 bytes.)

You must run this program from pure DOS, so follow these steps to use Disksave:

1. Open and print Disksave.txt. This file contains the list of function keys you use to perform your work.
2. Copy Disksave.exe to a floppy disk.
3. Boot to DOS.
4. Insert the disk with Disksave.exe in the floppy drive.
5. Enter **disksave** at the command prompt.
6. Press F2 to make an image file of the Master Boot Record (you're prompted for a path and filename).
7. Press F4 to make an image file of the boot sector (you're prompted for a path and filename).

Label the floppy disk with the name of the computer and put it away in a safe place. If you need to repair the MBR or boot sector, follow these steps:

1. Boot to DOS.
2. Place the floppy disk with the program and the image files in the floppy drive.
3. Enter **disksave** at the command prompt.
4. Press F3 to restore the MBR (you'll be prompted for the file location).
5. Press F5 to restore the boot sector (you'll be prompted for the file location).

If you're using fault tolerance, you can also use your Disksave floppy to turn it off. This is useful if Windows NT will not boot from mirrored disks. Press F6 to turn off FT. This breaks the mirror. However, Disksave has no way to turn the FT bit back on.

Dommon

Dommon.exe is a server-only utility that monitors the status of servers in a domain, and domain controllers in trusted domains. The software checks the secure channel status to the domain controller of the current domain, as well as to domain controllers in trusted domains. The software uses the current user's name and password, so if the user doesn't exist in any available domain, the queries fail. Administrators can also use Dommon.exe to disconnect and restore domain connections.

Dumpel

Use Dumpel.exe to dump an event log into a tab-delimited file. You can filter for certain event types (or filter out certain event types). This is a good way to keep an eye on certain applications, or even certain events in certain applications. For example, use it to gather information about specific events in Exchange Server (from the Applications Event Log).

Dumpel.exe works at the command line with the syntax **dumpel -f *file* [-s *server*] [-l *log* [-m *source*] [-en1 n2 n3...] [-r] [-t]** where

- **-f *file*** is the filename of the output file.
- **-s *server*** is the server that has the event log of interest.
- **-l *log*** names the log you want to dump (system, application, security).
- **-m *source*** specifies the source (for instance, Rdr, Serial) to dump records. You can supply one source (if you omit the switch, all events are dumped).
- **-en1 n2 n3...** filters for event ID *nn* (you can specify a maximum of 10). If the -r switch is omitted, only these record types are dumped. If the -r switch is used, all records except records of these types are dumped. You cannot use this switch without the -m switch.

- **-r** instructs whether to filter for or against (filter out) specific sources or records.
- **-t** separates individual strings with tabs (otherwise strings are separated by spaces).

It's common to use this utility to create a file you can import into a spreadsheet. This gives you an easy way to investigate problems and patterns of problems.

Floplock

This utility (commonly known as FloppyLock) controls access to floppy drives, which makes it handy for several reasons:

- Users can't introduce viruses via a floppy disk.
- Users can't load unauthorized software on their computers.
- Users can't take information out of the office via a floppy disk.

Before you leap out of your chair in excitement to install this, remember that it also means users can't use My Briefcase via the floppy drive. This is a downer if you like the idea that employees can take work home.

Floplock.exe is not installed automatically when you install the Windows NT Resource Kit. You must specifically install it—it installs as a service. After installation, open the Services utility in Control Panel to configure the startup type. (If startup is automatic, the lock on the floppy drives survives reboots.)

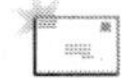

Note When you install the service on a workstation, users who are members of the Administrators and Power Users groups can continue to use the floppy drives. When you install the service on a server, only members of the Administrators group will be able to use the floppy drives.

Tip You can turn the service on or off from a remote computer.

Forfiles

I use a lot of batch files because I'm an old MS-DOS freak, and also because there are some functions I need regularly that are implemented easily via a batch file. If you perform tasks with batch files, Forfiles.exe is a command-line utility you can use in a batch file to have multiple files as targets of your commands. Before you say "I can do that already with a wildcard," I'll mention that Forfiles.exe works with trees, and you can't target files in subdirectories with a wildcard character.

The syntax for Forfiles is **forfiles [-p*path*] [-m*searchmask*] [-c*command*] [-d*ddmmyy*] [-s] [-v] [-?]** where:

- **-p*path*** is the starting path (the current directory is the default).
- **-m*searchmask*** sets the mask for searching (the default is *.*).
- **-c*command*** is the command to execute against each file (the default is "cmd /c echo @FILE").
- **-d*ddmmyy*** filters files with a date equal to or greater than the value of ***ddmmyy*.**
- **-s** recurses into subdirectories.
- **-v** runs Forfiles in verbose mode.
- **-?** displays help.

I've seen clients use this utility to print text files that exist in a tree of folders, and copy files in a tree to another location.

Getsid

Getsid.exe is a command-line utility that works only on Windows NT Server. Use it to compare the SIDs of two user accounts. This means you can compare a user's account SID between the PDC and BDC to see whether there's been any corruption in your database replication.

The syntax for Getsid is **getsid** ***server1 account*** ***server2 account*** where:

- ***server1,*** ***server2*** are the names of the Windows NT servers on which you expect the account to be found.
- ***account*** is the SID for the account.

Index Server

Index Server (only on the Microsoft Exchange Server Resource Kit) searches the contents of documents on your IIS server and creates an index. This lets users locate documents via queries (you'll need to create the query form). What's nifty about Index Server is that it can index formatted documents (including spreadsheets), so you can publish documents in their native format instead of converting them to HTML.

To install Index Server, look in the \Apps\Index directory of the Server RK CD-ROM (the files are separated into subfolders by platform). There are three self-extracting files to choose from:

- **Idxsvall.exe** for documents in every supported language

- **Idxsveng.exe** for International English
- **Idxsvenu.exe** for U.S. English

You can use Index Server for your intranet or for any drive you can access on the Internet with a Uniform Naming Convention (UNC) path.

Layout

This utility saves and restores the positions of desktop icons. It's probably not the most powerful, geeky utility ever written, but I love it. I have shortcuts all over my desktop, and I arranged them around my wallpaper (a picture of my granddaughter). I know exactly where each shortcut is on the desktop, and it takes only a nanosecond to locate and click the shortcut I need.

Every once in a while, something untoward occurs, and I have to reboot, which results in a desktop in which my icons are lined up in neat vertical rows along the left side of my monitor. I hate neat vertical rows; they intermix software shortcuts with system icons, which makes it hard for me to find what I need. It takes a long time to drag the shortcuts back to their original positions, and I rarely remember exactly where they were. As a result, I occasionally click the wrong icon or spend a long time searching for the icon I need.

Layout made my life easier—it's these little things that make working at a computer all day bearable. After I created the perfect desktop layout, I saved it. The next time the icons decide to align themselves down the right side of my granddaughter's face, I can restore my perfect layout effortlessly.

Layout consists of two files: Layout.dll (a shell extension) and Layout.reg (a registry import file). Here's how to install and use this nifty utility:

1. Copy Layout.dll from the RK directory to *%Systemroot%*\\System32.
2. Open Layout.reg from Explorer, which registers the DLL (see Figure C-3).
3. Create the perfect desktop layout.
4. Right-click the My Computer icon on the desktop and choose Save Desktop Icon Layout from the shortcut menu (see Figure C-4, on the following page).
5. To restore the layout after it's been destroyed, choose Restore Desktop Icon Layout.

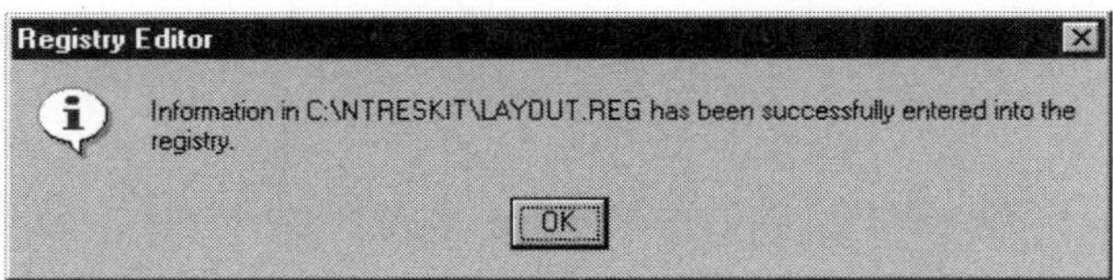

Figure C-3. *Register Layout.dll so you can use it.*

Figure C-4. *New commands on the shortcut menu let you save and restore your desktop layout.*

Save the layout again every time you add, remove, or move an icon. To remove the utility, you need to get rid of the registry entries. Here are the contents of the Layout.reg file:

```
[HKEY_CLASSES_ROOT\CLSID\{19F500E0-9964-11cf-B63D-08002B317C03}]
@="Desktop Icon Layout"[HKEY_CLASSES_ROOT\CLSID\{19F500E0-
9964-11cf-B63D-08002B317C03}\InProcServer32]
  @="Layout.dll"
  "ThreadingModel"="Apartment"

[HKEY_CLASSES_ROOT\Folder\shellex\ContextMenuHandlers\IconLayout]
  @="{19F500E0-9964-11cf-B63D-08002B317C03}"

[HKEY_LOCAL_MACHINE\SOFTWARE\Microsoft\Windows\CurrentVersion\Shell
Extensions\Approved]
  "{19F500E0-9964-11cf-B63D-08002B317C03}"="Desktop Icon Layout"
```

Local

You can ascertain the names of users in local groups on servers and domains with the command-line utility Local.exe. The syntax for Local.exe is **local *groupname* [*domainname* | *server*]** where:

- ***groupname*** is the name of a local group (the one you're curious about).
- ***domainname*** is the name of a network domain.
- ***server*** is the name of the network server that has the local group.

Enter **local** without parameters to get a help screen.

Caution If the group name has spaces, you must enclose the name in quotation marks.

Tip You can redirect the returned information to a file.

This utility is handy because it works with remote servers. Otherwise, it's just as easy to open the group icon from User Manager For Domains to see a list of members.

Netclip

This is another handy utility for network users. It's a GUI program that lets you see the contents of the clipboard on another computer. Call your friend down the hall, tell her to grab some information and place it on her clipboard, then open her clipboard and paste the data to a document in your own computer. It's faster and easier than copying files across the LAN. The data can be manipulated with any data format your installed software supports.

When you open Netclip it displays the local clipboard. To see the clipboard of a remote Windows NT computer, click the Connect button on the Netclip toolbar. Then enter the name of the remote computer you want to access (see Figure C-5).

There are two caveats:

- You must know the name of the computer, because there's no Browse button.
- The target computer must also have Netclip installed.

The clipboard for the remote computer opens (see Figure C-6), and you can grab the contents. Click Disconnect to shut down the connection to the remote clipboard.

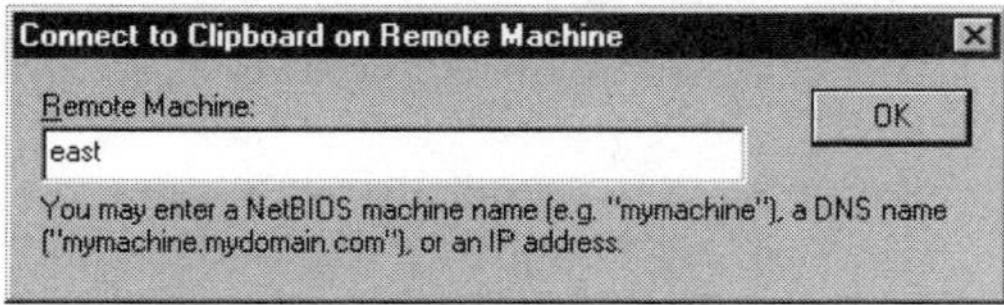

Figure C-5. *Enter the name of the computer that has the clipboard you want to open.*

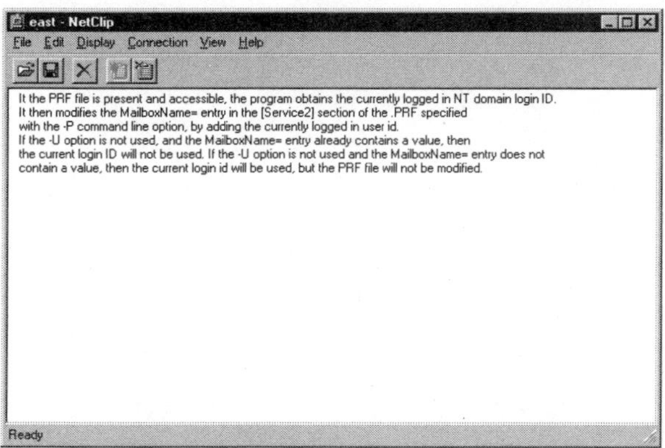

Figure C-6. *Select the data, then drag or copy it to the place you need it.*

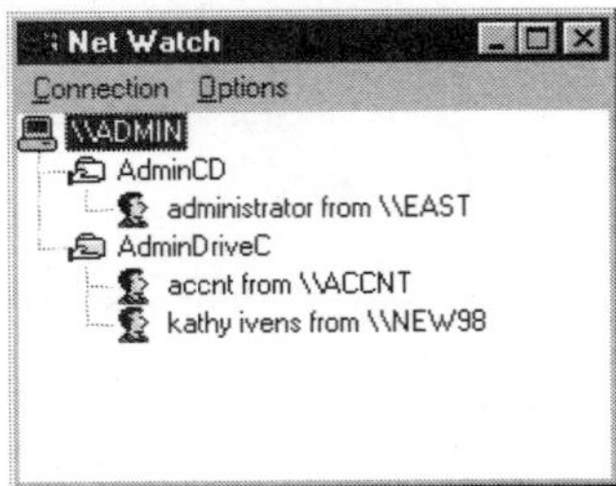

Figure C-7. *The local computer (named Admin) has several users accessing shares.*

Netwatch

Use Netwatch to see the users who are connected to shared folders, and to disconnect them if you wish. You can also use the software to stop sharing a folder. Best of all, you can monitor more than one computer at a time.

Caution You must be a member of the Administrators group of any computer you watch.

Open Netwatch from the Resource Kit item on the Programs menu (it's listed as Net Watcher on the Diagnostics submenu). When the software opens, it displays the shares on the local computer that are being accessed by remote users (see Figure C-7).

To view the shares on a remote computer, choose Connection from the menu bar, then choose Add Computer. In the Select Computer dialog box, select the computer you want to monitor (see Figure C-8).

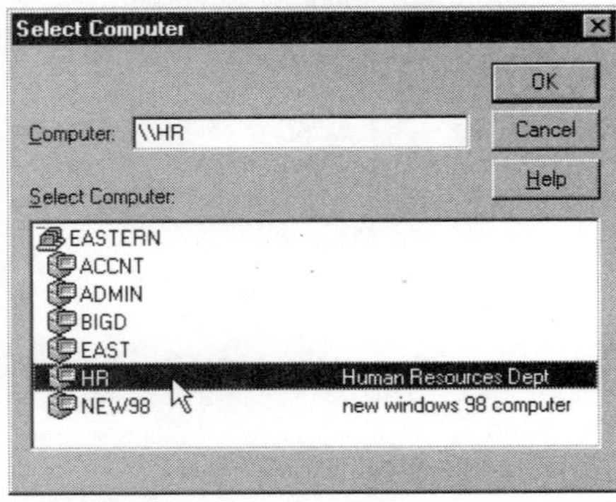

Figure C-8. *Choose the network computer for which you want to monitor the use of shares.*

Netwatch updates its display every 30 seconds, but you can press F5 to refresh the display if you need a quicker update.

Sclist

Sclist.exe is a command-line tool you can use to show the status of services on your local computer or on a remote computer. For example, it's a way to sit at your workstation and make sure all the services that should be running on the Exchange server are running.

The syntax for Sclist is **sclist [-r] [-s] [*MachineName*]** where:

- **-r** reports only running services.
- **-s** reports only stopped services.
- ***MachineName*** is the remote computer (if omitted, the local computer is the target of the report).

Tip The program reports to the screen, but you can redirect output to a file.

Shutdown

Use the command-line utility Shutdown.exe to shut down any Windows NT computer on the LAN. The software also works for restarting computers.

The syntax for Shutdown.exe is **shutdown [*computername*] [/l] [/a] [/r] [/t:*xx*] ["msg"] [/y] [/c]** where:

- ***computername*** is the remote computer.
- **/l** means a local shutdown.
- **/a** aborts a shutdown and it must run during the timeout period before shutdown is started (if you enter this switch, all other switches are ignored).
- **/r** restarts instead of shutting down.
- **/t:*xx*** sets shutdown for *xx* seconds (the default is 20).
- **"msg"** specifies a message to display (the message must be enclosed in quotation marks and cannot exceed 127 characters).
- **/y** answers any questions or prompts with "Yes."
- **/c** forces any running applications to close first (does not permit the software to ask if you want to save changes).

Whoami

People who log on to computers with a variety of names understand the usefulness of this command line utility.

Enter **whoami** at the command line to see who you are in the format *domainname\username*. If you're not logged on to a domain, the name of the computer is displayed instead of the domain name.

Appendix D

Web Resources for Information and Help

The Internet has plenty of places you can visit to learn about Microsoft Exchange Server and the Exchange client applications. This appendix covers some of the sites I've found to be helpful or interesting (or both).

The URLs I enumerate here were valid at the time I wrote this book, but I can't guarantee they will be totally accurate when you read this book. As far as Microsoft sites are concerned, you can always start at *http://www.microsoft.com* and work your way through the links.

Web Sites for Exchange Information

Here are some of my favorite Web sites that provide information, news, hints, and add-on utilities for Exchange Server and for the Exchange client software.

http://www.slipstick.com

This is, in my opinion, the best Microsoft Exchange Server/Outlook site on the Internet. It's run by Sue Mosher, an expert on Exchange Server and an internationally known expert on Outlook issues.

The site has a lot of nifty add-ons for Exchange Server (scripts and forms) and tons of add-ons and utilities for Outlook.

Sign up for the Exchange Messaging newsletter.

http://www.microsoft.com/exchange/

This is the home page for Microsoft's Exchange group. Start here to get information, news, and white papers about Exchange.

http://www.microsoft.com/exchange/developers/

The Microsoft Exchange Server Developer Forum is dedicated to providing information about the Exchange and Outlook development environments. The site provides links to sample applications and documentation. There are also links to visit the Web sites of developers who are creating applications with Exchange technology.

http://www.cdolive.com

CDOLive is dedicated to information about Microsoft Collaboration Data Objects. The site's mission is to "provide non-commercial information, sample code and links to third party add-ons to build solutions using Microsoft Collaboration Data Objects with Microsoft Outlook 98, Microsoft Exchange 5.5 Scripting Agent, and Microsoft Active Server Pages."

Microsoft CDO lets you build Groupware and Workflow solutions that use Exchange Server as the backbone. These solutions run on top of Exchange Server, using the Event Service (Microsoft Exchange Scripting Agent).

http://www.outlookexchange.com

This site is sponsored by ECMS and Micro Eye, and it's the place to go to find code, tips, and tricks for developers who work in the Exchange environment. ECMS is Enterprise Communications & Messaging Solutions, a group of evangelists (their own description) for implementing messaging and communications solutions based on Microsoft BackOffice technology. A group of developers in ECMS, called Notes Busters, declares that their mission is to create Exchange/IIS-based applications that nullify Lotus Notes' historical advantage in the area of messaging application development.

Micro Eye is a custom application development company that specializes in Exchange/Outlook solutions. (I met Randy Byrne, of Micro Eye, at a Microsoft Exchange Conference, and I was extremely impressed with the depth of his knowledge.)

The site is dedicated to taking some of the mystery out of customizing Outlook and Exchange, and any Exchange administrator who visits here will come away with lots of useful information. Be sure to check out the Outlook Code Example Page for snippets from Outlook experts—you'll find you can easily adapt them for your own Exchange enterprise.

There are articles you'll find fascinating and useful; they provide the hard-to-find help and documentation facts you're always searching for but can never seem to find. And, if there's a utility you absolutely must have for your own Outlook users, but you're struggling with the code, visit this site to find consultants with the expertise you need.

http://www.msexchange.org/exchlist/defaultframe.htm

The host for one of the best forum/mailing list sites on the Web, this is the place to go to ask questions and receive answers. Exchange administrators from all over the world use this site. Sign up today!

An enormous, searchable archive of mailing list postings, combined with a robust section of FAQs, pretty much guarantees you'll get the answer you're seeking.

http://www.egroups.com

Visit the message forums, news groups, and pages that have tons of good information. This site holds a plethora of data about Exchange, Microsoft Windows NT, and many other geeky subjects. Don't visit unless you have some spare time; you'll be clicking through all the pages on this site for a long time.

http://www.bopa.org

This is the home of the BackOffice Professionals Association. You'll find peer-to-peer support, technical problem solving, and access to plenty of information about technology. Members of BOPA include Microsoft Certified Professionals, analysts, developers, trainers, system administrators, Windows NT professionals, and BackOffice professionals.

http://www.exchangestuff.com

This site offers a large menu of choices for information, news, hints, links, FAQs, and other resources. This is another site at which you'll find you spend a lot of time, clicking your way through numerous valuable pages and links.

http://www.winntmag.com/exchange/

This is the home site for *Windows NT Magazine*'s *Exchange Administrator*, a monthly newsletter dedicated to solutions for Exchange and Outlook administrators. Also check the home page for *Windows NT Magazine* (*http://www.winntmag.com*), where you can find articles about Exchange Server.

http://www.exchangesoftware.com

This site is filled with add-ons, utilities, and information for the Exchange administrator.

http://www.swinc.com/resource/exch_smtp.htm

This site has tons of good information about Exchange and Internet Mail. If you're looking for answers to solve the intricacies and problems you face with the IMS, try this site first.

http://www.extracheez.com/boards/

This site's name apparently comes from the fact that the developers who put this site together find it helpful to send out for pizza with extra cheese during those all-night coding sessions. From the boards page, move to BackOffice, then to Exchange Server, where you'll find messages that contain questions you're probably asking—and plenty of expert answers.

http://www.amrein.com

This site, hosted by Amrein Engineering, has an almost overwhelming amount of information about Exchange. The home page displays so many choices you won't know where to begin. The site also offers a newsletter.

http://www.angrygraycat.com/goetter/widgets.htm

Here's the place to find widgets and do-hickeys to make your life as an Exchange administrator easier. The site is filled with sample code you can use to solve problems, add features, and write utilities.

Exchange User Groups

If you have a user group in your area, plan to attend meetings. It's a great way to learn from other administrators' experiences. Some user groups maintain Web sites, and you can frequently obtain articles, hints, and other useful information from those sites. This section enumerates a few of the user groups you might want to check out.

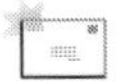

Note Many of the Exchange user groups are a Special Interest Group (SIG) of a larger computer user group.

Philadelphia BackOffice Users Group (PBOUG)

This group, which has been meeting regularly for several years, focuses on all the BackOffice applications, but meetings are scheduled on specific BackOffice topics, so Exchange Server meetings are fairly regular. The PBOUG meetings are held at corporate offices, where the BackOffice topic under discussion is running. Microsoft techies attend regularly. The group draws members and attendees from the three-state area that is proximate to Philadelphia. If you don't live in the Delaware Valley, visit them at *http://www.wolffdata.com/pboug/*.

Great Lakes NTug Exchange SIG

If you're near the Southfield, Michigan, Microsoft, you can attend this group's meetings. Otherwise, check out the group at *http://www.NTug.com/Exchange*. Meetings are held on the third Thursday of the month from 5 to 7 P.M.

NTPro Exchange User Group

NTPro is a Washington, D.C.-based professional association that provides education for computer professionals with an interest in Windows NT Server, BackOffice technologies, and related server and development issues. The Exchange User Group meets on the second Tuesday of the month at the Washington, D.C., Microsoft.

Northern California Exchange Users Group

This group meets every other month at Microsoft in Foster City. Foster City is just south of the San Francisco International Airport. There's no Web site (yet), but you can get information from Microsoft by writing to the company at 950 Tower Lane, Suite 900, Foster City, CA 94404.

San Diego Microsoft Exchange User Group

This user group meets on the first Thursday of the month at 6 P.M. Meetings are held at Stellcom Technologies. For information, call 619-646-7222.

Appendix E

Microsoft Exchange Add-Ons and Service Packs

Life as an administrator is easier if you add helpful utilities to your Exchange system, and if you keep up with bug fixes and new features from Microsoft.

Exchange Add-On Products

There are quite a few developers offering programs and utilities you can use with Microsoft Exchange Server and client software. In this section, I mention some that I've been impressed with.

- **Workgroup Overview** This is a program that copies the items from multiple user calendars to a public calendar on an Exchange Server. Usernames are displayed with each appointment, and private appointments have their subjects replaced with the word "Private." Available at *http://www.omaha.org/~adamh/projects.htm*.
- **Add Holidays** This is a form you can use to distribute lists of company holidays and other important dates to users. Available at *http://www.slipstick.com/exchange/olforms/holiday.htm*.
- **Microsoft Outlook Roving Client Utility** This utility makes it easy to implement Microsoft Outlook for clients who need to access their mail from different computers. Available at *http://www.redfox.co.uk/olclient/*.
- **Rover for Microsoft Exchange** This is another software program that permits roving clients to access their server mailboxes. Available at *http://www.compressmail.com/erwhite.html*.
- **Profile Maker** This is a suite of utilities that Exchange Server administrators will love. I've been impressed with this company's products for some time and the additional Microsoft Exchange features in their latest version are among some of the best, most needed utilities I've seen: gain additional mailboxes for users, instant and easy profile creation, and lots of other time-saving features. Get more information (and download a demo) at *http://www.autoprof.com/home.htm*.
- **Script Director** This is a deployment and administration tool for Exchange developers and administrators. You can use it to automate the installation of

scripting or routing agents. It works across multiple public folders and multiple mailboxes. Available at *http://www.microeye.com*.

- **Exchange Templates** These are pre-built messages you enter once, then send over and over. This saves time when responding to common queries. The program inserts personal information about the recipient so the templates don't seem to be templates. Available at *http://www.nsoftware.com/et.htm*.
- **Import to Personal Address Book** This is a utility (actually it's a clever Microsoft Word macro) that takes any list you can use for mail merge in Word and adds it to your Personal Address Book. This is available at *http://www.slipstick.com/exchange/imppab.htm*.

Service Pack 2

If you haven't yet installed SP 2 for Exchange Server, read the information in this section to see if you should (you should!). If you haven't yet installed SP 1, don't worry—SP 2 is cumulative.

Enhancements in SP 2

Service Pack 2 includes some enhancements you might find useful (or even necessary).

InterOrg Replication Utility

If you support multiple Exchange organizations this utility allows you to replicate public folder information and free/busy schedules between separate Exchange organizations. The replication can be one-way or bi-directional, and operates across both trusted and non-trusted Microsoft Windows NT domains.

Microsoft Outlook for Macintosh

The following enhancements are available for Outlook for Macintosh:

- Support for message signing and encryption using S/MIME version 2
- Support for viewing calendars created by Windows versions of Microsoft Outlook 97 and later
- Support for Mac OS 8.5

Other Enhancements

The following enhancements had been made available for download from Microsoft previously, and are included in SP 2:

- **Move Server Wizard** This utility allows you to move servers between sites and organizations.
- **Microsoft Importer for cc:Mail Archives** This enhancement lets users preserve important information that's stored in their cc:Mail personal e-mail folders.
- **Lotus Notes Connector** This enhancement permits replication of directories and exchange of messages with Lotus Notes systems.

Fixes in SP 2

The following table lists known problems and bugs that are fixed in SP 2. I've included the Microsoft Knowledge Base article for each so you can investigate any problem that you want to learn about (perhaps it seems familiar).

Problem	Knowledge Base Article
16-Bit Client Unable to Read Schedule+ Data	Q140404
16-Bit Outlook Can Only Open One Schedule+ Appt Book	Q143196
Outlook Hangs when Opening Another User's Calendar	Q172937
Authrest.exe Err Msg: Dynamic Link Library Not Found	Q177726
Admin.exe Dr. Watsons While Importing an Active Newsgroup	Q182319
Internet Options Tab Missing from Send Options Dialog Box	Q182716
MTA Event 2050 with Badly Encoded X.400 Message	Q183014
Interop Issue with Lowercase PAB Address	Q183104
Notes Client Gets Error Message: Error Loading Metafile	Q183290
Unable to Display Outlook Calendar After Move Mailbox	Q183517
Schedule + Won't Print Outlook Private Appointments	Q183650
Message Class Changed during Forward from Public Folder	Q184333
Cannot Reply to RTF Message Addressed to MS Mail Recipient	Q184457
cc:Mail Connector Sends Messages Twice Under Load	Q184524
MIME Type Extension Mapping Not Used for Attachments	Q184534
Messages Not Rerouted Between 2 X.400 Connectors in Site	Q184662
Kanji Outlook MS Mail Users Get NDRs Sending to Exchange	Q184681
Text Attachments Modified for Internet Mail	Q184718
Outlook & Exchange One-Off SMTP & Display Name Parsing	Q184957
AV in Dsamain.exe When Expanding or Scrolling Objects	Q185098
Recipient Address Corrupted on Messages to EDK Gateway	Q185592
Spinning Thread in Mad.exe During Routing Recalculation	Q185693
Directory Service May Stop Unexpectedly During Exception H	Q185933
Exchange Server MTA Always Uses RTSE Window Size 3	Q185934
Attached DBCS Message Not Displayed Properly	Q185986
NDR on Message from Outlook via Microsoft Mail Connector	Q186258
Location of Attachments Shifted When Message Forwarded	Q186343
Russian Outlook MS Mail User Gets NDR Sending to Exchange	Q186672
DBCS Attachment File Name Not Encoded If Using UUENCODE	Q187581
Message Content Changes When Sending via X.400 to UNIX	Q187643
Downloading Messages Using Outlook Express Crashes Store	Q187868
MTA Routes Mail to EDK Connector when Other Route Exists	Q187915
Unicode Message with TNEF Causes Information Store to Stop	Q187970

(continued)

(continued)

Problem	**Knowledge Base Article**
File Attachments in OWA Append 2 Extra Bytes CR/LF	Q187994
Adding Recipients To a Form May Change Display Name	Q188420
Delivery Report Discarded Over 1984 X.400 Connector	Q188597
Public Folder Slowness in Folders with Thousands of Msgs.	Q188631
Changing the State of Circular Logging Fails on a Cluster	Q188635
Folder Assistant Rule to Forward Messages May Fail	Q188647
Error for Incorrect Journal Recipient Is Informational	Q188772
Replying To or Forwarding Resent Message Causes NDR	Q188778
Information Store Crashes While Client Downloads POP3 Mail	Q188807
Cannot View Message Text on Black Background	Q188829
CDO Only Publishes Three Months of Free/Busy Data	Q188833
Public Folder Rule Fails Using Field From EFD	Q188969
NDR When Sending to Recipient From Offline Address Book	Q188979
IS Stops Unexpectedly Formatting a Binary Property Value	Q188989
Problems Occur When Incorrect Property Is Set on Message	Q189193
Scheduled Fax Which Includes Files Is Never Sent	Q189318
MTA Logs Event 9301 Though X.400 Connector Is Identified	Q189345
Exchange MTA Logs Event 1136	Q189753
French Admin Reports Blank Password on Newly Created Windo	Q189755
SMTP Message ID May Be Incorrectly Truncated	Q190041
12006 and 4117 Errors when IMS Receives an SMTP Message	Q190084
IIS Hangs When File Upload Is Cancelled from Browser	Q190361
Facilities Data Not Sent Out (by Exchange) with CALL ACC	Q190500
Connector for cc:Mail Converts Messages Larger Than 20 KB	Q190555
Corrupted MIME Encoding Causes Information Store to Crash	Q190556
Attachments with $ in the File Name May Be Renamed	Q190557
MoveUser Fails After Running ISINTEG	Q190722
Eseutil Fails with JetDuplicateKey Error	Q190918
NDR Returned When Message Includes Several Attachments	Q191163
Outlook Fails to Connect	Q191164
Notes Connector Crashes When Importing Too-Long Field	Q191286
Site Connector Not Usable Through a Firewall	Q191594
MTA Fails to Convert Message from 1984 X.400 System	Q191947
System Attendant (Mad.exe) Stops in ScSetDeleted	Q191956
Messages with Incomplete X.400 Addresses are NDR	Q192052
Information Store Access Violates When Freeing Memory	Q192053
High CPU Usage by STORE Displaying a Folder View	Q192065
Event Service with Internet Explorer 4.01 Hangs NT Shell	Q192066

(continued)

(continued)

Problem	**Knowledge Base Article**
NNTP Message ID Missing From Event Description	Q192203
Information Store Stops When Forwarding Internet Message	Q192204
Full Fidelity Not Maintained on Opaque-Signed Message	Q192205
IIS Crashes with ActiveX Component Using MAPI	Q192274
Dumpster Size Performance Monitor Value Wraps Prematurely	Q192324
JET Will Now Retry 16 Times on -1018 Error	Q192333
Messages NDR after Applying 5.5 SP or 5.0 Hotfix	Q192349
Backup Stops Because of Communications Error	Q192440
Setup Doesn't Add Permission to MSExchangeES Registry Key	Q192493
Slow Backup Performance with Single-Processor Servers	Q192513
DXA Appends 001 at End of Display Name in MS Mail GAL	Q192514
Cc: Field Moved to To: Field with MHS Extended Addressing	Q192519
MAPI Spooler Sends NDRs During Folder Synchronization	Q192533
Notes Connector Crashes Processing Voice Mail Attachment	Q192542
Cannot Log On with Account Containing Extended Characters	Q192582
IMS Incorrectly Archives Message If ResolveP2 Is On	Q192583
Paged Pool Memory Leak Caused by Attachment Processing	Q192592
Attachment File Name in 8.3 Format in cc:Mail User Inbox	Q192593
Message with Empty From: Field Stuck in MTS_OUT Queue	Q192594
Incorrect Date on Message Sent Through cc:Mail Connector	Q192595
Missing Transaction Log Yields "Unable to Find the File"	Q192657
cc:Mail Connector Ignores Export Custom Recipients Flag	Q192697
cc:Mail Connector Does Not Parse Attachment Name Correctly	Q192700
SBS Err Msg: Unable to Display This Folder...	Q192712
PerfMon Counters Unavailable After Applying 5.5 SP1	Q192742
Admin Program Quits Unexpectedly When Creating Newsfeed	Q192748
Server Hangs Running a Printing Service and Exchange INS	Q192792
Admin.exe Stops When Viewing Properties of Remote Server	Q192836
Full Offline Address Book Download with Differences Specif	Q192839
MS Mail Connector Doesn't Support Turkish Characters	Q192887
Dirsync Between Notes and OV/VM over Exchange Fails	Q192911
OWA Error 404 Opening Messages After Applying 5.5 SP	Q192930
PROFS Does Not Retain File Extension of Attachment	Q192932
Event 4123; Message Not Delivered	Q192939
Internet Mail Loses Message Body	Q192940
Internet Mail Service Does Not Allow Auto Forwarded Msgs	Q192982
Content Conversion Errors on OLE Embedded Objects	Q192983
Ability to Restrict Size of Headers Contained in Message	Q193035

(continued)

(continued)

Problem	Knowledge Base Article
Cannot Stop Information Store from a Command Prompt	Q193040
Information Store's Directory Query Returns LDAP Error	Q193041
MTA Stops; Events 2110	Q193049
NDR When Message Is Routed Between Multiple Connectors	Q193081
Unable to Reply to Messages After Hotfix Is Applied	Q193123
Security Context Deleted and Initialized at Same Time	Q193215
Per-Entity MTA Counters Not Working After Upgrade	Q193221
Euro Displayed Incorrectly After POP3 to MAPI Conversion	Q193256
DBCS Text in Bulleted List Not Displayed Properly	Q193258
OWA Stops when Replying to Message with Inline Image	Q193260
Meeting Update Generates NDR After Moving Server	Q193283
No MTA Support for ISO 8859-7 (Greek) Character Set	Q193345
Message Delivery Is Slowed or Stopped to SNADS	Q193346
Access Violation Occurs When Stopping Dirsync Service	Q193395
Address Book Views Not Updated After Correct Interval	Q193423
Error Msg: The Domain or User Name You Have Specified...	Q193437
Exchange Server 5.5 120-Day Evaluation Copy Expiring	Q193485
Outlook Web Access Stops on Corrupt Calendar Data	Q193557
KMS Database Conversion Fails During Exchange 5.5 Upgrade	Q193567
HOWTO: Determine the Logical Drives on a System	Q193623
Internet Mail Service Stops with Event Log Error 4116	Q193639
Bad Error Handling in CfolderRender::put_DataSource	Q193675
Dates Incorrect After Migrating cc:Mail DB6 Bulletin Board	Q193735
Dates Appear Incorrectly After cc:Mail Migration	Q193745
cc:Mail Connector Doesn't Deliver NDRs from Certain ADMDs	Q193761
Zero Byte Attachments Cause NDRs from Exchange 5.5 SP1	Q193762
Message Sent with X.400 One-Off Address Generates NDR	Q193780
Internet Mail Service Stops with Event IDs 4182	Q193782
DXA Does Not Handle Long MAC Mail Addresses Properly	Q193842
MTA Stops Processing Messages and Generates 9156 Events	Q193894
One Recipient Dropped on Exchange DL on Incoming Message	Q193961
MTA Queues Backup After MTA Logs 1133 State Check Warning	Q194031
Exchange 5.5 SP1 Upgrade Fails on Cluster Server	Q194128
Notes SMTP Addresses Are Truncated upon Reply	Q194191
POP3 Client's Reply Message to Exchange User is NDRd	Q194192
cc:Mail Migration Wizard Fails to Migrate cc:Mail User	Q194218
Alt 0216 Character Incorrectly Translated in SMTP & X.400	Q194321
Information Store Crashes Processing HTML Message	Q194337

(continued)

(continued)

Problem	Knowledge Base Article
NDR Returned for Deleted Mailbox when Message Sent to DL	Q194504
NDR When Message Contains 8-Bit Subject	Q194505
Deadlock While Purging Unused Indices	Q194506
Store Crashes while Processing Outbound SMTP Message	Q194560
Empty Subject Msg Can Cause NDR When Sent Through X.400	Q194651
Unable to Post a Reply to Exchange 5.5 Newsgroup Folder	Q194657
Message Sticks in MTA Queue While Other Messages Flow By	Q194750
Outlook Web Access Cannot Resolve Name	Q194839
Client Cannot Retrieve Message in Parts Using SSL	Q194998
Resource Failure Error on Computers w/ more than 1 GB RAM	Q195006
Internet News Service Sends Long “newnews” Command	Q195040
NDR When Replying All to Message Sent to Moved User	Q195124
Invalid Fetch Command Causes Information Store to Stop	Q195171
Premature MTA Fanout Inside a Site	Q195200
5.0 and 5.5 Internet Mail Services Do Not Do AUTH NTLM	Q195201
cc:Mail 8.01 Clients See Attachment Name Changed to Date	Q195203
5.5 SP1 Update Fails on 2nd Cluster Node with French PDC	Q195214
Outbound SMTP with 8-Bit Data in the Message Body	Q195215
Lsdiavm.exe Process Terminates with a Dr. Watson	Q195304
Admin Error When Viewing Internet Newsgroups Root Folder	Q195363
Attachments with Long Filenames Crash Client	Q195397
Notes Shortname Field Might Not Be Synchronized	Q195523
Rules Are Not Applied to SMTP Messages Received as [cc]	Q195583
MTA Stops and Numerous Events Appear in Event Log	Q195731
Store Crash when IMAP Append Is Aborted on 100 MB Network	Q195741
Notification Option Set Incorrectly During Migration	Q195852
Access Violation While Processing Long DBCS BinHex Files	Q195894
Address Space Not Updated When You Recalculate GWART	Q195905
Cannot Specify Domains to Relay to in Internet Mail Service	Q195969
Deadlock in STORE Due to a Stack Overflow	Q195971
Move Mailbox Fails with Client Operation Failed Error	Q195985
Directory Service Stops When Upgrading to 5.5 or 5.5 SP1	Q196043
DRAS Connector Fails Connecting to Multiple Sites	Q196045
Option to Zero Out Deleted Messages on Exchange Server	Q196169
Attributes Not Available to LDAP Users with Admin Rights	Q196491
PROFS and SNADS Connector Does Not Support Euro Symbol	Q196615
OWA Causes an Access Violation in MAPI	Q196670
Internet Mail Service Attachment Formatting Fails	Q196849

(continued)

Problem *(continued)*	**Knowledge Base Article**
Dirsync Service Stops Unexpectedly-Event 181 in Event Log	Q196892
Total Nick (Alias) Collisions Counter Not Incremented Properly	Q196893
Mailbox Receives Duplicate Messages after Server is Moved	Q196895
RTF Message Appears Incorrectly After Being Forwarded	Q197013
POP3 Clients Cannot Log In with CTA via Membership Server	Q197059
JET Retry Hotfix Makes Repair (ESEUTIL /P) Very Slow	Q197060
FETCH Using IMAP Client Fails to Retrieve SMIME Message	Q197130
Internet Mail Service Stops when Routing Messages	Q197142
Changes to Domain Names Cause Large Incremental Downloads	Q197280
MTA Can Stop After Generating an Event ID 9405	Q197281
Dirsync Does Not Correctly Convert Date to UTC Format	Q197291
Mode Command Does Not Function Properly with Chat Server	Q197292
Changing Calendar View Takes an Unusually Long Time	Q197293
IRCX Channel Name on Remote Server Appears Incorrectly	Q197376
MTA Generates 9301 Events on Incoming Connections	Q197378
Euro Symbol Displays "?" Sending Plain Text	Q197394
MTA Stops Processing Mail with Events 57	Q197398
Cannot Filter Junk E-mail on Blank "From" Field	Q197405
INETINFO Crashes Running HTTP-LOADSIM Against OWA	Q197406

Index

Note to the reader: Italicized page numbers refer to figures, tables, and illustrations.

Special Characters

A

B

E

L

M

N

Q

R

S

About the Author

Kathy Ivens has been a computer consultant since 1984, and has authored and contributed to more than three dozen books on computer subjects. She writes a monthly column in *Windows NT Magazine*, and is the editor of their weekly online newsletter, *UPDATE*. Before becoming an expert in computing, Ms. Ivens spent many years as a television producer, where she had fun producing sports and was mildly amused producing news and entertainment programs. Preceding that career she spent some time as a community organizer and also as a political consultant. She still doesn't know what she wants to be when she grows up.

The manuscript for this book was prepared and submitted to Microsoft Press in electronic form. Text files were prepared using Microsoft Word 97 for Windows. Pages were composed by nSight, Inc., using Adobe Pagemaker 6.5 for Windows, with text in Garamond Light and display type in ITC Franklin Gothic. Composed pages were delivered to the printer as electronic prepress files.

Cover Designer
Girvin Design

Layout Artist
Tara L. Murray

Project Manager
Sarah Kimnach

Tech Editor
Anooshirvan Ghazai

Copy Editor
Barbara Sutton

Proofreaders
William Oppenheimer and Abby Luthin

Indexer
Joan Green